MODERN LOGIC

the text of this book is printed on 100% recycled paper

MODERN LOGIC
An Introduction

Norman L. Thomas

BARNES & NOBLE BOOKS
A DIVISION OF HARPER & ROW, PUBLISHERS
New York, Hagerstown, San Francisco, London

L. C. catalogue card number: 66–23154

ISBN: 0-06-460103-X

Manufactured in the United States of America

78 79 80 12 11 10 9 8 7 6 5

ABOUT THE AUTHOR

Norman L. Thomas received his B.A. and M.A. degrees in philosophy from the University of California at Berkeley. His background includes three years as a Navy electronics technician in World War II, four years as a Naval aviator during the Korean War, four years teaching mathematics at San Ramon High School in Danville, California, where he also served as Chairman of the Mathematics Department, and nine years teaching philosophy at Bakersfield College. As Chairman of the Philosophy Department at Bakersfield, he introduced two lower-division courses in symbolic logic and was instrumental in the development of an expanding range of courses related to philosophy. Other assignments he has had in philosophy have been as a coordinator for the Extension Division of U.C.L.A., and as an Assistant Professor at Fresno State College. Currently, he is Associate Professor of Philosophy at Simpson College. He is a member of the American Philosophical Association and the History of Science Society. His publications include articles on ethics and the history of science.

To My Wife
Marjorie

Preface

An explanation of some aspects of modern deductive logic begins in this book with the presentation of a loose and generally intuitive discussion of some of the new terms and concepts that have appeared in the last fifty years or so, and develops from there into a more systematic approach similar to that found in many college texts currently in use.

The second and third chapters of the book are devoted to an essentially intuitive presentation of two deductive systems. After the reader has had ample opportunity to work with these systems—called here "Sets" and "Logical Deduction"—in terms related to his everyday experiences, the more rigorous systems—Propositional and Class Calculus—are introduced as what might be called axiomatizations of their intuitive counterparts.

These latter systems are discussed with as much rigor as it is possible to give within the confines of this format, and an application of one of them is then made to a case involving practical problems to demonstrate its utility as it is returned, in Alfred North Whitehead's words, ". . . from the upper regions of abstract thought . . . back to earth for an analysis of concrete fact."

A discussion of some additional matters in the philosophy of logic is given in the last chapter, wherein problems and difficulties that may have been glossed over or given only brief attention in previous chapters are clarified to the extent, at least, of making the questions a little clearer even though the answers may still need further correction and modification.

Some special items of interest included within this book are: the use of numbers to denote areas of a three-circle Venn Diagram, thereby avoiding the more cumbersome or less specific descriptions usually given; a new method of numbering columns on a Truth Table that indicates not only the columns compared but the sequence of steps taken; and a chapter on Switching Algebra that serves the double purpose of providing an introduction to the algebra of electrical switches and of demonstrating the way a theoretical system may be directly applied to the practical problems that face the technician or machine operator.

Exercises are included at the end of every major section and answers are given at the end of the book. [*Logic Workbook*, by J. W. Miller (New York: Oxford University Press, 1958) is recommended as a source of additional relevant exercises.]

I am indebted to many sources for the material within these pages. I would like to use this occasion to express my gratitude to some of them. I wish first to express my appreciation for the lessons I have learned from David Rynin, Benson Mates, John Myhill, and Donald Kalish, although I hasten to add that they are in no way responsible for the content and general organization of this text nor for any of the inadequacies or errors that may appear within it. I am also indebted to my teachers in the National Science Foundation's summer institutes in mathematics at Oberlin College in 1959 and the University of Santa Clara in 1960. Professor Lowell Dabbs of Bakersfield College provided a valuable service in helping me organize the original material and develop the outline form. The students in Philosophy 7: Logic at Bakersfield College were, perhaps, more helpful than they will ever know. I owe them—and hereby offer—a sincere expression of my thanks for their cooperation and interest in the rather loosely defined material that went through many corrections, additions, and modifications as it took shape as a course and as a book. Dr. Gladys Walterhouse of Barnes & Noble was most helpful with the comments, suggestions, and corrections she made as editor and in her sympathetic treatment of the material as it was given. I hope that my wife, Marjorie, who typed the entire original manuscript with all its symbols, diagrams, and difficulties, will find some recompense in the deep personal satisfaction that she deserves to share with me in the publication of this book.

Table of Contents

INDEX OF SYMBOLS USED IN THIS BOOK

Symbol	Meaning	Page introduced
$\cup$	Union	19
$+$	Union	137
	Parallel circuit	154
$\cap$	Intersection	19
$\times$	Intersection	137
	Series circuit	154
ab (variables conjoined)	Intersection	40
	Series circuit	159
$\{\ \}$	Set: listing	20
$\{x \mid \ldots\}$	Set: description	20
a'	Negation of set a	22
	Symbol of complementarity	137
	Opposite pole of switch a	157
1	Universal Set	22, 27
	Closed circuit	155
0	Null or Empty Set	23, 27
	Open circuit	155
$\{1\}$	Element of a set	20, 27
(1)	Area number	26, 27
A	Universal Affirmative proposition	37
E	Universal Negative proposition	37
I	Particular Affirmative proposition	37
O	Particular Negative proposition	37
s	Subject term of conclusion	42

Symbol	Meaning	Page introduced
p	Predicate term of conclusion	42
m	Middle term	42
I, II, III, IV	Figures of syllogism	42
$\cdot$	Conjunction	62
	(Defined)	125
$\vee$	Disjunction	62
	(Primitive)	124
$\supset$	Implication	64
$\boldsymbol{\supset}$	(Defined)	124
$\equiv$	Equivalence	64
	(Defined)	125
( ), [ ], { }	Grouping symbols	65, 124, 137
$-p$	Negation of variable p	65
	(Primitive)	124
①	Table Value column	68, 70
(x)	Universal Quantifier	98
$(\exists x)$	Existential Quantifier	99
$\subset$	Set Inclusion	113
$\boldsymbol{\subset}$	(Defined)	137
C	Implication	134
A	Disjunction	134
K	Conjunction	134
E	Equivalence	134
N	Negation	134
$=$	Identity	137

MODERN LOGIC

1

Introduction

Courses currently given under the name of "Logic" range from a classical presentation of Aristotelian reasoning to an extremely rigorous development of mathematical or symbolic logic. Or a logic course may be directed towards an intellectual discussion of deductive and inductive inference, rhetoric, Mill's canons, and the basic tenets of syllogistic reasoning.

This text will be primarily a course in symbolic logic. Other subjects will be introduced and given some treatment, but an essential aim of the course is that of carrying the student along the first level of understanding of the new logic and the new mathematics and showing him some applications of these innovations to specific problems of science or engineering. We do not expect to ignore the major systems of the past although we may be accused of manhandling them somewhat.

Rhetoric—the study of debate and argumentation—is not a subject that is closely enough related to symbolic logic to warrant bringing it into this text.

Syllogistic or traditional logic must be treated in some detail if for no other reason than the fact that it existed for so long as the *only* logic and may therefore be considered to have left deep impressions on any system that has developed since. It is possible that traditional logic speaks in terms that are as close to our normal conversational images as any other formal system, either from the past or in use today. We are not giving "history for history's sake," then, but history for the sake of knowing where the ideas came from so that we will be better able to ferret out mistakes that are due to the particular origins.

A. DEDUCTIVE AND INDUCTIVE REASONING

One important distinction to be made in the beginning is that between Deductive and Inductive Reasoning.

A familiar usage of Deductive Reasoning is in the solution of mathematical problems. It is particularly well illustrated in the development of a proof in geometry. But we will also find Deductive Reasoning being used in our ordinary language, although it may not in this case be recognized as reasoning at all. If, for example, someone tells you, "George is not a Freshman so he may not wear a beanie," you would rarely stop to consider that statement as an instance of reasoning. But if we make certain modifications and additions—being careful to retain the original meaning of the statement—we could put it in a form such that it may indeed be recognized as an instance of Deductive Reasoning:

George is not a Freshman.
No one but a Freshman (no non-Freshmen) may wear beanies.
Therefore, George may not wear a beanie.

This argument is valid and in this form may be shown to be so by our established systems of logic.

It is valid, you might say, but it is also trivial. Why go to all that trouble with a sentence that can be seen on inspection to be valid given the establishment of certain rules of campus dress? Our answer is that we want, for our Deductive Reasoning, to clearly establish forms of correct reasoning—which may be done in simple cases such as the one above—and then we may go on to use these forms in problems that are a good deal more complex. (For an extensive discussion of the meaning of "validity" as distinct from the meaning of "truth," see Chapter 6.)

Let us say at this point that we are taking Deductive Reasoning to be that kind of reasoning which seeks to discover whether or not a given conclusion is actually entailed by certain premises, assumptions, axioms, or presuppositions. Some examples may help to illustrate this definition.

One very common form used in Deductive Reasoning is the following: If *A* occurs, then *B* will occur; and *A* occurs. Therefore, *B* occurs. There are two premises and a conclusion here. The premises are (1) If A occurs, then B will occur, and (2) A occurs. The conclusion then is B occurs.

(A special case of that form might be: If we win the game, then we win the series; and we win the game. Therefore, we win the series.)

We recognize, of course, that that argument form will also apply to a somewhat more complicated condition. We may use that form, for example, to show that the following is valid: If *R*

and *S* occur, then *G* will not occur; and *R* and *S* occur. Therefore, *G* does not occur.

For another standard deduction, consider a case from high school mathematics: In plane geometry we are given, to begin with, a number of axioms. Let us take two of them. (1) The whole is equal to the sum of its parts. (2) A quantity may be substituted for its equal. Now, if we consider a line segment, AB (the meaning of "line segment" to be given by definition), that is divided into two parts, x and y, such that $x = y$, we may prove that $2x = AB$ in the following manner:

$x + y = AB$, because the whole is equal to the sum of its parts, and x and y are the parts of AB.
$x + x = AB$, because x is equal to y, and a quantity may be substituted for its equal; so we may replace y with x.
$x + x = 2x$, by an axiom of arithmetic (all axioms of arithmetic are assumed in plane geometry).
$2x = AB$, by substituting $2x$ for $x + x$ in the second step.

These examples should help us to understand more clearly what is being done in Deductive Reasoning. We are, essentially, setting up certain assumptions or axioms and some basic argument forms that are then applied to more and more complicated conditions. Beginning with a few of the most simplified statements we can make, we use our reasoning to make connections and relationships between these statements and carry them all out to their full implications.

In the examples above we are making deductions that are extremely simple; so simple, in fact, that the student may feel irritated or indignant at being forced to go through such tortuous proceedings to get to a conclusion that was quite obvious in the first place. As the philosopher Schopenhauer said, "It is like having one's legs broken so that he can be taught to walk on crutches."

A better metaphor than that of Schopenhauer's, however, might be that of training an aviator to fly by his instruments. Under normal conditions of clear weather and empty skies a pilot may fly by instinct and natural reactions to information given him by all of his senses. But when he is in a storm or heavy clouds and can barely see the tips of his wings he can no longer rely on his intuitive understanding of the situation about him. It is a well-recognized fact among aviators that while flying in the clouds it is possible to feel as if you are in a tight climbing turn when, as a matter of fact, you are flying straight and level, or, on the other hand, to be actually in a tight spiral towards the ground even though your senses tell you you are in the comfortable condition of straight-and-level flight.

Because of such deceptions produced by intuitive knowledge, therefore, it is essential that the aviator learn a kind of flying that is based upon a deliberate denial of his intuitive feelings. If he is to learn a special kind of flying that will make him a professional pilot capable of flying an airplane under a much wider range of circumstances, then he must learn to "walk on crutches" as if his legs were broken. That is, he must learn to have absolute dependence upon his instruments even when they are contradicting much of the evidence of his senses.

Deductive Reasoning, whether in logic or in mathematics, has some of the characteristics of instrument flying. The basic assumptions and rules of operation we work with are analogous to the instruments and their usage in an airplane. And it is as necessary *and* as productive for us to stay strictly within the limits of those assumptions (axioms) and rules as it is for the aviator to observe and fly by the instruments on his panel.

If the Deductive Reasoning process seems unnecessarily cumbersome in the handling of the elementary problems we have mentioned, we may be assured that this apparently cumbersome approach is the only one that will handle the complicated problems that occur in the examination of more profound issues. But the real assurance, of course, comes only by using the deductive procedure as in working out problems of geometry or algebra or logic and thus discovering for oneself its utility and power.

Inductive Reasoning offers us less certainty than Deductive Reasoning and more in the way of various degrees of probability. In Deductive Reasoning we are simply carrying out the implications of our assumptions and rules of operation to get results that may be unclear to begin with but that are, indeed, already implied by our rules and assumptions. But in Inductive Reasoning we are working with predictions of the future, generalizations concerning wide areas of unobserved instances, and theories pertaining to so-called regularities in nature.

For a definition of Induction we may say that it is that kind of reasoning that seeks to produce a true statement about all members of a group of things or events on the basis of an examination of a limited number of individuals within that group.

Statements such as the following are examples of Inductive Reasoning: "He gives a quiz every Friday morning—at least that is what he has done all semester so far," "That's a box of bad apples—I've looked at ten of them and found a worm in every one I checked," and "There is a good possibility we will have rain if the wind is from the south—that is generally what happens."

It should be noticed here that the procedure in each of those examples is to make some statement concerning certain general conditions or supposed regularities based upon observations of individuals or individual circumstances. The statements indicate attempts to discover some regularity or generalization on the basis of particular occurrences carefully observed and enumerated. Alfred North Whitehead calls it trying to "see what is general in what is particular."

The inductive process is closely related to what is called the scientific method. It is the process of reasoning that is fundamental to the activities of the scientist. But its main characteristic, as one can see by the examples, is probability, rather than certainty. "No empirical science," says P. W. Bridgeman, "can ever make exact statements." *

The probabilities that we talk about may, of course, be extremely high. The example that has been made classic by the writings of David Hume in the late eighteenth century is the one that concerns the statement, "The sun will rise tomorrow." The observations we have made since the first days we began to observe at all have included instances of the sun rising at the beginning of every period of approximately 24 hours each. It always has risen in the past and it always will in the future, we are convinced. But without meaning to bicker over trivialities or to claim the unreasonable, we may still point out that our knowledge of the sun rising tomorrow is not the absolutely certain knowledge we have of the conclusion that is deduced in the following operation: $97 \times 58 = 5626$. It is, to be sure, highly probable that the sun will rise tomorrow, and it would be freak-

* *The Logic of Modern Physics.*

ish for one to act as if the sun were not going to rise tomorrow; but we must recognize that that prediction is a probability which we have come to believe by Induction and that it does not contain the kind of certainty which we may find in any deductive argument.

Deduction gives us conclusions that are certain because these conclusions are nothing more than the implications of our assumptions. Induction, on the other hand, gives conclusions that are only probable. But Deduction is based upon assumptions and rules that are, as much as possible, divorced from experience. It is a study of forms and operations that are deliberately purged of references to the world of sensory perception. (The way this definition developed is the subject of most of the remainder of this chapter.) And Induction, on the other hand, is most intimately associated with experiences and sensory activity. The fundamental steps in the inductive process are observation and experience.

Bertrand Russell discusses the extremes of this relationship as being between facts of experience and pure logic: "In pure logic, no atomic fact [simplest kind of fact we may experience] is ever mentioned: we confine ourselves wholly to forms, without asking ourselves what objects can fill the forms. Thus pure logic is independent of atomic facts; but conversely, they are, in a sense, independent of logic. Pure logic and atomic facts are the two poles, the wholly *a priori* and the wholly empirical. But between the two lies a vast intermediate region. . . ." *

It hardly needs saying, therefore, that the scientist or philosopher or anyone else interested in discovering things about the universe he lives in will find both Inductive and Deductive Reasoning indispensable to his investigations. Deduction enables us to carry out the implications of our assumptions to their fullest extent without being influenced by the often misleading perceptions of our immediate experiences. And Induction is our way of seeing generalizations and categories in the world of our experience. For anyone who would like to look further into this topic, there are a number of excellent books and articles written on the distinction between the two activities, Deduction and

* Bertrand Russell, *Our Knowledge of the External World.* (New York: New American Library, Mentor Books, 1956), p. 49.

Induction, and the relationships they have to each other. A recent work that gives a fully adequate and readable discussion of the matter is *A Philosopher Looks at Science*, by John G. Kemeny.*

Our major interest in this text, of course, will be in deductive systems and, particularly, in logic as a deductive system. But logic will not be the only deductive system discussed. The student will also find, especially in this first chapter, a number of references to various systems of mathematics—particularly geometry. The reason for this is, as one might guess, that following the approach of modern logic and mathematics we will be looking at logic purely as a deductive system and, since geometry is another deductive system, the latter may be used on many occasions to illustrate certain aspects of the former.

B. TRADITIONAL DEDUCTIVE SYSTEMS

What will here be called traditional logic is that system invented by Aristotle in the fourth century B.C. Traditional logic is —using our own terminology—a rigorously developed system of class relationships that depends primarily upon the meanings given to words through language usage. Or, to temper the jargon with a familiar example, traditional logic is a study of the syllogism, which is a formal argument appearing in the following manner:

All men are mortal.
All Greeks are men.
———————————
All Greeks are mortal.

From Aristotle through St. Thomas Aquinas in the thirteenth century up until the nineteenth century,† the syllogistic logic was

* John G. Kemeny, *A Philosopher Looks at Science* (Princeton: D. Van Nostrand Co., Inc., 1959).

† There were logical systems other than the syllogistic system of Aristotle that were introduced during that period. The Megarian and the Stoic logics, for example, were developed almost concurrently with that of Aristotle around the fourth century B.C. But even though these non-Aristotelian systems had certain superiorities to that of Aristotle, syllogistic logic was overwhelmingly the dominant system in the Western world until the late nineteenth century. For a discussion of the power and completeness of the Stoic-Megarian logic, see *Stoic Logic* by Benson Mates (Berkeley: University of California Press, 1961).

the principal system taught in European schools and revered by philosophers as the rational approach to the realities of God's world. There were attempts made—notably by the philosopher Gottfried Wilhelm Leibniz in the seventeenth century—to introduce a more thorough symbolization into our language and thus produce a system that would have more of the characteristics of a mathematical discipline. But the accomplishments made by Leibniz were not enough (even to Leibniz himself) to give serious threat to the logic invented by Aristotle.

In the nineteenth century there appeared a number of developments that may be said to have seriously challenged the concepts of the traditional deductive systems. A new kind of geometry was introduced, for example, that made a considerable impact on the world of mathematics. Although for many years there had been doubts expressed about certain postulates and procedures of Euclidean geometry, Euclid's *Elements* was as well established in the schools as Aristotle's syllogism. Just as Aristotle's logic maintained itself so long as the pre-eminent system of logic, so did Euclid's *Elements* remain the only geometry text to be used in the schools for over two thousand years. And both systems were founded on essentially the same beliefs in the nature of reasoning and of the real world. One finds in both systems the clear implication that the subject matter they are working with and the reasoning that is handling it are realities of nature that may be grasped and manipulated by mind and thought. An axiom of his geometry was true for Euclid because it said something about the very being and structure of the universe. "The whole is equal to the sum of its parts" was a truth founded in the rational structure of matter and revealed to man because he is the only rational animal. And the way in which Euclid's axioms and postulates were associated with one another—the very process of deduction—followed laws of procedure that were conceived as being woven into the cloth of nature, part of the natural and inevitable pattern of the cosmos.

C. MODERN SYSTEMS OF LOGIC AND MATHEMATICS

Beginning in the nineteenth century, this was no longer to be the case for *any* deductive system. What had been axioms or self-evident truths of the traditional systems were now being called assumptions. "Postulate" was being given its literal meaning and applied to *all* the basic affirmations of the standard systems of deduction.

To elaborate on this a bit, let us consider more specifically some aspects of the development of non-Euclidean geometry.

In the earlier part of the nineteenth century Nicholas Lobachevsky, followed later by Bernhard Riemann, challenged one of Euclid's postulates and substituted contrary postulates that were used to construct other geometrical systems. These other systems then were shown to have all the validity and coherence of that of Euclid although they brought up questions that had been almost inconceivable before that time. The new systems that developed out of this action—called, quite naturally, non-Euclidean geometries—were destined to become leading influences in the development of an entirely new concept of the nature of deductive systems.

A basic step in the construction of the original non-Euclidean geometries was that of denying a postulate that was considered to be essential in Euclidean geometry. The "parallel postulate" found in Euclid's system states that through any point outside a given line, one and only one line can be drawn parallel to the given line. That is, there is one distinct line—no more and no less —parallel to line *l* through point *p*.* There had been a number of mathematicians before Lobachevsky who had indicated their suspicions of this postulate—believing that it was not a postulate at all but a theorem that should be proved on the basis of some of the other postulates and axioms. But no one was ever able

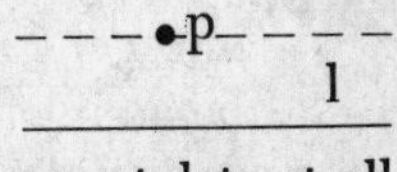

* "Euclid's parallel postulate" is a name commonly given to the fifth postulate of Euclid's *Elements*. In reading the postulate itself we see no mention of parallel lines: ". . . if a straight line falling on two straight lines make the interior angles on the same side less than two right angles, the two straight lines, if produced indefinitely, meet on that side on which are the angles less than two right angles." However, because of the fact that this postulate is the fundamental assumption on which the Euclidean theory of parallels is constructed—the assumption that is needed, for example, to prove the basic theorem that says a transversal cutting two parallel lines will produce equal alternate interior angles—it is common practice to denote Euclid's Postulate Five as the "parallel postulate." (This postulate has appeared through the ages in a number of different forms including the one given above.)

either to find proof for it or to completely remove all doubts as to whether it should be proved or not—that is, whether or not it really was a statement that could be "accepted as true without proof."

Nicholas Lobachevsky, then, was in one sense simply carrying on in the tradition of the skeptical mathematicians of the past when he proposed that *more* than one line, in fact, an infinite number of lines could be drawn through the point *p* that would not intersect line *l*.

If we think of this proposal within the narrow limits of the world immediately available to our senses, it may seem to be little more than mere fantasy. Extending the lines to a great distance, it appears, would make it inevitable that all but *one* of the lines through point *p* would eventually intersect line *l*. But if we let our imaginations roam into the world of unlimited vastnesses and extensions possible in such universal measurements then we become aware of the fact that we actually have no criteria for deciding whether lines with extremely small angles between them would intersect the given line or not. There is nothing in *experience*, we discover, that makes such an idea impossible. Also, if we define "parallel" simply in terms of non-intersection, there is nothing about the definition of the word that would make Lobachevsky's parallel postulate a contradiction.

Whatever the practical case, Lobachevsky proposed that there *could* be additional parallels through *p* and then went on to see whether or not he could build up *another* geometrical system—other than the traditional one of Euclid's—using this new parallel postulate.

And, to the consternation of the traditional mathematicians, he did construct a new geometry that had all the rigor and elegance of Euclid's system even though it contradicted one of the basic "truths" that had for the most part been considered as an indestructible building block on which the immense and immutable edifice of a "true system of thought" had been erected.

Bernhard Riemann at a later time also questioned the Euclidean parallel postulate, but he gave as an alternative the proposal that there are *no* lines that can be drawn through point *p* that would be parallel to line *l*. That is, he began with the proposition that every line through point *p* would eventually intersect line *l*. We can see that if we were standing on a sphere (which, coincidentally enough, we happen to be), then if every line on that sphere were considered to be a segment of a great circle (that is, a line drawn on a plane that passes through the center of the sphere) then, indeed, a line through any given point on the sphere would intersect any other given line on the sphere.

Such an intuitive description might also be given of Lobachevsky's postulate using a rather unusual but well-defined surface called a pseudosphere, which looks something like the diagram on the right.

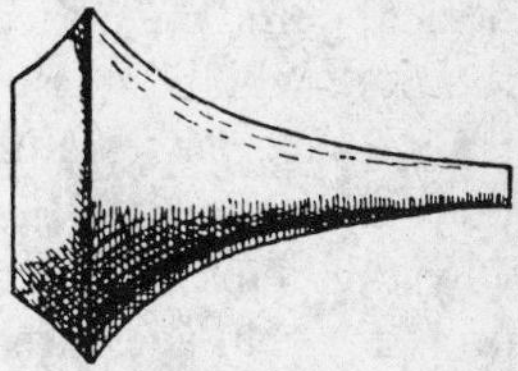

From Roberto Bonola, *Non-Euclidean Geometry*, Dover, 1955.

If the universe itself were formed like a sphere or a pseudosphere, then the geometries of either Riemann or Lobachevsky would be the mathematical system we would use to analyze characteristics of the universal space. And, considering the immensity of the universe and the vast measurements with which we have not the slightest familiarity, we should not be surprised to find that when Albert Einstein began to work in physics with extreme speeds and distances he discovered that Euclidean geometry—which had always been perfectly adequate for analyzing the limited spaces of our experiences before—was no longer adequate for the analysis of these greater magnitudes. Einstein, in fact, did turn to Riemannian geometry for the mathematical concept that was most useful and meaningful in the problems in theoretical physics that he was investigating.

But to restate our purpose in this discussion: We mean to use the development of non-Euclidean geometry as an illustration of a major point made in the monograph *Axiomatics*, by Robert Blanché.* In the traditional systems the connection between form and content was so close that the division between them was, for the most part, indiscernible. The axioms, definitions, and theorems of traditional logic and mathematics were closely related to "practical knowledge" gained through diagrams and tangible constructions in three-dimensional space. But in the modern logical and mathematical systems, as we have already seen in the discussion of Deduction and Induction, there *is* a clear dis-

* Robert Blanché, *Axiomatics* (New York: The Free Press of Glencoe, 1962).

tinction made between theory on one hand and practice on the other—between abstract reasoning based on the simplest sorts of postulates and symbols (primitive symbols, as they are called), and material facts based upon items of knowledge from our experience.

"A geometrical theorem had always been thought of as at one and the same time a piece of information about things and a mental construction, a law of physics and a part of a logical system, a truth of fact and a truth of reason. From these paradoxical pairs, theoretical geometry nowadays entirely relinquishes the first, which is assigned to applied geometry. There remains, for the theorems, simply truth, separated and so to speak atomic: their truth is solely their integration into the system, and that is why theorems incompatible with one another can both be true, provided that they are related to different systems." *

This modern approach to mathematics and logic was brought about, to some extent, as a result of the attack upon the belief in the certainty, the fundamental truth, and the reality of Euclidean geometry, and the consequent discovery that other mathematical systems could be devised that were just as valid and even as *useful* as the two-thousand-year-old traditional geometric system. Such discoveries led to the formulation of a completely new attitude and orientation in the field of formal deductive systems. Now it is no longer claimed that the postulates and axioms of mathematics and logic are the basic *a priori* truths that give us fundamental facts about the universal space we live in, but that they are, instead, simply assumptions that we make in order to devise a system that will generally prove to be useful in handling some particular aspect of experience that we do not yet understand. Edna Kramer said, in *The Mainstream of Mathematics*,† "For ordinary everyday purposes, the Euclidean system is the simplest, and hence we use it, not because it is the 'absolute' and only truth, but because it makes our work easier. The Riemannian system happens to be the simplest for use in the Einstein theory."

In other words, we may say that another philosophical position is being proposed today with respect to the truths of the axioms and postulates (assumptions) that are used in a mathematical

* Blanché, *op. cit.*, p. 5.

† New York: Oxford University Press, 1952, p. 261.

system. In the classical mathematics, it was supposed that the axioms were basic, irrefutable expressions of something absolute and eternal in nature. Plato considered them to be of the higher level of knowledge of the "real world" that was known by reason alone, and not through observation of the world as given by our senses. (The world we know by sensory perceptions, the world we experience, is according to Plato simply a poor reflection of the real world that may be known by our reason. There is only one kind of knowledge, he said, and that is knowledge of the absolutes. Information given by our senses can be really understood only by referring to that *unique* set of truths that may be revealed by reason.) The axiomatic system of Euclid was, for over two thousand years, considered to be the epitome of knowable truths. "As certain as Euclid" was a phrase that was used, and one of the motivating hopes of philosophical and scientific research was that other knowledge could be achieved in the worlds of physics, politics, and ethics that would be as certain and as secure as that which was contained in Euclidean geometry.

The attitude of logicians who follow the nineteenth century, on the other hand, is one that rejects the immutability and eternality of the axioms and postulates that are used in a mathematical system. It is still the case, of course, that these fundamental statements are taken as the necessary basics for the development of any system. But now they are called assumptions instead of axioms (accepted premises, rather than self-evident truths), and their truth, in the mathematical sense, is solely a matter of their meanings within a given system—the theorems that may be produced by carrying out their implications through the deductive procedure. "The logical status of the postulates is clear: far from being asserted as truths which are productive of other truths, they are merely adopted as hypotheses for the purpose of deriving some given set of propositions, or in order to find out what consequences are implied by them." * For us they are simply reasonable assumptions—or, better: assumptions for reasoning.

From the classical point of view, there was *one* deductive system that was everlastingly true; and the goal of the mathematician or philosopher was to get some vision of this system

* Blanché, *op. cit.*, p. 27.

and to progress, through modification and correction, to a more and more precise statement of the truths it contained.

From the modern viewpoint, any deductive system is true only insofar as the assumptions are consistent with one another and certain rules of operation are not violated as the implications of the assumptions are investigated.

It must still be remembered, of course, that the first complete system of mathematics was developed and existed for centuries as a system that was actually intimately related to the facts and experiences of the natural world. Euclid made great strides in the direction of a completely formalized system. But that formality was impressed upon a knowledge that was very closely connected to the world of experience. As is frequently pointed out in modern logic and mathematics texts, many of the most fundamental procedures of operation in Euclid's geometry are founded on reference to diagrams and other spatial experiences that are of a purely intuitive character.

The modern method of building rigorous deductive systems therefore, can never be said to have developed "out of whole cloth." The new philosophy of logic and mathematics is the product of innumerable attempts over long periods of time to give the traditional systems greater rigor and consistency. But the traditional systems themselves were first firmly established in the mind of man by reference to intuitive understandings and facts of experience, and the development of reference to pure deduction and abstract reasoning, isolated as much as possible from experience, was something that came after there was already some system to work on.

In consideration of such facts it would be reasonable to conclude that in the teaching of the new system to students yet unfamiliar with terminology and procedures, it may be well to pay some attention to the history of deductive systems as we look for the procedure that will serve us best in presenting the new logic to the student who knows nothing about it. That is, it may make the learning easier and the grasp of the system eventually more profound if we should begin with a great deal of reference to intuitive understandings that come from our everyday use of the language and from manipulations of things in our environment, and go from there, then, to a greater rigor that becomes more and more demanding as the text progresses. When the stage is thus set and the student is ready we may then be able to introduce a strict and rigorous deductive system without so severely shocking him that he finds himself transfixed before an eerie world of vacant symbols, mechanical procedures of operation, and empty theorems wrought by tedious mental gymnastics.

It is our hope that by the time the student reaches the unit on rigorous deductive systems he will have enough training in and familiarity with the new ideas and vocabulary to be able to involve and enjoy himself in the development of a neat, complete, coherent, and self-sustaining deductive system of logic.

In this culmination of our efforts we will be, in effect, axiomatizing a system that has been accepted in an intuitive way already. That is, we will be searching for the axioms—assumptions or presuppositions—that underlie the entire system. We will look for the fundamental propositions that are the foundations on which our deductive systems are constructed.

D. AXIOMATIZATION

The question as to why we want to axiomatize a system at all is answered in a quote from L. Susan Stebbing: "Abstraction is necessary to ensure generality." It appears that when a system is separated from the world of intuition and experience—when it is developed with only the bare minimum of reference to the simplest of intuitive concepts—it thereby gains a maximum of general applicability. The smaller the number of so-called self-evident truths that are used (what we now more carefully call assumptions), the greater the possible application of the completed system to the things of an empirical world. When we start with nothing but a few brief assumptions, the system we develop out of these assumptions has application to a wider variety of independent experimental studies: physics, astronomy, chemistry, biology, and even psychology.*

---

* Books that may be referred to for illustrations of the point made here are: Thomas Bartee, *Digital Computer Fundamentals* (New York: McGraw-Hill Book Co., Inc., 1960); Samuel Goldberg, *Probability: An Introduction* (Englewood Cliffs, N. J.: Prentice-Hall, Inc., 1960); Kemeny, Snell, and Thompson, *Introduction to Finite Mathematics* (Englewood Cliffs, N. J.: Prentice-Hall, Inc., 1956); J. Eldon Whitesitt, *Boolean Algebra and Its Applications* (Reading, Mass.: Addison-Wesley Publishing Co., 1961).

Therefore, even though the original system may come to us as quite acceptable and complete because of its relationships to our own experiences and our intuitive understandings, we can make it relate to *more* areas of our experience by, paradoxically enough, detaching the system from experimental knowledge as much as possible—that is, by minimizing our references to experience and concentrating on reason alone.

To take another quotation from Alfred North Whitehead: "Nothing," he said, "is more impressive than the fact that as mathematics withdrew increasingly into the upper regions of ever greater extremes of abstract thought, it returned back to earth with a corresponding growth of importance for the analysis of concrete fact." *

In the last part of this text will be found a chapter devoted to the application of an abstract deductive system to the world of practical experience. In that chapter we are using a system called the Calculus of Classes—or Boolean Algebra—to handle problems that appear for the electrician and the computer technician as they couple switches together in an electrical circuit.

The deductive system that is used in the chapter devoted to application is a system that will appear in its first presentation, in Chapter 2, as an essentially intuitive discipline closely related to and connected with matters of our daily experience. This discipline—the study of sets—will be presented with very *little* rigor and a great deal of reference to ordinary language and everyday experiences. But in the second part of Chapter 4 we will give an axiomatization of the system of sets and thus formalize it to such an extent that it will be ready for application to many areas of experience and particularly those that demand a tight system of logic or mathematics.

---

* A. N. Whitehead, *Science and the Modern World.*

2

Sets and Syllogisms

As with any other concept of mathematics or logic, the concept of a set appears most meaningful when considered with respect to things of everyday experience. If we should speak of the set of **all zyzyx**, which is composed of arf, bog, and fleegle, we could, as logicians, work with this and other sets of similar nature with perfect consistency and even a kind of understanding. But a more meaningful set for the unindoctrinated would be, say, the set of **all red-headed male students in Bakersfield College**. This is a meaningful, comprehensible, and determinable set for anyone who wants to take the trouble to carry out an investigation. For anyone who knows English, the set of **all major vowels in the English alphabet** is an understandable and determinable set (*a*,*e*, *i*,*o*,*u*); and for those who know simple arithmetic, the set of **all positive integers less than four** may be indicated by naming its members (1,2,3).

We consider things in terms of sets in one way or another throughout our daily life. But we do not generally describe these sets with any attempt at rigor or over-all consistency. The set of **all movie stars** we may intuitively reduce to the set of **all male movie stars**, the set of **all female movie stars**, and then, perhaps, **the set of all dog movie stars**. But this latter set may introduce for us the problem of distinguishing between male and female dog stars and we then realize that the set of **all female movie stars** may be too gross a definition for our purposes. It rarely happens, however, that at this juncture we retrace our steps and carefully correct our definitions so that we can be rigorously precise and accurate in our denotations of the sets we want to use. More than likely the problem is taken care of with "You know what I mean."

But the mathematician, the scientist, the logician, the computer-programmer cannot depend on such a simple solution. It is, in fact, just that problem of the machine *not* knowing what you mean that makes it necessary to develop a language of sets that may be used in a rigorous examination of the relations between given sets and in the communication between man and machine for the solving of problems concerning sets.

Therefore, for those reasons and for many others that will appear as we go further through the text, we are going to introduce here some of the basic concepts, terms, and operational procedures that have been devised for the manipulation of class or set symbols. If at times it appears that we are being unnecessarily careful in our definitions, it might make it easier to imagine that we are trying to stay at least one step ahead of a fantastically complex machine that obeys our instructions *to the letter* and must, therefore, be given instructions that are meaningful to the letter.

A. THE SET

Any collection of objects that have some property common to all of them can be defined as a set. Examples already mentioned are the set of major vowels and the set of positive integers less than four.

The concept of a set is such a normal one that its very simplicity may be responsible for some of the confusion in the minds of those who are first introduced to the idea. When one says, "my family," for example, he is generally considering a group of individuals that make up a specific set. If "immediate family" is implicit in his statement, then he might describe the set as consisting of his father, his mother, and whatever siblings he might have. Then, if he were asked to clarify the point a little further, he might also admit that *he* belonged to the set, my family; and a complete collection of individuals all being within a defined group (or having a common characteristic) would then have been denoted by one title.

The first-string members of the college football team can all be taken together as a set composed of eleven individuals. The planets of our solar system make a set of nine individuals. And (as we will soon see it is useful to say) all the present Presidents of the United States is a set composed of one individual.

B. SET NOTATION

Each of those sets mentioned may then be given a symbol so that it can be manipulated in a regular mathematical fashion. We might, for example, say my family would be denoted as the set F;

the football team as *T;* and **the planets of the solar system** as *P*. We would then be ready to use these sets in any formal system that may be devised.

1. UNION AND INTERSECTION. The simple function of denoting the sets is not enough. We also find it useful to be able to combine the sets with various interrelationships. If, for example, we define a Set *A* as **all college students,** Set *B* as **all football players,** and Set *P* as **all people over 21 years of age;** then we want to be able to combine these sets in a way that will enable us to denote other sets like **all football players over 21 years of age, all college students and people over 21 years of age, all college football players,** and the like.

Such additional sets *can* be indicated through the use of two concepts represented by two simple symbols. The concepts are Union and Intersection, and the symbols are $\cup$ and $\cap$, respectively.*

In normal conversation we speak of cars and we speak of donkeys. We might, for example, speak of **those students who own cars** (thereby designating a particular set, *C*), and of **those students who own donkeys** (another set, *D*). But we might also speak of **those students who own cars or those students who own donkeys**—thereby denoting a third set which is simply a combination of the first two. Any student who owns either a car or a donkey *or both* is a member of the third set. And the idea expressed in this case is exactly the idea of the Union of the two sets. When we bring

---

* A comment must be made here about terminology and symbol usage that should be remembered and referred back to later on in the text as the issues get more complicated. There is as yet no generally accepted, standard notation that the student may expect to find in use throughout all logic texts. Even within the same text it is often necessary to use two or three different symbols for the same concept in order to keep the material in line with developments that have taken place in special aspects of the subject of logic. The following table, then, is introduced to show other common ways of indicating Union and Intersection—or, as some would have it: class sums and class products.

Given two sets, *a* and *b:*

Union	$a \cup b$	$a + b$	$a \vee b$	
Intersection	$a \cap b$	$a \times b$	$a \cdot b$	ab

Further comments on kinds of notation will be made as additional symbols are introduced.

the two sets, Set *C* and Set *D*, together in Union, we mean to designate all the things or people or elements that are in *C* *or* in *D* *or* in both. This new set, then, is indicated by $C \cup D$.

Similarly, we may speak of a set consisting of *just* those students who own cars *and* donkeys, that is, students who own a car and a donkey. A student to be a member of this set must own both; and this is the set we say is formed by the Intersection of the two given sets. This set will be designated as $C \cap D$.

Consider carefully this aspect of what we are doing here: two sets are given by designating some particular description an individual must fulfill in order to belong to each set (those students in Set *C* are those who own a car, those in Set *D* own a donkey); then two *additional* sets are formed by combining the given sets in two ways (car *or* donkey, car *and* donkey)—each way carefully described to stand for a particular kind of combination.

Let us take a few more examples. If *A* is the set of all vowels and *B* is the set composed only of the letters a through e, what is the set $A \cup B$? This set would consist of all the vowels {a,e,i,o,u} *plus* the given letters {a,b,c,d,e}, or, noted as a single set, {a,b,c,d, e,i,o,u}. (Once we've named the vowels *a* and *e* we don't have to mention them again, of course.) How about $A \cap B$? This would be composed of *just* those letters that are in *A* *and* in *B*, or {a,e}.*

Given Set *G* {Lynn, Brian, Cheryl, Tim} and Set *H* {Lynn, Cheryl, Donna, Melinda}. Then Set $G \cup H$ is {Lynn, Brian, Cheryl, Tim, Donna, Melinda} and $G \cap H$ is {Lynn, Cheryl}.

Suppose Set *A* is all integers 1 through 7, and Set *B* is all even integers 4 through 9. What, then, is $A \cup B$? $A \cap B$?

One way of designating a set without simply listing all its members (and this is particularly useful in mathematics) is to use braces and a vertical bar to describe everything (all *x*) having some *particular* quality. For example, $\{x \mid x^2 = 25\}$ would be read "The set of all x such that x^2 equals 25," which is, of course, the set {5, −5}. The *x* before the bar simply tells you to consider everything in the universe (in this particular case, all numbers in the universe) and the $x^2 = 25$ says to pick out of this universe just those numbers which, when squared, will give 25. $\{x \mid 1 < x < 5,$

---

* Braces { } are being used here to include all the elements and only those elements that are assigned to the given set.

x is an integer} is read, "The set of all x such that x is greater than 1 and less than 5 and x is an integer," which is {2,3,4}. Likewise, {x | x is a prime number less than 8} would be {1,2,3,5,7}.

2. UNIVERSAL SET. It may have been noticed in the last section that when we wanted to speak of a set we would do something to give limitations to the things we were considering as possible members of the sets. In one case it was clear that we were speaking of different kinds of college students; in another case, of the letters in the alphabet; and in another, of numbers.

If one is to use the set concept with care and rigor, it is generally necessary to specify the things or elements that are within the realm of consideration for the sets being defined, that is to give our area, range, or Universe of Discourse.

In our first two examples, our Universe of Discourse was {x | x is a college student}; the other Universes might have been said to be {x | x is a letter of the English alphabet} and {x | x is a real number}.

It is not always the case that a *limited* Universe of Discourse is designated. Sometimes the expression {x | fx} is used and "For *all* *x* . . ." is given literal meaning; as some philosophers claim it is meaningful to say, "Everything is matter," or "For all *x*, *x* is matter." But for most of our purposes when we want to speak of a set of some kind, we will want not only to designate those things that *do* belong to the set, but also to make it possible and meaningful to say something about those elements that are not members of the set. That is, we specify a Universe of Discourse so that when we say, "Set *a*," we are indicating one particular area in a given space—which might be represented as in the diagram.

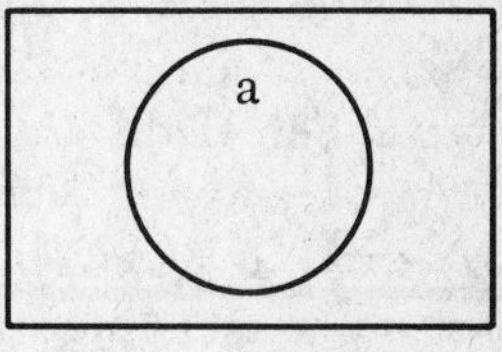

Then those things outside the circle (but in the rectangle) will be things that are not in *a*. The rectangle itself will stand for the Universe of Discourse or all those elements being considered as we begin defining our sets.

The definition of a set implies a Universe of which that set is a part. If the Universe is not defined, then we take it to be the Universe of all things. Otherwise, we positively describe our Universe as all integers, all letters of the English alphabet, and so forth.

3. NEGATION. Since it will be useful, as will soon become apparent, to be able to speak of those things *not* in *a* as well as those things that *are* in *a*, we will designate not-*a* as a set in itself; that is, *a*′.*

Under these conditions, the Universe of Discourse may be given as the entire universe of all things or it may be defined as consisting only of college students, or real numbers, or men who have taken the oath of office of President of the United States of America. (If it is not perfectly clear exactly what the Universe is, then it must be made clear by specifically defining its scope—by asserting what area the Universe is supposed to cover.)

The negations of a set within the Universe will then indicate entities corresponding to whatever limits we have established. Suppose we say our Universe of Discourse is men who have taken the oath of office of President of the United States of America. For the sake of brevity we will call members of this Universal Set "United States Presidents." Now let us define Set *A* within this Universe as consisting of all United States Presidents who took the oath of office after the year 1860. Then not-*A*, or *A*′, is seen immediately to be all United States Presidents who took the oath of office before the year 1860. Set *A* would include all Presidents from Abraham Lincoln through the one serving today, and Set *A*′ would include all presidents from George Washington through James Buchanan.

If we said our Universe of Discourse was $\{x \mid x$ is a positive integer$\}$, and Set *A* was composed of positive integers from 1 through 10, or $\{x \mid 1 \leqq x \leqq 10$, x is an integer$\}$; then Set *A*′ will be all positive integers except those from 1 through 10, or $\{x \mid x > 10$, x is an integer$\}$.

Sometimes it is useful to mention the Universe of Discourse itself as a set, and this is called, appropriately enough, the Universal Set. If the Universe was $\{x \mid 1 \leqq x \leqq 10$, x an integer$\}$, if Set *A* was $\{x \mid 1 \leqq x \leqq 5$, x an integer$\}$, and if Set *B* was $\{x \mid 6 \leqq x \leqq 10$, x an integer$\}$, then the Union of *A* and *B*, $A \cup B$, would be all integers 1 through 10, or the Universal Set. The Universal Set will be denoted here by the symbol "1"; thus in the above, $A \cup B = 1$.

4. NULL SET. Another set that finds a use in modern logic is the Null Set or Empty Set, which is designated by the symbol

* Other designations for not-*a* commonly in use are: $\bar{a}$, $-a$, $\sim a$.

"0." This set, as the name implies, is the set that has no members. But the introduction of a kind of set that has no members calls for a modification of the description of a set given on p. 18. At this point, about the best we could do is to redefine a set as being, let us say, a categorical description given to one element or a collection of elements, or a categorical description that refers to no elements whatsoever. It may be seen here, however, that the difficulties inherent in giving such a definition might make it better simply to avoid the attempt at a definition at all and leave the word "set" as a basic and undefined term, and depend upon the illustrations we have given to make its meaning intuitively clear.

Although it may not be immediately apparent how a set with no members can be useful in logic, the student is asked to bear with us for a while with the assurance that uses will begin to appear as more operations are developed and explained. Some examples of the Empty Set could be the set **all bathing beauties on the moon**, or **all right-wing supporters of the Liberal candidates**, or **all numbers that are both greater than 5 and less than 3.**

If Set A is $\{x \mid 1 \leqq x \leqq 4\}$ and if Set B is the collection $\{x \mid 6 \leqq x \leqq 9\}$, then the Intersection of A and B would be the Empty Set. Symbolically, $A \cap B = 0$.

Using the foregoing terminology, it may now be seen that the set $A \cap A'$ is the Empty Set, or $A \cap A' = 0$, and the set $A \cup A'$ is the Universal Set, or $A \cup A' = 1$.*

Let us look at some illustrations of the use of the Universal Set and the Null Set. Suppose we denote a Universe as follows:

$$1 = \{x \mid 1 \leqq x \leqq 9, x \text{ is an integer}\}$$

We may also denote that Universe by listing rather than describing its elements:

$$1 = \{1,2,3,4,5,6,7,8,9\}$$

We may, then, consider certain sets within this Universe as follows:

---

* The Null, or Empty, Set is an invention of modern logic and is not found at all in traditional logic. This fact will be the cause of several problems of reconciliation between the two that will begin to become apparent in Section C of this chapter.

$A = \{1,2,3,4,9\}$	Listing
$B = \{x \mid \sqrt{x} = 2\}$	Description
$C = \{x \mid x \geqq 5\}$	Description
$D = \{1,3,5,7,9\}$	Listing
$D = \{x \mid x \text{ is an odd number}\}$	Description

$A \cup C$ may be determined from the above first by listing the elements of C: $\{5,6,7,8,9\}$, and then by denoting that set which is composed of elements in either A or C or both: $\{1,2,3,4,5,6,7,8,9\}$. This, we see, is the Universal Set and may be indicated as such: $A \cup C = 1$.

The use of the symbol "1" to stand for the Universal Set could, perhaps, cause confusion if care were not taken to distinguish clearly between the use of that symbol as denoting a number—a number that may be an element in one of our sets—and its use to denote the Universe out of which the sets are taken.

In this book, whenever the symbol "1" is found standing alone we will consider it to be referring to the Universal Set or a Universe of Discourse. The symbol "1" used as an element of a set, on the other hand, will always be found contained within braces. It is possible for us to say then that our Universal Set has three elements in it indicated as follows: $1 = \{-1,0,1\}$.

The symbols "1" and "0" within braces indicate elements of the Universal Set, and there should be no confusion between that usage and the one wherein they stand for the Universal and Null Sets respectively.

Returning to the previous example, suppose we take the Intersection of Sets B and C, or $B \cap C$. The elements in C, we said, are $\{5,6,7,8,9\}$; and we may see there is only one element in B, that is, $\{4\}$. (B is a Unit Set.) So the Intersection of B and C is the Null Set. $B \cap C = 0$.

The student may consider also the following relationships of any given set to the Null Set and the Universal Set:

$$a \cap 0 = 0$$
$$a \cup 0 = a$$
$$a \cap 1 = a$$
$$a \cup 1 = 1$$

Set a may be supposed to have some finite number of elements in it as an aid in recognizing the validity of the Unions and Intersections given above.

5. VENN DIAGRAMS. John Venn is another figure of the nineteenth century who played a role in the development of modern logic. Our concern with his work here will be directed towards the diagrams he used to explain his logic problems. As we were doing on p. 21, he used circles to indicate sets and a rectangle for the Universe of Discourse. In his diagrams, however, the sets would be drawn overlapping one another to show all possible combinations that might take place between them. Three sets, *a*, *b*, and *c*, would be indicated as below:

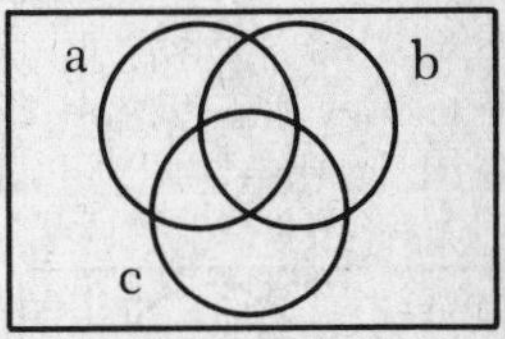

In this manner Venn could visually illustrate combinations of *a* and *b*; *b* and *c*; *a* and *c*; *a*, *b*, and *c*; and each of these with the Universe apart from the other sets.

The Venn Diagrams will be used along with the symbolic notation that has been introduced to give a picture of the operations that we will be performing with sets.

a. Shading Method. To picture Union between two sets, say Set *a* and Set *b*, we want to use the Venn Diagrams to show the area within the Universe that is denoted by $a \cup b$. This means the area that takes in all those things that are either in *a* or in *b* or in both *a* and *b*. Using shading to denote this area, the Venn Diagram would appear as on the left below.

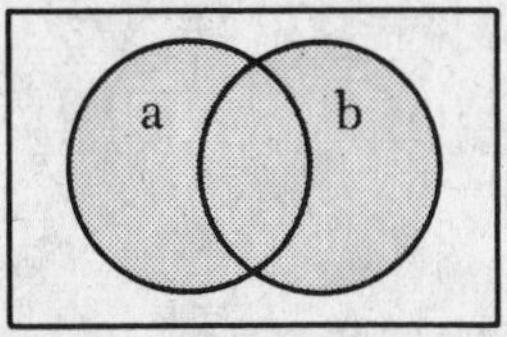

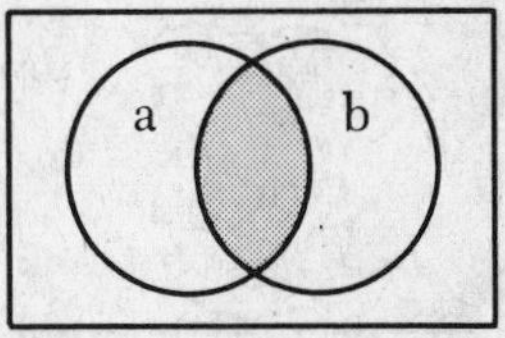

Thus $a \cup b$ is the entire area included within the two circles and represents all elements (if indeed there *are* any) that are in *a* or in *b* or in both *a* and *b*.

The Intersection of *a* and *b*, or $a \cap b$, is just that area composed of things which are both in *a* and in *b*. The Venn Diagram for Intersection is shown on the right above.

Three sets brought together in Union, that is $a \cup b \cup c$, would be indicated in the diagram on p. 26 (top left).

Anything that is either in *a* or in *b* or in *c* or in any combination of these three sets may be said to be an element of the set $a \cup b \cup c$.

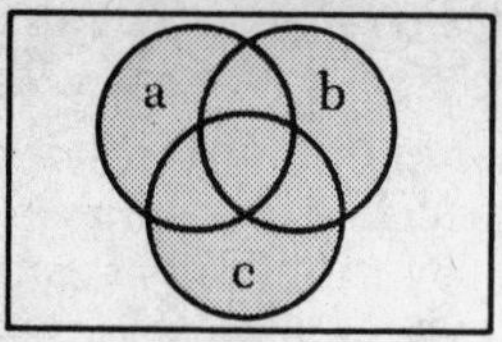

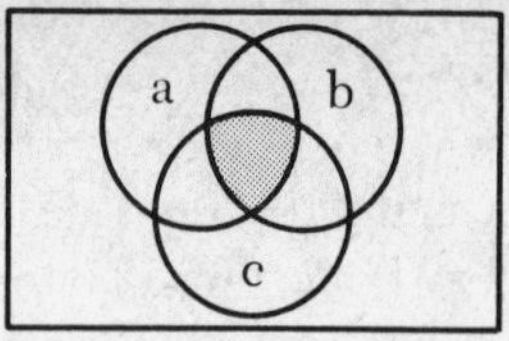

The Intersection of the three sets, $a \cap b \cap c$, is diagrammed above on the right. This shows that only those elements, each of which belong to all three sets, are members of $a \cap b \cap c$.

There are, of course, complications that may be introduced into this system of set combinations. For example, we might consider the Union of two sets and this Union in Intersection with a third set. That is, $(a \cup b) \cap c$. Or, again, we may be looking for the set $(a \cap b) \cup c'$.

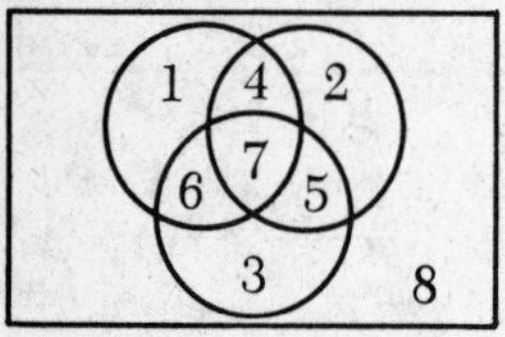

b. Area Numbers. To help in the definition of these areas, we will assign numbers to each part of a three-circle Venn Diagram as on the left.

$a \cup b$ may now be seen to be the area (1,2,4,5,6,7), c is the area (3,5,6,7), and $(a \cup b) \cap c$ is the area (5,6,7)—picking out the numbers common to the sets $a \cup b$ and c. The diagram used to indicate this set is on the left below.

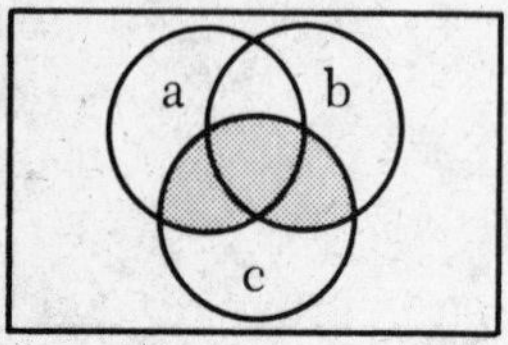

$(a \cup b) \cap c$

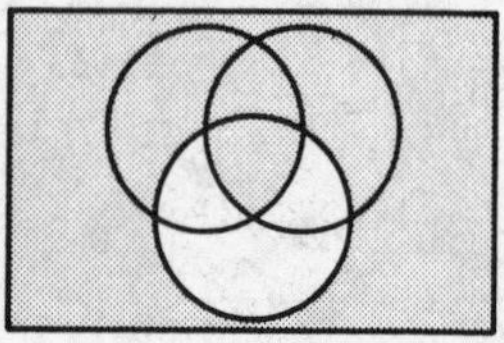

$(a \cap b) \cup c'$

The set $(a \cap b) \cup c'$ may be handled in the same way. $a \cap b$ is the set (4,7), c' is (1,2,4,8), and the Union of these two sets is (1,2,4,7,8). This latter set, then, would be pictured by Venn Diagrams as on the right above.

It may be well to call attention to the fact that the numbers are used only to designate the areas we are referring to; they tell us nothing about the elements that may be included in those areas. Suppose, for example, we were dividing the first string of the football team into groups or sets such as Set A, those players weighing over 200 pounds, Set B, those players over six feet tall, and Set C, **those players who are married.** Then the Universal Set would have exactly eleven members in it, although the number designation for the Universal Set would still be (1,2,3,4,5,6,7,8). $A \cap B$ might have five members, although the number designation would be (4,7). The Venn Diagram is a picture, or graph; the number designation tells us what part of the picture illustrates the set being considered.

On p. 24 we recognized the possible confusion between the usage of the symbols "1" and "0" as Universal Set and Null Set on the one hand or elements in a set on the other. And here, with area numbers, we have a third possible use for the symbol "1"—that is, to designate the space $a \cap b' \cap c'$. In this case, when we want "1" to stand for an area number it will always be enclosed within parentheses. So in a Universe, 1, we may have an element {1} in the space (1) of a Venn Diagram—each symbol representing a different concept.

The Venn Diagrams and the number designation system may be seen to be useful in determining certain properties of relationship between complex collections of sets. For example, if we wish to know whether or not $a \cup (b \cap c)$ is the same set as $(a \cup b) \cap (a \cup c)$, we find the area numbers for the first set: $a =$ (1,4,6,7); $b \cap c =$ (5,7); $a \cup (b \cap c) =$ (1,4,5,6,7).

Then we find the area numbers for the second set: $a \cup b =$ (1,2,4,5,6,7); $a \cup c =$ (1,3,4,5,6,7); $(a \cup b) \cap (a \cup c) =$ (1,4, 5,6,7).

By this simplified and intuitive method we can show that those sets are identical to one another. The question here may have been put in ordinary language as follows: Is the set composed of **antelopes, or bears and chickens** the same set as **antelopes or bears, and antelopes or chickens?**

Taking another example, does $(a \cup b)'$ equal $a' \cap b'$?

$$a \cup b = (1,2,4,5,6,7)$$
$$(a \cup b)' = (3,8). \qquad \text{The first set.}$$

$$a' = (2,3,5,8)$$
$$b' = (1,3,6,8)$$
$$a' \cap b' = (3,8) \qquad \text{The second set.}$$

Again, the two given sets are shown to be identical to one another. In this case the question might have been: Is the set composed of **those people who are not athletes or Boy Scouts** the same as that composed of **those who are not athletes and those who are not Boy Scouts?**

Let us go over this material on Venn Diagrams and the area numbers and consider again its purpose. It has been introduced as a way of handling both general and particular problems relating to sets.

If we want to show the general relationships of one, two, or three sets to each other and to the Universe, we draw a Venn Diagram to indicate all possible areas wherein they may (and where they may not) share common elements. When we shade in some given complex set, e.g., $(a \cap b) \cup c'$ we give a precise description of the area wherein there may be elements: in a but not in a and c unless also in b; not in c alone; and so forth. We do not have to know anything about the specific elements in the individual sets to make this general picture of the way elements in the sets *may* be related.

The number designation system is used in the Venn Diagrams only to simplify our procedures of shading. Without the number system we would be forced into the use of some cumbersome methods such as, for example, shading in one area in one diagram and another area in another diagram, then drawing a third diagram to produce a shaded area that is the combination of the first two. But the number system gives us the simple approach of matching numbers between designated sets and using the final group of numbers to designate the areas to be shaded in.

If it is simply the case of determining equivalent sets, of course, the shading step need not even be taken.

After a complex set has been indicated by the Shading Method, it is an easy task to use it for finding out information about particular elements. Suppose, for example, we want to describe a particular kind of television program. Let us say we wish to isolate that set of programs that have the following characteristics:

> **Those that are entertaining and those that are either not violent or have redeeming educational features.**

We symbolize this set as $E \cap (V' \cup R)$.

Using the number designation system we find the area of the Venn Diagram that will picture this set:

$$E \cap (V' \cup R)$$
$$(1,4,6,7,) \cap ((1,3,6,8) \cup (3,5,6,7))$$
$$(1,4,6,7,) \cap (1,3,5,6,7,8)$$
$$(1,6,7)$$

The diagram is a picture of the set designated by the area numbers (1,6,7).

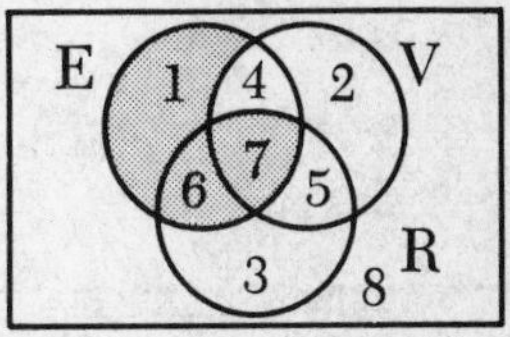

The diagram may now be used to answer questions such as, "If a program is violent what specific additional characteristics must it have to be included in our complex set?" We see in answer to this that (7) is the only shaded area within the *V* circle, which means the program must be, in addition, both entertaining and educational. We may see also by area (3) that even those programs with educational features are not included if they are not entertaining. And entertaining programs that are violent and not educational are not included, as is shown by the blank space of area (4).

We have here a specific example of the way in which Venn Diagrams and the number designation system may be used to show how relationships between particular, named sets may be better understood.

This system of shading a Venn Diagram helps us to gain accuracy and precision in the use of our language. Not only have we become better able to say exactly what we mean but we are now also able to *discover* exactly what it is we are saying—by tracing the necessary implications through our diagrams.

In our final example let us become even more particular in our determination of sets by naming precisely the elements that belong to each set we use.

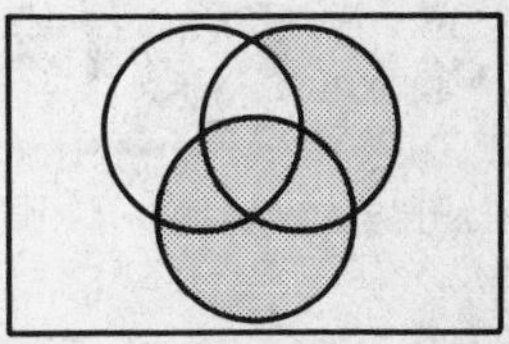

Given the Venn Diagram for $(a' \cap b) \cup c$, we may work out the following area designation:

$$a' = (2,3,5,8)$$
$$a' \cap b = (2,5)$$
$$(a' \cap b) \cup c = (2,3,5,6,7)$$

Let us see how this would work with actual elements by supposing our universe to be the following people (who may be the students in a small logic class):

$1 =$ {Earl, Frank, Gloria, Harriet, Inez, Jean, Ken, Lee, Mat, Nancy, Pete, Rosemary, Sam}

These people may be considered as belonging to three sets in the universe and distributed in their membership as follows:

Artists: {Earl, Frank, Gloria, Nancy}
Band Members: {Gloria, Harriet, Inez, Jean, Ken, Lee}
Choir: {Ken, Lee, Mat, Nancy}

Entering the initials of their names on a Venn Diagram to picture this distribution, we produce the figure given below.

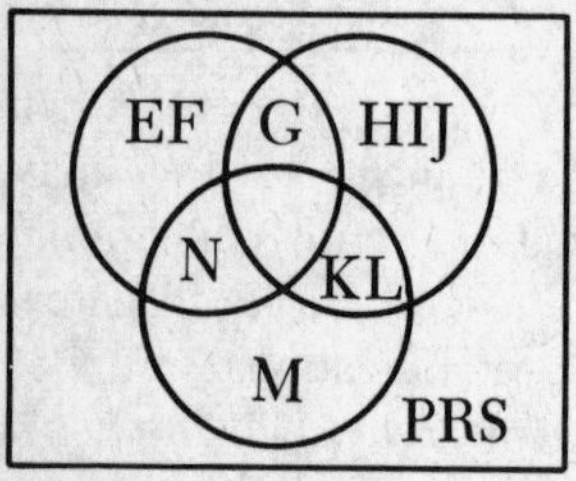

Now if we are asked to find those people in the band who are not artists or those people who are in the choir, we know we want the set $(A' \cap B) \cup C$, which will be, as we determined above, (2,3,5,6,7). Listing the elements in this area, we have {H,I,J,K,L,M,N}. If, on the other hand, we wanted those who are not both artists and choir members plus those band members who are in the choir, our set would be $(A \cap C)' \cup (B \cap C)$. The members of this set are found in the following manner:

$$(A \cap C) = (6,7)$$
$$(A \cap C)' = (1,2,3,4,5,8)$$
$$(B \cap C) = (5,7)$$
$$(A \cap C)' \cup (B \cap C) = (1,2,3,4,5,7,8)$$

This set, then, would include everyone but Nancy, who is listed in area (6).

c. Elimination Method. In work introduced in the next section we will find another system of diagramming to be more useful than the Shading Method. It may be explained as follows:

Instead of using the positive approach of the Shading Method—instead, that is, of shading in those areas of the Venn Diagram that have or may have members—the Elimination Method directs our attention to those areas that do *not* or can *not* have elements in them by *crossing out* the space referred to. By this system we denote a space in the Venn Diagram that *must necessarily* be empty of elements. In using this method we are concerned with statements such as $a \cap b = 0$, which may be given as "The Intersection of a and b is empty." We will diagram such a statement by crossing out the intersection of a and b with horizontal lines.

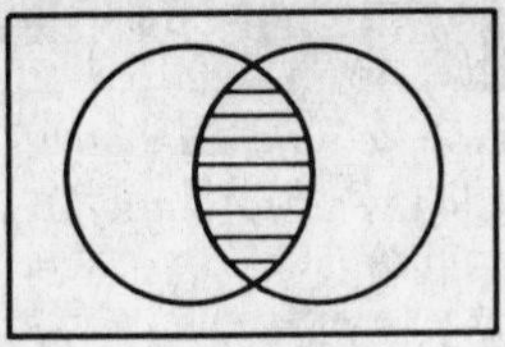

$a \cap b = 0$

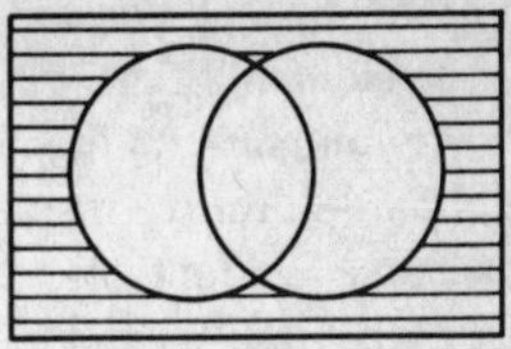

$a' \cap b' = 0$

For another example, consider the expression $a' \cap b' = 0$. The intersection of a' and b' is the area outside the two circles. The horizontal lines, then, indicate that that area is empty.

It may be helpful to consider particular cases of such combinations. If we wanted to symbolize the statement, "No beatniks are executives," we could first restate it in the form, "The Intersection of the two sets, **beatniks** and **executives**, is an Empty Class," and express it in symbols, then, as $B \cap E = 0$. Given the rather unusual statement, "No non-Martians are not Earthmen," this could be restated as, "The Intersection of the set **non-Martians** with the set **non-Earthmen** is empty," and this would be symbolized as $M' \cap E' = 0$.

The difference between the two methods should be carefully considered: By the Shading Method we mark on the Venn Diagrams those areas that have or may have elements in them—we give positive indications concerning the membership of a set. The Elimination Method, on the other hand, tells us specifically only which sets do *not* have elements. Whether or not there are any elements at all that exist outside the set being eliminated is not brought into question.

6. SUMMARY. Through an examination of examples it was seen that a set may be said to be a collection of items (elements, members, units, individuals) wherein one distinct property or characteristic is recognized as being common to all these items. It is a group of individuals that are seen *as* a group by specifying some property common to all of them. (Or, in the case of the Null or Empty Set, it is a categorical description that refers to no elements whatsoever.)

Whenever the particular members or elements of a set are named or listed, braces are used to indicate the fact that they are all the members and the only members of that given set. A common mathematical usage is that of braces and a vertical bar to describe a property or properties of elements of a given set.

The Universe of Discourse is that group or species or kind of things or elements that we limit ourselves to in defining our sets. It may be all numbers or all animals or all celestial bodies or all of any definable group. In speaking specifically of sets, the Universe of Discourse is identical to the Universal Set.

Specifying our Universe in this manner allows us to consider the negation of a set, or just those elements that are *not* in a set we have designated. The negation of a set a, that is, not-a, is symbolized a'.* The Empty Set is that set with no elements or members. A set in Union with its negation is equal to the Universal Set. A set in Intersection with its negation is equal to the Empty Set.

The Venn Diagram is a picture of the relationship of a set or sets to each other and to the Universe of Discourse. Sets in Union or Intersection may be pictured by shading representative areas of a Venn Diagram. The number designation is a system used to denote the areas of the Venn Diagram referred to by the set symbols. The Elimination Method, as opposed to the Shading Method, eliminates (with horizontal lines) a designated set that is specifically described as having no members.

The basic ideas of sets that have been introduced will now be used in the discussion of the syllogism of traditional logic. The concepts and terminology of sets were not in any way a part of traditional logic, but the simplifications involved in the ideas of a set language should help to give a broader and more meaningful picture of traditional logic to someone of modern temper and education, while at the same time modifications of traditional logic that have appeared in the last one hundred years are being introduced to bring the system up to date.

---

* The negation of a set is called, in some cases, the Complement of the given set. This term will be used more frequently in the material that comes later in the book.

LOGIC EXERCISES

1. List the members of the following sets:

   A = your parents.

   B = your male parents.

C = all states of the United States that border on the Pacific Ocean.
D = the subjects you are currently studying.
E = all two-digit numbers that can be made with "4" and "5."
F = all positive integers less than 20 that are divisible by 3.

2. Describe the following sets:
   $G = \{2,3,4,5, \ldots ,16\}$
   H = {Roosevelt, Truman, Eisenhower, Kennedy}
   $J = \{2,4,6,8\}$
   K = {The Moon}
   L = {a moon}

3. List the members of the following sets:
   $M = \{x \mid x^2 = 9\}$
   $N = \{x \mid 2 \leqq x \leqq 5, \text{ x is an integer}\}$
   O = {x | x is the president of your college}
   P = {x | x is a planet of our solar system}
   $Q = \{x \mid x^2 - x = 12\}$

4. (a) Given Set R as {1,3,5,7,9} and Set S as {2,3,4,5,6} what is $R \cup S$? $R \cap S$?
   (b) If Set T is all college students, Set W is all football players, and Set X is all people over 21 years of age, describe the sets:
   $T \cup X$ $T \cap X$ $W \cap X$ $T \cup (W \cap X)$

5. Given Set A: Math, Physics, Philosophy, German
   Set B: English, Humanities, Philosophy, French
   Set C: Philosophy, Latin, German, French, Eskimo

   What is the set $(A \cap B) \cap C$?
   $A \cup (B \cap C)$?
   $(A \cup B) \cap C$?
   $A \cap (B \cap C)$?
   $A \cup B \cup C$?

6. Given as the Universe: {Ann, Bob, Charlie, Dianne, Elvis}
   And the following sets: A {Ann, Bob, Charlie, Dianne}
   B {Bob, Charlie, Elvis}
   C {Ann, Dianne}

   List the sets:
   $A \cup B$ $A \cap B$ $B \cap C$ $A' \cup C$ $C' \cup B$ $C' \cap B$

7.

Student	Age	Height	Sex	Class	Party
v	22+	6′1″	m	soph.	Demo.
w	19+	5′2″	f	soph.	Rep.
x	14+	5′5″	m	soph.	Rep.
y	20+	5′6″	f	fresh.	Demo.
z	48+	6′5″	f	lifer	Bull-Moose

Using the chart above and given the following sets:

A: {Students under 21} *D:* {Non-Democrats under 6′ tall}
B: {Students over 21} *E:* {Female Democrats}
C: {Non-Republican females}

Designate the sets indicated below: (Show the sets by using Union and Intersection and list the members of each.)

1) Students who are either over 21 or Non-Republican females.
2) Students who are both under 21 and Non-Democrats under 6′ tall.
3) Students who are not Non-Republican females but who are under 21.
4) Students who are not over 21 but who are Non-Demos. under 6′ tall.
5) All those students who are either not under 21 or who are not Non-Rep. females.

8. Given a Universe composed of all values for x where x is an integer and $2 \leqq x \leqq 7$:

A: $\{x \mid x > 5\}$ B: $\{x \mid x \leqq 4\}$ C: $\{x \mid \sqrt{x}$ is an integer$\}$

List the members of the following sets:

$A \cup B$ $(A \cup B) \cap C$
$A \cup B'$ $(A \cup B) \cap C'$
$C \cup A'$ $B \cup C'$
$A \cap B$ $A' \cap B'$

9. Use Venn Diagrams to show:

$a \cup b$ $a \cap b$ $a' \cup b$
$a' \cap b'$ $(a \cap b)'$ $(a \cap b) \cup a'$

10. Draw a Venn Diagram for each of the following. Use area numbers to define the set indicated.

a) $a \cup (a' \cap b \cap c)$ c) $(a \cap b \cap c) \cup (b \cap a' \cap c')$
b) $(a \cup b') \cap (a' \cup c)$ d) $(a \cap b) \cup (a \cap c) \cup (b \cap c)$

11. Use Venn Diagrams to determine whether the following equations are valid:
a) $a \cap (a \cup b) = a$
b) $a' \cup b' = (a \cap b)'$
c) $a \cup (a' \cap b) = a \cup b$
d) $(a \cup b) \cap (a' \cup c) = (a \cap c) \cup (a' \cap b)$
e) $(a' \cap b') \cup (a' \cap b) \cup (a \cap b') = 1$
f) $(a \cap b)' = a' \cap b'$

12. Use the Elimination Method in giving Venn Diagrams for the following:
a) $(a \cup b) = 0$
b) $(a \cap b) = 0$
c) $(a' \cap b') = 0$
d) $(a' \cup b') = 0$
e) $a' \cap (b' \cup c) = 0$
f) $[b \cap (a \cup c)] \cup (a \cap c) = 0$
g) $a \cap b' = 0$

SET COMBINATIONS

Sport	Minimum Players	Equipment	Place	Type
1. Football	22	Ball	Outdoor	Spectator
2. Poker	2	Cards	Indoor	Participant
3. Golf	1	Clubs, Ball	Outdoor	Participant
4. Spin-the-Bottle	4	Bottle	Indoor	Participant
5. Basketball	10	Ball	Indoor	Spectator
6. Russian Roulette	1	Gun	Indoor	Participant

SETS	ELEMENTS
A = Sports that use a ball.	?
B = Indoor participant sports.	?
C = Sports involving fewer than ten players.	?
D = Outdoor participant sports.	?

Using Union, Intersection, and negation, indicate the following sets symbolically; then list their elements:

13. Sports that use a ball or are indoor participant sports.
14. Indoor participant sports that use a ball.
15. Sports that do not involve fewer than 10 players or that use a ball.
16. Sports that use a ball and are either outdoor participant or indoor participant sports.
17. Either sports that do not use a ball but do involve fewer than ten players or those that are not indoor participant sports, or both.

C. THE SYLLOGISM

The syllogism is the cornerstone of traditional logic. Everything of major importance that Aristotle had to say concerning logic was stated in terms of the syllogism, and it was as a result of the efforts that were made to break away from the restrictions of the syllogism that radical innovations were produced by the founders of Modern Logic. We will, therefore, spend some time in examining a few major items of syllogistic reasoning. The purpose of this examination will be to familiarize the student with certain aspects of the traditional logic: the limited area it covered; the large number of basic principles that had to be accepted; the terms and concepts that were used and, in an appreciable number of cases, are still in use today; and the essential rigor that was involved in the discipline. Also, in this examination the student is expected to exercise his ability in the handling of some of the set theory procedures learned in the last two sections.

It must be clearly understood that the set theory procedures are not a part of traditional logic. These procedures are used here primarily for the purpose of simplifying the presentation of the ideas of syllogistic reasoning and aiding in the analysis of these ideas. The student should always be aware of the distinction between traditional and modern logic. The concepts of set analysis, Venn Diagrams, Null and Universal Sets, and the symbols used in notation are all no more than two hundred years old. The use of syllogisms, as has been said, dates back over two thousand years. Some of the material that has been introduced in the foregoing sections will not be discussed in any further detail until we get to the chapters dealing with the calculus of classes near the latter part of the text.

1. KINDS OF PROPOSITIONS. A standard syllogism is composed of three propositions: a major premise, a minor premise, and a conclusion. The following is a typical syllogism:

All monks are paupers. (Major Premise)
Some saints are monks. (Minor Premise)

Some saints are paupers. (Conclusion)

Each of the propositions in a syllogism may be presented in one of four possible ways:

1) Universal Affirmative, such as the major premise of the example, where *all* of a given class are mentioned.

2) Universal Negative, as in "No monks are paupers," where *all* of a class are *excluded* from some other class.
3) Particular Affirmative, as in the minor premise and conclusion of the example, where *some* of a class are described as being in another class.
4) Particular Negative, as in "Some saints are not paupers," where *some* of a given class are *excluded* from another class.

These propositions are generally designated with the capital letters *A, E, I,* and *O,* respectively.

The symbols and terminology used here will be referred to frequently in further discussion. It is important, therefore, that the student make a positive effort to understand and remember these terms and their usage. A traditional mnemonic device for remembering the letters as they are associated with the propositions is to consider the Latin words for "to affirm," written as AffIrmo, and "to deny," written as nEgO; thereby giving first the affirmative then the negative Universal and Particular Propositions.

Somewhat as an aside, it should be noted that the two premises and the conclusion of the syllogism were designated by a common term, "proposition." Here we find used one of the terms that in modern logic serves to distinguish between sentences (words used in some grammatical pattern), and the meaning expressed by the sentences. Perhaps the best explanation of this would be found in an example. When in English we say, "The dog is big," and a Frenchman says, "Le chien est grand," it is clear that we are both *saying the same thing;* but it is also quite obvious that, in another sense, one said something (made an utterance) totally different from that spoken by the other. This situation is handled in modern logic by making a distinction between the words used and the ideas mentioned. In this case each party was using words of his own language to mention an idea—or proposition—that had a common meaning for both speakers.

We will, in this text, consider the *sentences* used in our logic problems and exercises as expressing *propositions,* or particular meanings. Our examples may then be given in French, German, or Eskimo, and as long as the words are translatable, everything should remain meaningful and valid.

2. REPRESENTATION OF PROPOSITIONS BY SET NOTATION. If a proposition may be expressed with any collection of symbols having *that meaning*—as we said a proposition could be expressed using sentences of any language—then a proposition may also be expressed using *logical symbols* which *have that meaning*. If, for example, I want to say that all apes are brave (that is, express that proposition), then I might let *A* equal the set **all apes,** and *B* equal the set **all who are brave,** and thus take a step towards symbolism by saying **All A is (are) B.**

The concepts of sets that have been introduced, however, give us an even more general and useful means of expressing all four of the propositions from traditional logic, even though, because of the fact that these propositions have undergone a bit of evolutionary change as the ideas have become clearer and more specifically defined, the symbols used in modern logic have meanings that are not exactly those of traditional logic.

To begin with, let us consider carefully what is being said by the sentence **All A is B. Everything that is in A is also in B** is obviously the intended meaning of this statement. It may seem possible to say that a Venn Diagram would illustrate this statement by shading in $A \cap B$.

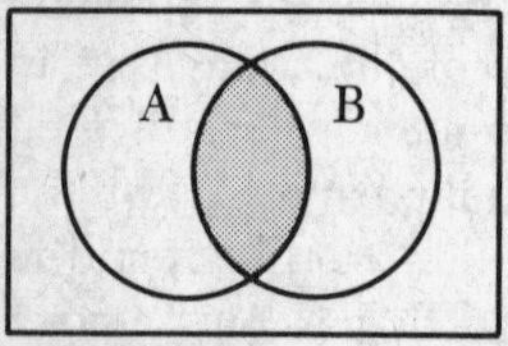

The only part of *A* which has any members is that part which is also part of *B*.

But suppose there isn't anything in A? Suppose we said, "All ghosts are scary"? If there are no ghosts what has happened to the Venn Diagram illustration of our proposition? The shading method is a way of representing sets that *have* elements; it appears inconsistent when we begin to speak of sets that are empty.

Furthermore, suppose there are *other* things that are *also* elements in *B*. As our diagram pictures it, only those things that are in *A* may be considered to be in *B*.

A peculiarity (from our point of view) of traditional logic is that all sets mentioned are considered automatically to have members or elements in them—as if it were said to be ridiculous to suppose that someone might want to reasonably discuss a set that has no members.

But modern logic recognizes that there are indeed meaningful statements which may be made and arguments which may be carried out using sets that have no members. **All dishonest logic students will be punished** is a meaningful proposition even though there never have been and never will be members in the set **dishonest logic students.**

In modern logic, therefore, the Universal Affirmative proposition is handled somewhat differently from the way it is in traditional logic. Instead of meeting the situation directly and talking about sets that *have* members, we approach the problem from the rear, as it were, and use our symbols and diagrams to describe—precisely and carefully—those sets in the Universe that do *not* and *can not* have elements in them by the terms of the *A* proposition.

We express the proposition **All A is B** in this approach by saying, "There is nothing in the Set *A* that is not also in Set *B*." Or, using our set terminology, "The Intersection of *A* with those elements *not* in *B* (B') is empty." Symbolically, $A \cap B' = 0$.

In the Venn Diagrams we use the Elimination Method to picture the idea as shown.

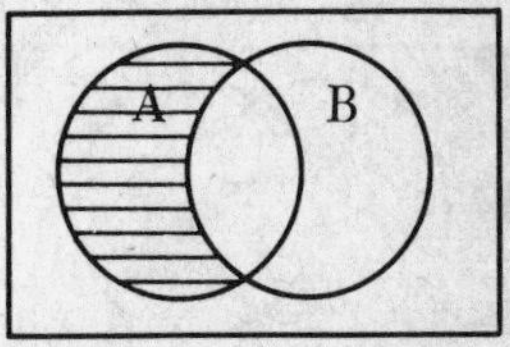

These symbols and this graphic illustration make the meaning of our original proposition clear and pronounced. They tell us that **All apes are brave** means nothing more or less than the proposition that there are no members of the class of **apes,** *A*, who are not also members of the class of **brave things,** *B*.

This is very important. Notice that nothing was said about other classes that brave things might belong to or about whether there were any additional classes that belong to *B* other than *A*. Since we wanted to indicate the area that is empty, we used horizontal lines to cross out the area to be eliminated. A thorough understanding of the meaning of the proposition will make it clear why we used this rather cumbersome symbolism to express it.

In the syllogism mentioned on p. 7, one of the premises told us that there are no members of the class of **men** who are not also of the class of **mortals.** That is, $A \cap B' = 0$, where *A* is the class of **men** and B' is the class of **those who are *not* mortal.** We say then that the class of **all things that are both men and not-mortal** is an Empty Class.

The fact that the Null or Empty Class is not a concept found in traditional logic—as mentioned on p. 23—must be kept in mind here. For the most part, the Null Class of modern logic may be used quite meaningfully in expressing ideas of traditional logic. But, as we will soon see, it is because of the very fact that there was no allowance made for a Null or a Universal Class that traditional logic developed some rather clumsy and useless kinds of valid syllogisms.

Because we will, in this work with syllogisms, be dealing only with Intersection and not with the Union of sets, we will begin to use the conventional device of simply putting the set symbols adjacent to one another to designate Intersection. That is, $a \cap b$ will be indicated ab, as is done to show multiplication of two unknowns in algebra.

Returning to the syllogism, we now have a notation that has been seen to be capable of expressing Universal Affirmative propositions, viz., $ab' = 0$; so let us go on to symbolize the remaining three kinds of propositions with the set theory notation.

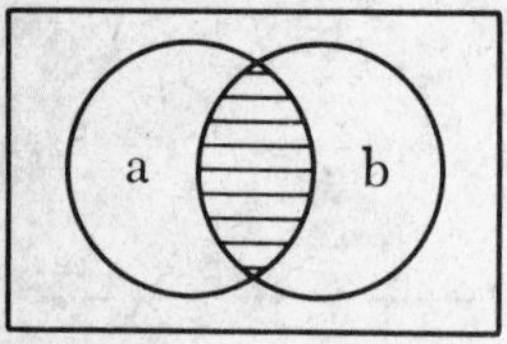

Universal Negative propositions—those of the kind, No *a* is *b*—may be indicated as $ab = 0$. The Intersection of a and b is the Empty Set. There are no elements that are both in a and in b. By Venn Diagrams, using the Elimination Method, we have the diagram on the left.

Particular Affirmative propositions—Some *a* is *b*—are indicated by $ab \neq 0$. The Intersection of the two sets is not empty (see the diagram on the left below).

A cross is used to indicate there *is* an element in this set composed of the Intersection of a and b.

Particular Negative propositions—Some *a* is not *b*—are indicated by $ab' \neq 0$. The intersection of a and not-b is not empty (see the diagram on the right below).

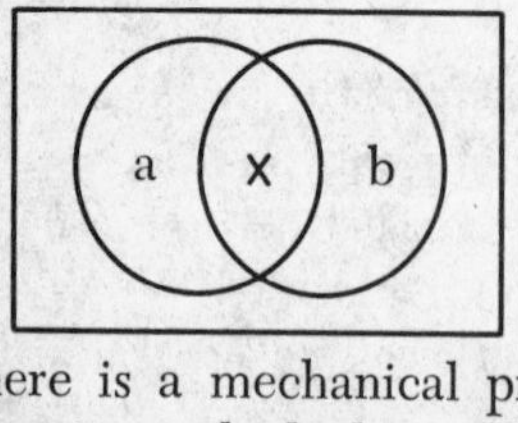

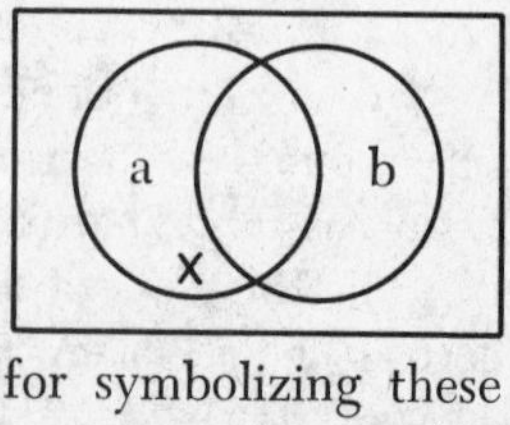

There is a mechanical procedure for symbolizing these four propositions which the student may want to memorize. In an *A* proposition the subject remains exactly as it is stated: for "All *a*

. . .", the "a" (the subject) appears unchanged in the symbolic expression. The predicate of an A proposition, however, is always negated. For ". . . is b," the "b" is given a prime and shown as b'. "All a is b," then, is symbolized $ab' = 0$.

For the E, I, and O propositions all the letters remain exactly as they appear in the original statement. (In the O proposition, "Some a is not b," the "not" appears as a prime sign after the b: $ab' \neq 0$.) The Universal Propositions are always equalities; the Particular Propositions are always inequalities.

These expressions for the A, E, I, and O propositions—$ab' = 0$, $ab = 0$, $ab \neq 0$, and $ab' \neq 0$, respectively—will be used along with the traditional notation as we go on with a further discussion of the syllogism of traditional logic.

3. RULES OF VALIDITY. Each of the three parts of the traditional syllogism—the major premise, the minor premise, and the conclusion—may be expressed as an A, an E, an I, or an O proposition. Consider a syllogism such as the following:

All astronauts are brave.	$AB' = 0$
Some husbands are astronauts.	$HA \neq 0$
Some husbands are brave.	$HB \neq 0$

The major premise in this syllogism is an A proposition, the minor premise is an I proposition, and the conclusion is an I proposition. Taking another syllogism:

No simians are lecturers.	$SL = 0$
All rhetoricians are lecturers.	$RL' = 0$
No rhetoricians are simians.	$RS = 0$

In this case the major premise is an E proposition, the minor premise is an A proposition, and the conclusion is an E proposition.

(The modern set notation is given to the right of these syllogisms only for the purpose of providing more practice in its usage. Such notation, as has been said before, has been in use for no more than the last hundred years or so and it is not to be considered as a notation that was used or even known by logicians who lived before the middle of the nineteenth century. It is not to be taken as an aspect of what we are calling here the traditional logic.)

Each of the given arrangements of propositions into a syllogism is called a *mood.* If a syllogism is composed, as in the first example, of a Universal Affirmative proposition given as the major premise, a Particular Affirmative proposition given as the minor premise, and a Particular Affirmative proposition given as the conclusion, then the mood of the syllogism is said to be *AII*—using the letters that are traditionally used to denote propositions.

The mood of the second syllogism is *EAE;* Universal Negative, Universal Affirmative, Universal Negative.

A further analysis of the syllogism may be made by considering the subject and predicate of each proposition as *terms.* In the last example, simians, lecturers, and rhetoricians are terms of the syllogism. We have, for convenience, symbolized these words by using the letters S, *L,* and *R.* (The standard notations for the terms of syllogisms where no specific qualities or classes are given are *p, m,* and *s*—similar to the variables *x, y,* and *z,* used in algebra.) These terms are given special names just as the premises are given names in the syllogism. The traditional way of denoting the terms is to say that the subject of the conclusion is the minor term, the predicate of the conclusion is the major term, and the term that appears once in the major and again in the minor premise is called the middle term.

This procedure of naming terms will perhaps be more meaningful to the student if we point out that the terms of the conclusion are always to appear in the same order: All *s* is *p.* The letter "*s,*" then, stands for the subject and "*p*" stands for the predicate of the conclusion. The letter "*m*" stands for the middle term appearing in the major and minor premises. Furthermore, the *s* will also always be found as a term in the minor premise and the *p* will always be given as a term of the major premise.

In the last example, then, the minor term is rhetoricians, the major term is simians, and the middle term is lecturers.

There are four possible arrangements of the terms in a syllogism. Using *p* for the major term, *m* for the middle term, and *s* for the minor term, these arrangements may be made as follows:

I	II	III	IV
mp	*pm*	*mp*	*pm*
sm	*sm*	*ms*	*ms*
sp	*sp*	*sp*	*sp*

The arrangements given above are standard in traditional logic and are called the figures of the syllogism: First, Second, Third, and Fourth Figures.

The total number of syllogisms that can be constructed may be calculated by recognizing again that each of the premises—the major premise and minor premise—and the conclusion may be given as any one of four kinds of propositions: *A, E, I,* or *O.* For each kind of proposition in the major premise there are four kinds that may be used in the minor premise. Four in each, then, will give 4×4 or 16 possibilities. And for each of these 16 possible arrangements in the premises, the conclusion may take one of four possible forms; so all together we have 4×16 or 64 different possible syllogisms when considering only the various propositions that may be used. That is, we have 64 different *moods* that may be constructed. But we also know that each *mood* may appear in one of four possible *figures.* In taking this last series into account, then, we have 4×64 or 256 possible syllogisms.

a. Traditional Tests For Valid Syllogisms. Only a few of these syllogisms are valid, however. We can see how obviously invalid syllogisms may be formed if we consider the following examples:

All monkeys are playful.
No monkeys are students.

No students are playful.

All apples are fruits.
Some fruits are oranges.

Some oranges are apples.

All cats are animals.
All animals are sentient beings.

All sentient beings are cats.

The conclusions of the above syllogisms may, on inspection, be seen to be absurd even though the premises could be accepted as true. When we thus have a case of true premises producing a false conclusion we may recognize a case of invalid argument. (The meaning we are giving to the terms "truth" and "validity" will be discussed in the final chapter.)

We find the need, then, for a set of general rules that will enable us to distinguish the valid from the invalid syllogisms in the collection of all possible syllogisms.

The rules of categorical syllogisms * are given in various forms that depend upon the particular logic text referred to. We will here present these rules as a set of seven requirements for the valid categorical syllogism:

1. No conclusion can be deduced from two negative premises.
2. If one premise is negative, the conclusion must be negative.
3. If both premises are affirmative, the conclusion must be affirmative.
4. The middle term must be distributed (see below for an explanation of this word) at least once in the major or minor premise.
5. Any term distributed in the conclusion must also appear as distributed in the major or minor premise.
6. No conclusion may be deduced from two Particular premises.
7. If one of the premises is Particular, the conclusion must be Particular.

The word "distributed" has a special meaning here. A term is said to be distributed in a proposition if the entire group or class is being referred to. For example, all *a* is *b* is a case in which *all* the elements in the class *a* are referred to, whereas it is not necessarily true that all the elements of *b* are brought into consideration. That is, in the expression All men are mortal, it can be seen that we are referring to the entire class of men, so that class is distributed. But we are not, obviously, referring to the entire class of mortals, so that class is undistributed. In No *a* is *b*, we are saying something about *all* the elements in *a* (that the class *a* does

* The categorical syllogism is distinguished in traditional logic from what is therein called the hypothetical and the disjunctive syllogisms. The hypothetical syllogism is of the form, If *a* is *b*, and if *b* is *c*, then *a* is *c*, and the disjunctive syllogism appears as, Either *a* is *b* or *a* is *c*; *a* is not *b*; therefore *a* is *c*. The categorical syllogism makes a clear affirmation or denial of membership or nonmembership of elements of one set within another set through the connective verb "to be." It may be argued that this distinction between three types of syllogisms can only be made on the basis of superficial characteristics. [See R. M. Eaton, *General Logic* (New York: Charles Scribner's Sons, 1959), pp. 79–80. See also R. J. McCall, *Basic Logic* (New York: Barnes & Noble, Inc., 1952), pp. 46, 132.]

not share any elements with class b), and we are saying the same about *all* elements of the class b (that it shares no members with a). In the proposition **Some a is b** we are not saying anything about either *all* of the class a or *all* of the class b; so neither term is said to be distributed. In an O proposition, **Some a is not b,** only some of the class a is being mentioned, so a is not distributed; but all of the class b is being referred to (that is, there are some things in a that are not in any part of the class b), so b is distributed.

A rule of thumb that may be used to distinguish between distributed and undistributed terms is: The distributed terms of a syllogism are the subjects of Universal propositions and the predicates of Negative propositions.

Coming back to the question of valid syllogisms, the only justification we have for the seven rules of categorical syllogisms listed above is a kind of agreement we can come to when we examine particular constructions of valid and invalid syllogisms.

Take, for an example, the syllogism:

All Dyaks are head-hunters.	$DH' = 0$
All model agents are head-hunters.	$MH' = 0$
All model agents are Dyaks.	$MD' = 0$

We recognize this to be an invalid syllogism because even if we took the premises to be true (using a carefully-generalized definition of "head-hunters") we would still find that the conclusion obviously does not follow from the premises. In analyzing this syllogism and others similar to it we see the one relevant thing they have in common is an undistributed middle term. So we say, as we did in Rule Four, "The middle term must be distributed at least once in the major or minor premise." Our general rule, then, is conceived out of an analysis of several particular instances of one kind of invalid syllogism, much in the manner of Inductive Reasoning. Our deductions with syllogisms are described here as being founded on inductive inferences. This is in keeping with the thesis proposed by John Stuart Mill in his book *A System of Logic.** (A student interested in this topic would find Mill's book to be an excellent source of ideas for further consideration.)

* John Stuart Mill, *A System of Logic* (London: Longmans, Green and Co., 1911).

Let us take another example:

Some recreation is profitable.	$RP \neq 0$
Dances are recreation.	$DR' = 0$
Dances are profitable.	$DP' = 0$

The above is an *IAA* syllogism in the First Figure. Its invalidity is a representation of the condition prohibited by Rule 7: The major premise is Particular but the conclusion is Universal.

For our last example let us consider:

No Rurales are savages.	$RS = 0$
Some Rurales are townspeople.	$RT \neq 0$
Some townspeople are not savages.	$TS' \neq 0$

In examining this, an *EIO* syllogism in the Third Figure, we find it is an apparently acceptable deduction and may be considered valid. In applying the seven rules to this syllogism we see that it violates none of them, and this is sufficient proof of its validity by the standards of traditional logic.

Considering the fact that these rules were—in essence—developed by Aristotle and modified, corrected, and amended by many other powerful and philosophical minds in over two thousand years of syllogistic exercise, it is not unreasonable to suppose that they will suffice for the determination of validity in most cases of syllogistic reasoning. Even if we describe them as having been developed simply as generalizations out of particular cases (rather than, as the traditionalists would have had it, developed out of cognitive perceptions of truths inherent in nature), we may still say that they are about as reliable as any generalizations can be. Exceptions will be made to these generalizations, and reasons for these exceptions will be given in terms of modern logic later in this chapter, but it must be recognized that the traditional system, which includes the work of many geniuses of the past who have given it their support, may still be relied upon for the analysis of syllogisms within the fairly wide area prescribed by our limitations.

In most cases—it may be said—a valid syllogistic argument can be determined by the traditional rules of categorical syllogisms, and these are the rules, then, that we will now apply to all the various possible syllogistic forms in order to distinguish the valid from the invalid.

Listed below are twenty-four forms of valid syllogisms—the twenty-four kinds of syllogisms (out of a possible 256)—that are not eliminated by any of our seven rules of categorical syllogisms:

FIRST FIGURE	SECOND FIGURE	THIRD FIGURE	FOURTH FIGURE
AAA	*AEE*	**AAI*	**AAI*
**AAI*	**AEO*	*AII*	*AEE*
AII	*AOO*	**EAO*	**AEO*
EAE	*EAE*	*EIO*	**EAO*
**EAO*	**EAO*	*IAI*	*EIO*
EIO	*EIO*	*OAO*	*IAI*

Those syllogistic forms marked with an asterisk are special forms that are called valid but "weakened" in the traditional logic. That is, if we say, All *m* is *p* and All *s* is *m*, we then expect to conclude All *s* is *p*. But in *AAI* of the First Figure our conclusion is, Some *s* is *p*. For the traditional logician this was simply a matter of not taking all you could get out of your premises. In modern logic, however, the conclusion Some *s* is *p* would be unacceptable. This will be discussed in the next section, which is a presentation of some more modern approaches to syllogistic logic.

As we have noted, all of the syllogisms listed above were found to be valid by a careful application of the seven rules to each syllogistic form. When one is presented with a syllogistic argument using ordinary language (such as All politicians are married; no saints are married; no saints are politicians), the seven rules may be applied directly to this specific case to determine if it is a valid syllogism. Or, of course, this specific syllogism may be analyzed to determine its mood and figure and then checked with the list above to determine whether it is valid.

b. Modern Tests For Valid Syllogisms. A three-circle Venn Diagram may be used to test for validity in a syllogism. We introduced earlier in this chapter a way of symbolizing propositions so that diagramming is possible. All *m* is *p* is symbolized $mp' = 0$, and the Venn Diagram for this proposition is as given on the right above.

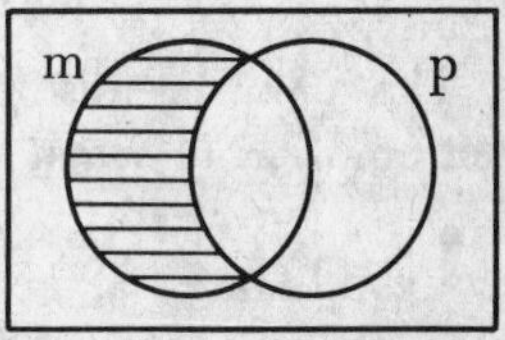

The other three propositions—Universal Negative, Particular Affirmative, and Particular Negative—are given in symbols and on Venn Diagrams on p. 40.

Let us take a valid syllogism from p. 47 to illustrate the Venn Diagram procedure of testing for valid syllogisms. A syllogism in the Second Figure of mood *EAE* is listed as valid, so we will state such a syllogism using m, p, and s as variables:

No *p* is *m*.	$pm = 0$
All *s* is *m*.	$sm' = 0$
No *s* is *p*.	$sp = 0$

We express this in a three-circle Venn Diagram by considering one proposition at a time. The major premise is Universal Negative so we block out with horizontal lines the area (4,7) on the diagram. The minor premise is a Universal Affirmative proposition relating s to m so we block out the area (3, 6), using vertical lines to distinguish these areas from the ones already blocked out.

As a final step, we check to see if the situation described by the conclusion is actually indicated in the diagram. The conclusion says, No *s* is *p*, or "The intersection of s and p is empty;" and when we look at the Venn Diagram we see that the area sp, or (6, 7), is crossed out. The validity of our syllogism is then confirmed.

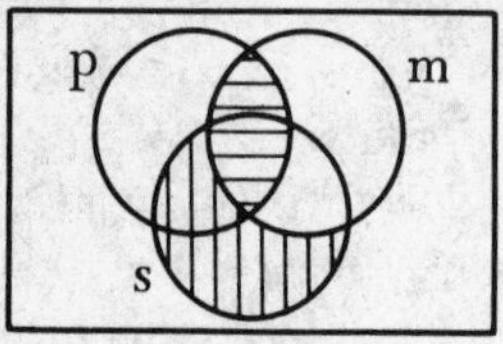

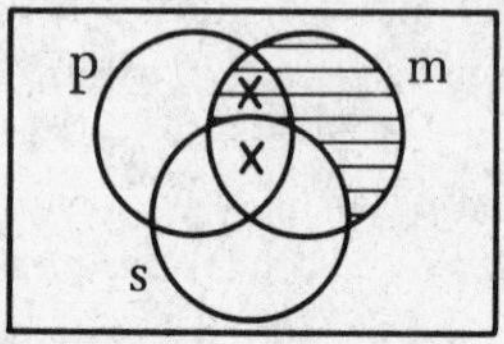

For another example, let us take *IAI* in the Fourth Figure.

Some *p* is *m*.	$pm \neq 0$
All *m* is *s*.	$ms' = 0$
Some *s* is *p*.	$sp \neq 0$

The major premise tells us that the intersection of p and m is not empty. But when we go to place an x in the area indicating intersection we discover there are actually two areas that meet the condition: (4) and (7). One thing that we can do in this case, then, is to put an x in *both* (4) and (7), and go on to the next step. Directing our attention to the minor premise, we cross out the area ms' or (2,4). But when this is done, we find we have eliminated the area (4) in which we had marked one of the x's. So by following closely the rules we used in discussing sets we may see that the conclusion $sp \neq 0$, or Some *s* is *p*, actually does follow from the premises given. The validity of the syllogism *IAI*, 4 is thus verified by Venn Diagrams.

For an illustration of one of the major distinctions between traditional and modern logic in the interpretation of propositions and syllogisms, we will take a syllogism with a so-called weakened conclusion as our next example.

Consider the syllogism of mood *AEO* in the Second Figure:

All *p* is *m*.	$pm' = 0$
No *s* is *m*.	$sm = 0$
Some *s* is not *p*.	$sp' \neq 0$

Here we have a Universal major and minor premise and a Particular conclusion—whereas a Universal conclusion could be drawn from those premises (thus giving *AEE* in the Second Figure, which is listed as valid).

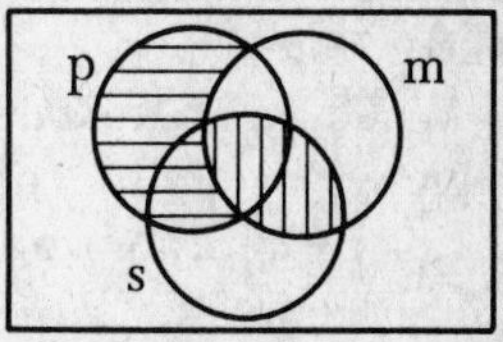

On the Venn Diagram we show All *p* is *m* by marking horizontal lines through area (1,6). No *s* is *m* is indicated by vertical lines through (5,7). But the conclusion Some *s* is not *p* does not appear in our completed diagram. It is true that there is a place, area (3), wherein an *x* *could* be marked to show Some *s* is not *p*, but there are also areas wherein we could place *x*'s to show Some *m* is not *p* or Some *m* is *p*.

The Universal Negative proposition, No *s* is *p*, is clearly indicated, but, again, that is another syllogism: *AEE*, 2.

Here we have illustrated the difference between the interpretations of Particular propositions given in the traditional and the modern logic. As was pointed out earlier in this chapter, in traditional logic a Particular proposition is considered to be referring simply to some members of a group that may more generally be described by a Universal proposition. The latter, of course, is always considered to be referring to a nonempty group —that is, a group that has at least one member.

In modern logical notation we speak of classes that may or may not have elements in them when we use Universal propositions. Therefore, we never allow our notations or diagrams to imply the necessary existence of any elements in using the Universal propositions. On the other hand, we see Particular propositions as propositions that *do* refer to an existing element or elements and we draw our diagrams, therefore, so that we do illustrate the existence of such object or objects.

Or, to state it in another way, we are saying in modern logic that we want to be able to speak of classes that may or may not have members in them without arriving at a conclusion that seems necessarily to imply the existence of such members. For example, a syllogism involving an Empty Class such as the following:

All birds are flyers.
No mermaids are flyers.

Some mermaids are not birds.

leaves us with a conclusion that requires the existence of at least one mermaid for it to have any meaning at all. But if we had concluded No mermaids are birds, we would not have depended upon the existence of any elements "mermaids" for the meaning of our statement or the validity of the syllogism.

When we have taken these limitations assumed by modern logic we naturally reduce the list of syllogisms considered to be valid. By refusing to accept a weakened conclusion as a valid inference we now have only 15 valid syllogisms.

To further explain this interpretation of Particular propositions and to look for deeper insight into the meaning of syllogisms themselves, let us take as our final example a syllogism with two Particular premises and a Particular conclusion. Consider the syllogism *III*,4.

Some *p* is *m*.	$pm \neq 0$
Some *m* is *s*.	$ms \neq 0$
Some *s* is *p*.	$sp \neq 0$

This syllogism may immediately be seen to be invalid by Rule 6, but let us see how it would work out on Venn Diagrams. Our major premise tells us there is at least one element in area (4) or area (7). Since this seems to leave the matter to our own discretion, let us put an x in area (4), which action will meet exactly the requirements called for by

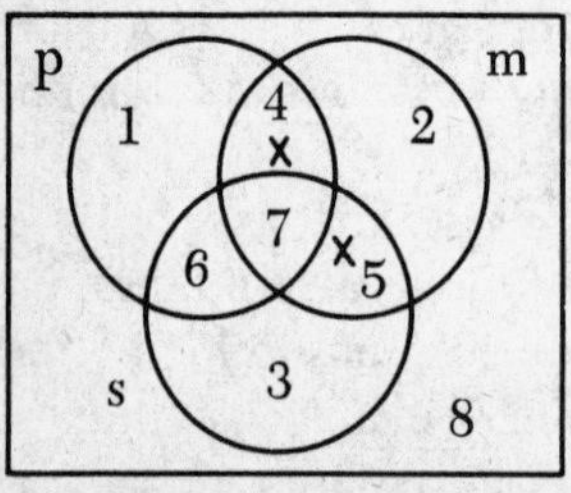

the major premise. By the same token, since the minor premise tells us there is at least one element in area (5) or area (7), let us meet this requirement by putting an x in (5). Of course, as we have said before, we *could* have put an x in either (4) *or* (7), and in either (5) *or* (7), but there are no stated conditions that make it impossible for us to put the x's in (4) and (5); so, making a willful and arbitrary expression of our individualism, we take the most unco-operative step possible.

Then we look to see if the Venn Diagram we have filled in properly expresses the sense of the conclusion: **Some *s* is *p*.** Of course, it does not. The diagram would have to show an x in either (6) or (7) for the conclusion to be correctly illustrated and we have set it up in such a manner that that conclusion is *not* shown.

An important lesson to be learned from this is that the major and minor premises of a valid syllogism must inescapably produce those conditions described by the conclusion. If it is even *possible* to set up the conditions described by the major and minor premises without at the same time (by the same action) setting up the condition described by the conclusion, then the syllogism is invalid.

Another way to say this—a way that leads us directly into the next section on Antilogisms—is to say that the denial of the conclusion in a valid syllogism must produce an inconsistency between the premises and the conclusion, because if the syllogism is valid, the conclusion must *necessarily* follow from the premises. The syllogism given above, then, is an example of an invalid syllogism wherein the denial of the conclusion (i.e., **no *s* is *p***) would not necessarily produce an inconsistency with the premises.

The use of Venn Diagrams gives us a simple way of finding valid syllogisms. Nothing more needs to be memorized or assumed in performing this test of validity than the basic procedural rules used in our discussion of sets. And, as will become more apparent later in the book, the elimination of the syllogisms with weakened conclusions actually produces a much clearer and more coherent picture of sets, groups, and classes and their relationships to one another than is given by the traditional system of syllogistic reasoning.

Another modern test for valid syllogisms, the test by Antilogisms, is one that follows from a discovery made by Christine

Ladd-Franklin in 1883. Mrs. Ladd-Franklin recognized that in a valid syllogism we think of the major and minor premises as leading to or *implying* the conclusion. Given, we say, these two premises as true, then this conclusion must follow. Of course, if we are given a true conclusion we can *not* say that the premises are necessarily true, or that a true conclusion implies true premises. A valid implication between the premises and the conclusion cannot be reversed. Each implication, then, must be checked as a single case.

But if we negate the conclusion of a valid syllogism, we have an inconsistency between the premises and the conclusion, and this relationship (inconsistency) is what is called a *symmetrical* relationship. That is, the premises are inconsistent with the conclusion and the conclusion is inconsistent with the premises. (The relationship of implication is *asymmetrical* because it cannot be given both ways: i.e., the premises implying the conclusion does not mean that the conclusion implies the premises.)

Mrs. Ladd-Franklin's work presents us then with a new simplification of syllogistic reasoning. By negating the conclusion of a valid syllogism we are given a set of premises and a conclusion that are inconsistent, and since inconsistency is a symmetrical relationship we may reduce the procedure of testing for valid syllogisms to four steps.

This kind of test is called the test by Antilogisms. An Antilogism, then, is a set of three inconsistent propositions, or an *inconsistent triad.* If, as we mentioned above, the conclusion is necessarily implied by the two premises in a valid syllogism, then the denial of the conclusion of a valid syllogism must necessarily produce an inconsistency among the three propositions.

If we present our syllogisms in set notation, the four steps we take to test for an inconsistency may be given as follows:

1. Negate the conclusion by changing an equation (Universal proposition) to an inequation (Particular proposition) or an inequation to an equation.*
2. Check all three propositions (major premise, minor premise,

* The equations in our set notation are $ab' = 0$ and $ab = 0$, and the inequations are $ab \neq 0$ and $ab' \neq 0$; that is, the Universal Affirmative, the Universal Negative, the Particular Affirmative, and the Particular Negative propositions respectively.

and the *modified* conclusion) to see that there are two equations (Universals) and one inequation (Particular).

3. Examine the two *equations* (not necessarily the major and minor premises) to see if there is one term that appears in both equations, once without a prime sign, or positive, and once with a prime sign, or negative.
4. Examine the terms that appear in the inequation to be sure that they have the same values (positive or negative) as they do in the equations.*

To illustrate the application of these rules, let us take the syllogism *AEE*,2, which we know by the list on p. 47 to be valid.

All *p* is *m*.	$pm' = 0$	$pm' = 0$
No *s* is *m*.	$sm = 0$	$sm = 0$
No *s* is *p*.	$sp = 0$	$(sp = 0)$
		$sp \neq 0$

This syllogism is made to appear in the form given above on the right as we perform our four tests of validity using the method of Antilogisms.

Following the rules, we first changed the conclusion from an equation to an inequation and put parentheses around the former to remind ourselves to eliminate it from consideration during the other three tests.

In applying Rule 2 we check all propositions to see that we have two equations (the major and minor premises) and one inequation (the modified conclusion).

---

* A full explanation of these rules could be given only after the student has completed some work in Boolean Algebra or the Class Calculus that is presented in Chapter 4 of this book. After such material has been studied it is recommended that the student refer to the book *Fundamentals of Symbolic Logic* by Ambrose and Lazerowitz (New York: Holt, 1962) for a detailed explanation of the derivation of these rules. A brief explanation of Mrs. Ladd-Franklin's work is given by J. Jørgensen in his *Treatise of Formal Logic* (New York: Russell and Russell, Inc., 1962), Volume I, p. 261: "Mrs. Ladd-Franklin has shown . . . that the asymmetrical copula 'implies' can be replaced by the symmetrical copula 'is inconsistent with' in conjunction with a negation. '*X* implies *y*' thus means the same as 'is inconsistent with not-*y*' and the whole of syllogistics can by means of this symmetrical copula be reduced to a single formula or 'inconsistency': viz., $(ab = 0)(b'c = 0)(ac \neq 0) = 0$."

Following Rule 3, we examine the two equations to see that there is a common term, m, that appears once positive and once negative.

Rule 4 then tells us to examine the inequation to see if the terms, s and p, appear with the same values (in this case, positive) as they do in the equations.

The syllogism has met the conditions prescribed by the rules and may then be said to have been cleared as valid by Antilogisms.

Let us take a slightly different case for our next example.

$$\begin{array}{c} mp' = 0 \\ ms \neq 0 \\ \hline (sp \neq 0) \\ sp = 0 \end{array}$$

Consider the syllogism *AII*,3. The Antilogism for this is indicated above. Here Rule 1 has already been effected, and we now find the third proposition (ignoring the conclusion in parentheses) to be an equation, and the inequation is seen to be the second proposition. But this should present us with no problem so far as the rules are concerned. Rule 2 calls for two equations and one inequation—which requirement is met.

Rule 3 says the two equations ($mp' = 0$ and $sp = 0$) must have a common term appearing once positive and once negative—and this is the case.

And Rule 4 requires that the terms appearing in the *inequation* must appear with the same values as they do in the equations—and this requirement also is seen to be fulfilled. So the syllogism *AII*,3 is cleared as valid.

For our final example, consider *EOO*,3. Once again we find

$$\begin{array}{c} mp = 0 \\ ms' \neq 0 \\ \hline (sp' \neq 0) \\ sp' = 0 \end{array}$$

the modified conclusion, $sp' = 0$, as an equation and the minor premise as the inequation. There *are* two equations and one inequation. There *is* a common term appearing once positive and once negative in the equations. And m appears as positive in both the equation and the inequation. But s appears primed, or negative, in the inequation and unprimed, or positive, in the equation.

So Rule 4 is violated in the case of the minor term and the syllogism may be described as invalid.

The student should be careful to note that what we have shown in this operation using Antilogisms is that the denial of the conclusion in a valid syllogism has produced an inconsistency in the propositions that made it up. Our tests are aimed at displaying this inconsistency in the major premise, the minor premise, and the *modified* conclusion—which tells us then that the original syllogism (with the unmodified conclusion) is valid.

The three propositions used in the Antilogism do not constitute the valid syllogism. The valid syllogism is composed of the major and minor premise and the unmodified conclusion. By showing that the denial of the conclusion led to an inconsistency we have validated the given syllogism.

This test by Antilogisms—using as it does the same modern interpretations of propositions as is used in Venn Diagrams—will also show syllogisms with weakened conclusions to be invalid. In any of the methods of modern logic we are committed to the concept of a Particular proposition as one that expresses the actual existence of one or more elements in a given group or set, and to the concept of a Universal proposition as one that expresses the relationship between classes or groups that may *or may not* have members or elements in them. Therefore, an Antilogism will show a Particular conclusion in conjunction with two Universal premises to be invalid just as the Venn Diagrams did. There is no such thing as a weakened conclusion in modern logic.

4. CONCLUSION. The syllogistic logic that has been presented here is only a small fraction of the material that may be given in a traditional course in logic. A glance at any one of a number of texts that give a fairly extensive coverage of syllogistic reasoning * will reveal additional topics such as conversion, obversion, and the reduction of syllogisms; the naming of syllogisms as Barbara, Celarent, Darii, and so forth; and the development of

* For example: Raymond J. McCall, *Basic Logic* (New York: Barnes & Noble, Inc., College Outline Series, 1952); Joseph G. Brennan, *A Handbook of Logic* (New York: Harper and Bros., 1961); Monroe C. Beardsley, *Practical Logic* (Englewood Cliffs: Prentice-Hall, Inc., 1950); Philip Wheelwright, *Valid Thinking* (New York: The Odyssey Press, 1962).

such topics as the hypothetical syllogism and various kinds of dilemmas.

But we have not meant to produce a comprehensive discussion of syllogisms here. We have meant to give some idea of the traditional approach essentially for the purpose of relating it to modern logic and showing how a modern approach may be used in the analysis of syllogisms. In addition, of course, this discussion of syllogisms has provided further practice in the handling of sets and has therefore served the purpose of giving the student more familiarity with ideas that will be in use throughout the remainder of this book.

We will proceed in our next chapter with the more or less intuitive presentation of some additional aspects of modern logic. The subject of sets will be placed to one side for a while as we develop some topics related to Propositional Logic; but the student will find all the terms and concepts that he has learned in the material on sets brought to the foreground again when he arrives at the work in Class Calculus and Boolean Algebra. What we hope to have achieved here is the meaningful introduction of some new ways of looking at things. The student is expected to have learned a few new analytical procedures and to have added to his vocabulary a few new terms that will prove to be useful in the material to follow.

LOGIC EXERCISES

Identify the following propositions as Universal Affirmative, Universal Negative, Particular Affirmative, or Particular Negative.

1. Lions are mammals.
2. Snow is not white.
3. Some atoms are unstable.
4. The lemming destroys itself.
5. Some who are not peaceful are civilized.

Translate the following into the symbolic notation of sets.

6. Moons are satellites.
7. No earthquakes are predictable.
8. Some movies are three-dimensional.
9. The fuel cell is not a heat engine.
10. Many movies are not for children.

11. No *a* is not *b*. (use "*b′*" for "not *b*.")
12. Some that is not *b* is *a*.
13. All that is not *a* is *b*.
14. All *a* is not *b*.
15. No *a* is *b*.
16. In problems 6 through 10, which terms are distributed and which are undistributed?

Determine which of the following syllogisms are invalid and tell which of the rules of the categorical syllogism are violated by the invalid ones.

17. No buses are scooters.
Some buses are Volkswagens.
Some Volkswagens are scooters.

18. All politicians are married.
None who are married are sagacious.
None who are sagacious are politicians.

19. All men's bathing suits are topless.
No ladies' bathing suits are men's bathing suits.
No ladies' bathing suits are topless.

20. All swans are white.
Some cows are white.
Some cows are swans.

21. Some *m* is *p*.
Some *s* is not *m*.
Some *s* is not *p*.

22. All *m* is *p*.
Some *m* is not *s*.
Some *s* is not *p*.

23. All *p* is *m*.
All *m* is *s*.
Some *s* is not *p*.

Draw Venn Diagrams for the following syllogisms and tell whether they are valid or invalid.

24. All policemen are moralists.
No sadists are moralists.
No sadists are policemen.

25. No fathers are mothers.
Some mothers are veterans.
Some veterans are not fathers.

26. No *m* is *p*.
All *s* is *m*.
No *s* is *p*.

27. All *p* is *m*.
No *s* is *m*.
Some *s* is not *p*.

28. Some *p* is *m*.
All *m* is *s*.
Some *s* is *p*.

Use Antilogisms to determine whether the following are valid or invalid. Tell which rule is violated by the invalid syllogisms.

29. No bushmen are golfers.
All executives are golfers.

No executives are bushmen.

30. Some of our guests are people.
All people are animals.

Some animals are our guests.

31. All mothers are patient.
Some shoppers are mothers.

Some shoppers are patient.

32. Some who are not athletic are not playboys.
No nonsportsmen are not athletic.

Some sportsmen are not playboys.

33. All gamblers are not trustworthy.
Some who are trustworthy are not pleasant.

Some who are pleasant are not gamblers.

3

Truth Table Logic

One of our most important concerns in modern logic is for meanings given to the words and symbols used in an argument. Continual effort is made to give rigid and precise meanings to the symbols that are used in logical analysis. Intuitive meanings are suppressed and explicit meanings are formulated and clarified with as much precision as possible.

In the discussion of traditional logic we noticed that the use of a Universal Affirmative involved the assumption that the class mentioned actually had at least one element in it. When one made a statement such as All A is B, it was *taken for granted* that everyone was assuming there *are* things that have the quality *A*. All animals are brave, or All angels are benevolent, should not even be argued, the traditionalists might have said, if there were *not* at least one such thing as an animal or an angel.

Anyone with the slightest intelligence "knows" that you don't argue about classes that have no members. If you are interested in a serious discussion, claim the traditionalists, let us keep within the area of common sense.

Under most conditions—where analysis is not extremely profound—we may depend upon this mode of communication with the conviction that we will be able to get the rather simple and straightforward information across to our correspondents without difficulty.

But if we mean our logic to handle some of the most complicated problems that may be conceived in this complex world of ours—if we mean to communicate on a level of profundity far beyond that of the superficial conversations we carry on in our daily lives or even beyond the relatively limited range of data with which the traditional logicians were concerned, then we must introduce a rigor into our definitions that will give us a solid basis for the analysis of the complicated problems that we may be faced with.

A. SENTENTIAL CONNECTIVES AND TRUTH TABLES

In a first step towards this disciplined and modified use of the language, we will take four common connectives used in the construction of a sentence or proposition (we will be using these terms as synonyms in this part of the book). Each of these sentential connectives will be associated with a limited but clear and precise meaning. We will admit that they may have other meanings as they are used in ordinary language, but we will see if we can discern *one* specific meaning for each of them (*one* meaning that is commonly recognized as being associated with the term) and then attempt to give a precise statement of that meaning for use in our system of logic.

1. CONJUNCTION. Take, to begin with, the connective *and.* When we use *and* in a compound sentence we generally mean for the sentence to be true only if both the clauses connected by *and* are true. For example, if I say, "The singer was six feet tall and he wore no shoes," my statement is recognized as being true if and only if the singer *was* six feet tall in accordance with the first clause *and* he was barefoot as stipulated by the second clause. Someone else might indicate a mistake I have made by saying, "No, you're wrong. He was *not* six feet tall," which is a reasonable way of making a denial, and which shows that my whole statement could be denied by simply denying one of its parts.

A sentence of this kind where the principal connective is *and* is called a Conjunction. Each of the parts of a Conjunction is a Conjunct. A Conjunction is true, we say, if both the Conjuncts are true, and is false if *either* of the Conjuncts is false.

2. DISJUNCTION. Another common sentential connective is the word *or.* This is a word that in actual usage is commonly given either of two meanings. We may, for example, say, "Either he will attend the meeting or his wife will," and mean for our statement to be true if he attends, if his wife attends, or if they both attend the meeting. On the other hand, we could also use the connective *or* in a sentence such as, "The burglar was either a man or a woman." In this case, according to the common meaning that would be given to such a statement, the truth of either one of these phrases excludes the possibility of the other being true. "The burglar was a man" could be true, or "The burglar was a woman" could be true, but—except for situations connected with a carnival, perhaps—it is impossible for both those phrases to be true.

The first usage mentioned above is said to involve the inclusive sense of the word *or*. The second usage involves the exclusive sense of *or*. In our work here we will use the first, or inclusive, sense of *or*. That is, we will say that a sentence using *or* is true if either or both parts of the sentence are true.

Our logical terminology for the connective *or* is Disjunction. A sentence or proposition whose principal connective is *or* is a Disjunction and each part or clause in a Disjunction is called a Disjunct.

3. TRUTH TABLES. Before continuing with a description of the remaining connectives let us consider a simple way of illustrating the rigorous definitions we are giving to these terms. The method we will consider is that of the Truth Tables. Given a sentence with two parts to it such as the Conjunction or Disjunction above, we know that either part *may* be true *or* false. If we consider the parts of the sentence together, they may both be true or both be false or one true and the other false. Our question here is, "What is the truth value of the sentence *as a whole* in the case of the truth or falsity of either of its parts?"

The Truth Table gives us a way of making a clear, shorthand answer to that question by directing our attention to each of the four possibilities, one after the other. Any sentence with two parts (or clauses) to it may be examined on a Truth Table that is set up in the manner of the one above.

p	*q*	
T	*T*	
T	*F*	
F	*T*	
F	*F*	

In the table *p* and *q* stand for the clauses of the sentence. For example, *p* could represent The singer was six feet tall, and *q* could represent He wore no shoes. The letters *T* and *F* below stand for the truth values of the clauses. The table, then, is an illustration of all possible combinations of truth values for a sentence containing two parts or clauses.

Suppose we take the Conjunction George is here, and Mary is happy. *G* will represent the first clause, *M* the second. We may then determine a truth value for the sentence as a whole: first, for the case wherein George *is* here and Mary *is* happy (i.e., where both

G	*M*	*G* and *M*
T	*T*	*T*
T	*F*	*F*
F	*T*	*F*
F	*F*	*F*

of the Conjuncts are true—the first line of the Truth Table). Then a truth value may be determined for the second case wherein George is here and Mary is *not* happy—the second line on the table; and third, where George is not here and Mary is happy—the third line; and, fourth, where George is not here and Mary is not happy—the fourth line on the Truth Table.

If we refer to what has been said earlier about Conjunction, it can be seen that the Truth Table shows clearly the idea given in our description: the sentence "George is here and Mary is happy," is considered to be true only in the first case, viz., wherein *both* of the Conjuncts are true, and it is false in the remaining three cases.

D	*P*	*D* or *P*
T	*T*	*T*
T	*F*	*T*
F	*T*	*T*
F	*F*	*F*

The same procedure may be followed for Disjunction. Consider the sentence **We will have a dance or we will have a party.** If *D* stands for **We will have a dance,** and *P* stands for **We will have a party,** then the Truth Table may be constructed as on the left.

The table illustrates the description we gave of inclusive Disjunction. If either one or both Disjuncts are true, the sentence as a whole—the Disjunction—is true.

To make our work a little easier, now that we know with some degree of precision what we mean by each of these connectives, we may use a symbolic representation for such precise meanings. For Conjunction (*and*) we will use a centered dot; "p and q" will then be noted $p \cdot q$. For Disjunction (*or*) we will use a wedge: "p or q" will be $p \vee q$.* The student may recognize certain similarities between these connective symbols—Disjunction and Conjunction—and Union and Intersection as the latter were used in the chapter on sets. Union, in set terminology, refers to a set that includes elements from either one set *or* the other set or both of two given sets, just as Disjunction, the connective symbol that is read "or," is true if either one clause *or* the other clause or both clauses of the disjunction are true. Intersection, as it is used in speaking of sets, refers to a set composed only of those elements that are in both the first *and* the second of two given sets; and a sentence described as a Conjunction is true if and only if both the first *and* the second clauses of the conjunction are true.

---

* Other symbols that are used for Conjunction are $\wedge$, &, ■.

4. IMPLICATION. Another sentential connective that is commonly used is that of Implication. An ordinary expression of Implication is found in sentences using the words "if . . . then." If it is raining, then the ground is wet. If the catalyst is present, then the reaction will take place. If a man answers the phone, it's my brother.

A sentence written as an Implication is meant to convey information of the following type: If the first part (the antecedent) is true, *then* the second part (the consequent) is also true. Therefore, in a case wherein the antecedent *is* true and the consequent is also true we say the sentence—the Implication—is true. But if the antecedent is true and the consequent is false, then, we say, the Implication is false.

Let us take an example. Suppose someone predicts, "If it rains, then we'll lose the cotton crop." "If it rains" is the antecedent, and "we'll lose the cotton crop" is the consequent. The prognostication is obviously quite true if it does rain and we do lose the cotton crop—i.e., when the antecedent and the consequent are both true. And the sentence is obviously false if the antecedent is true (it does rain) and the consequent is false (we do not lose the cotton crop).

On the right is an illustration of these two cases on the Truth Table. We also introduce here the truth values of the Implication in the two additional cases wherein the antecedent is false.

p	q	p implies q
T	T	T
T	F	F
F	T	T
F	F	T

To explain the last two lines of the Truth Table consider the following:

Suppose I say, "If you study hard, then you will get good grades." If you *do* study hard and you *do* get good grades, then what I have said is true. Of course, if you do study hard and you do *not* get good grades, then what I said was false. But if you do *not* study hard, then it really doesn't make any difference to the truth value of my proposition whether or not you get good grades. What I said *may* still be true—or, of course, it may be false. But if we are going to make all possible allowances (as we say a man is innocent until proved guilty) we may suppose that whether you did or you did not get good grades, you have not challenged the *truth* of my statement. That is, if you deny the antecedent—if you fail to take the first step of my hypothetical statement—then what I said may be considered as having been unassailed, or *true* until proved otherwise. Whether you did not study hard and you *did* get good grades or you did not study hard and did *not* get good grades, the statement that began "*If* you study hard . . ." will remain true as proposed.

For our purposes here it is necessary to give a truth value to every possibility (antecedent true, consequent true; antecedent true, consequent false; antecedent false, consequent true; and antecedent false, consequent false). The most reasonable truth value assignment to make in the last two cases, then, we say, is that of calling the Implication true.

In brief, it may be said that an Implication is true in every case except where the antecedent is true and the consequent is false.

The symbol we will use for Implication is the horseshoe. "If p, then q" will be rendered "$p \supset q$". This may, of course, be spoken, "p implies q." *

5. EQUIVALENCE. The Equivalence is usually used in ordinary language for the specific purpose of clarification. "He will push button A if and only if the red light flashes" may be used as an example. We are saying here, "If the red light flashes, then he will push button A; and he will *not* push button A if the red light does not flash." The sentence will be true, we are pointing out, not only if the red light flashes and he does push the button, but also if, since the red light does not flash, he does *not* push the button. The two instances wherein the sentence is made false are, first, if he pushes the button even though the light does not flash, or if he fails to push the button when the light *does* flash.

p	q	p if and only if q
T	T	T
T	F	F
F	T	F
F	F	T

The Truth Table for Equivalence gives a clear and immediate illustration of the sense of what has been said above.

The Truth Value for a sentence expressing Equivalence is true when the truth values of the clauses are like one another and false when the clauses are opposed to one another.

The symbol for Equivalence is $\equiv$. The sentence $p \equiv q$ may be read then as "p if and only if q" or "p is equivalent to q." †

* Another symbol in use for this connective is $\rightarrow$.

† Another symbol for equivalence is $\leftrightarrow$.

CONJUNCTION			DISJUNCTION	IMPLICATION	EQUIVALENCE
p	q	$p \cdot q$	$p \vee q$	$p \supset q$	$p \equiv q$
T	T	T	T	T	T
T	F	F	T	F	F
F	T	F	T	T	F
F	F	F	F	T	T

In summary, let us look above at the four connectives that have been introduced and the Truth Table value—or, as we will call it, the *Truth Value* for each of them.*

6. NEGATION. The last symbol (other than the grouping symbols) to be introduced into this system is that of Negation. The Negation of a phrase or statement is its direct or immediate contradiction. The Negation of We will win is We will not win. The negation of Sugar is sweet is Sugar is not sweet. In ordinary language we usually give the effect of Negation by inserting "not" into the phrase or sentence or by preceding the expression with "It is not the case that. . . ." Of course, we may also use a contradictory verb for this purpose; as the Negation of John will succeed, may be given as John will fail. But symbolization of sentences of this type must be done with particularly careful attention given to the meaning of the words.

We will use a straight dash to stand for Negation, and this dash may be used before an individual letter—indicating a clause or simple proposition—or a combination of letters—indicating a complex proposition. In the latter case the combination of letters must be enclosed by parentheses, ( ), brackets, [ ], or braces, { }. Following are some of the ways in which Negation may appear: $-p$ $-(p \vee q)$ $-[-(p \supset -q)]$ $-\{[-(p \cdot q) \vee -q] \cdot -p\}$.

The Negation of any phrase or sentence may then be indicated on the Truth Table in a manner following the two examples on p. 66. The Negation of p is simply the reverse of the truth values assigned to p in the left-hand column. The Negation of

* It should be noted here that the arrangement of T's and F's in the left-hand columns of a Truth Table is somewhat arbitrary. There are some books (e.g., Brennan's *Handbook of Logic, op. cit.*) that begin at the top row with F's instead of T's. This, of course, would change the Table Value of the connective symbols and may lead to some confusion in going from one text to another. The arrangement presented here is the one that appears to be most commonly used in current logic texts.

p	q	$-p$	② $-$	① $(p \vee q)$
T	T	F	F	T
T	F	F	F	T
F	T	T	F	T
F	F	T	T	F

$(p \vee q)$ is found by first showing the Table Value for $(p \vee q)$, and then writing the opposite value in each case below the negative sign. The column below ②, then, shows the Table Value for $-(p \vee q)$, which is *FFFT*.*

The example $-(p \vee q)$ is a representation for such a sentence as the Negation of The princess will tell the king or the queen will tell the king. That Negation may be indicated in ordinary language by It is not the case that the princess or the queen will tell the king. We will save explanation of this example until the student has become accustomed to the more complicated sentence structure.

Let us take a few examples of translations to symbols from ordinary language:

The party will be given or Lynn will not dance.	$P \vee -D$
If the radio does not work, he will send a carrier pigeon.	$-R \supset C$
Not *p* but *q*.	$-p \cdot q$
p if *q*.	$q \supset p$
Not *p* and not *q*.	$-p \cdot -q$
It is not the case that both *p* and *q*.	$-(p \cdot q)$
Not either *p* or not *q*.	$-(p \vee -q)$
p is a necessary condition for *q*.	$q \supset p$
p is a sufficient condition for *q*.	$p \supset q$
p only if *q*. (Set up truth tables for $p \supset q$ and $q \supset p$ to verify this symbolization for yourself.)	$p \supset q$

* Other symbols for negation are $\bar{p}$, $\sim p$, p'.

LOGIC EXERCISES

Find the Table Value for each of the following:

1. $-(p \cdot q)$
2. $-(-p \cdot q)$
3. $-(p \supset q)$
4. $-(p \supset -q)$
5. $-(p \vee -q)$
6. $-p \equiv -q$
7. $-(p \equiv q)$
8. $p \supset -p$
9. $p \cdot -p$
10. $p \vee -p$

Symbolize the following sentences:

11. If you do not vote, you are not a good citizen. (V,G)
12. The car was black and did not have a California license. (B,C)
13. It is not true that either classes are dismissed or the swimming pool is open. (C,S)
14. It is not the case that either we do not win the game or we break up our team. (W,B)
15. The meeting will take place if the president arrives. (M,P)
16. The meeting will take place only if the president arrives. (M,P)
17. Whenever it is raining the dog is wet. (R,D)
18. It is purple polka dot, but still not attractive. (P,A)
19. If we go to the movie, we will have popcorn and soda pop. (M,P,S)
20. Either we will go swimming or if we do not go swimming we will go horseback ridng. (S,H) (Be careful of your grouping symbols here.)

B. USE OF THE TRUTH TABLES

1. EXAMINATION OF ARGUMENTS. The Truth Table and the four basic connectives (five, if we consider Negation) may now be used in the examination of arguments that might appear to us in ordinary conversation. An argument may be composed of a series of statements (clauses or simple propositions conjoined by the connectives into sentences) and a conclusion that is *implied* by these supporting statements.

A simple argument may be something like the following: If John is at work, we'll have bacon in the morning. John is at work. Therefore, we will have bacon in the morning.

Putting the above argument into symbols, we have:

$$W \supset B.\ W.\ \text{Therefore, } B.$$

To go a little further in our symbolization, we may recognize that the first two sentences are meant together to *imply* the conclusion. That is, the first two sentences connected as a Conjunction (with an *and* between them) imply B. A more complete symbolization of that argument, then, would be $[(W \supset B) \cdot W] \supset B$. Here we are saying that *if* it is true that W implies B, *and* W is true, *then* B is true. Everything enclosed in brackets is part of the antecedent of an Implication. An argument, then, appears here as a Major Implication wherein both the antecedent and the consequent may be composed of Conjunctions, Disjunctions, Equivalences, or Implications.

W	B	[(W ⊃ B) ①	· ②	W] ①	⊃ ③	B ②
T	T	T	T	T	T	T
T	F	F	F	T	T	F
F	T	T	F	F	T	T
F	F	T	F	F	T	F

Once we have the argument in the above form it is a relatively simple matter to *determine its validity* by means of a Truth Table. The Truth Table above illustrates for us the validity of the argument based upon the specific meanings we have given to the symbols of connection we are using.

This Truth Table may be considered as a device that gives us an answer to the question, "Does $[(W \supset B) \cdot W]$ actually imply B?" We find the answer in the vertical line of *T*'s that is indicated by the number 3 in the circle above the second sign of implication. The *T*'s tell us that that Major Implication is always true.

We arrived at such an affirmative answer by first determining the Table Value for $W \supset B$ and by comparing that Table Value *through a Conjunction* with the Table Value of *W*. These first two Table Values are indicated by the 1's above the columns. We then look at the column indicated by the number 2 as the Table Value of the antecedent of an Implication that has *B* as a consequent. The Table Value of this Major Implication, then (found by comparing the Table Value of the antecedent with the Table Value of the consequent), is the Table Value of our argument.

The *argument* is valid, we say, because in any combination of truth values of the basic parts of the argument, the premises always imply the conclusion.

But many of the propositions in a reasonably complicated argument are not like the simple expressions we have been examining. They may be, instead, combinations of combinations of clauses united by the connectives, and sometimes even combinations above that.

The sentence **If your aunt died, your cousin would inherit the ranch,** is a simple Implication: $D \supset I$. A further qualification may be added, however, such as If your aunt died or she married again, then your cousin would inherit the ranch. This latter sentence has the additional complication of a Disjunction in the antecedent and must then be symbolized $(D \vee M) \supset I$. And an even further complication will arise if we negate the above conditions by saying, It is not the case that if your aunt died or she married again, your cousin would inherit the ranch. The symbolization of this would require brackets as an additional set of grouping symbols: $-[(D \vee M) \supset I]$. The parentheses enclose the antecedent of our Implication and the brackets enclose the total Implication—which is negated.

Suppose we consider the above example simply as one sentence of the following argument: It is not the case that if your aunt died or she married again, your cousin would inherit the ranch. And your aunt did not marry again. Therefore, your aunt died and your cousin does not inherit the ranch.

The above argument is symbolized:

$$\{-[(D \vee M) \supset I] \cdot -M\} \supset (D \cdot -I)$$

The Truth Table that will be needed to test the validity of the argument will be larger than the one we have already considered. In this argument we have three different clauses instead of two as in the one before. Our Truth Table, then, will have to have more lines on it in order to indicate all the possible combinations of Truth Values for these clauses.

The simple procedure of writing out the possible combinations will tell us how big the Truth Table must be, but there is a rule of combinations in mathematics that tells us the number of possible combinations we can get in a situation like this. That rule is: The number of combinations is equal to the value of 2 raised to the power n, where n represents the number of different clauses (letters) in the argument. In this case we have three different letters, so 2 raised to the third power is 8. We should, then, have eight lines in our Truth Table.

p	q	r	
T	T	T	
T	T	F	
T	F	T	
T	F	F	
F	T	T	
F	T	F	
F	F	T	
F	F	F	

The table to the right is one on which any argument with three different letters may be examined. We have used p, q, and r as variables in an attempt to make it clear that this is the standard set-up for examining a three-clause argument and that *any* letters may be substituted for the variables p, q, and r.

At this point the procedure of working out Truth Tables inevitably becomes more complicated, thus making it necessary for us to develop some means of analysis that will keep us from finding ourselves hopelessly entangled in columns of Table Values. The plan described below may seem complicated and unclear at first, but after reading the description and following through with an application to an example its value should begin to become apparent.

Beginning with a single clause or proposition such as p or a complex proposition such as $-p$ or $p \cdot q$, we determine the Table Value and put an empty circle above the column of *T*'s and *F*'s. Then we look for the clause or proposition that is associated with our first proposition through a sentential connective. If this second case is a clause or a simple proposition, we find its Table Value and put a circle above this second column and then put the number 1 in both circles to indicate we are comparing these two columns to find the Table Value for this more complicated proposition involving another connective symbol. After finding this latter Table Value we put an empty circle above that column and go on to look for the proposition that is associated with it through some other sentential connective. Whatever the complexity of the next proposition, we begin by labeling its simplest parts with the next number following the last one we have used. Again, the parts that are compared are given the same number in their respective circles as the comparison is made and the Table Value is determined. Then when the Table Value of the second complex proposition is found, the next higher number is entered into the circle above that column and also in the circle above the column of the previous complex proposition. The Table Value is entered in a column below the connective joining these two complex propositions and a circle is drawn above the connective and the column.

This procedure continues until the major sentential connective is examined and the highest number used is placed in a circle above the Table Value column of this major connective.

Let us now consider an example to see if all that explanation in theory can be brought to life by a case in point.

We will go back to the example symbolized on p. 69 and substitute the letters *D* for **Aunt died,** *M* for **Aunt married,** and *I* for **Cousin would inherit** in place of *p, q,* and *r* on the Truth Table.

			③	①	②	①	⑤	③	⑥	④	⑤	④
D	*M*	*I*	$\{-[(D$	$\vee M)$	$\supset$	$I]$	$\cdot$	$-M\}$	$\supset$	$(D$	$\cdot$	$-I)$
T	T	T	F	T	T	T	F	F	T	T	F	F
T	T	F	T	T	F	F	F	F	T	T	T	T
T	F	T	F	T	T	T	F	T	T	T	F	F
T	F	F	T	T	F	F	T	T	T	T	T	T
F	T	T	F	T	T	T	F	F	T	F	F	F
F	T	F	T	T	F	F	F	F	T	F	F	T
F	F	T	F	F	T	T	F	T	T	F	F	F
F	F	F	F	F	T	F	F	T	T	F	F	T

In the Truth Table above we begin with the proposition, $D \vee M$, find its Table Value and put a circle above the Disjunction symbol. Then we look for the clause or proposition to which this first proposition is connected and find that to be *I*, a simple proposition. We fill in the Table Value for *I* by simply copying that Table Value given under *I* in the column to the left, and we put a circle above this new column. Then we indicate the fact that we are comparing the first and second propositions as an implication by putting a 1 in each of the circles above the respective Table Values. An empty circle is drawn above the new Table Value—found under the first Implication symbol—and we go on to the next step. At this point we find that the entire proposition for which we have found the Table Value (which we now label ②) is to be negated. So we write out the Negation of this latter Table Value under the sign of Negation that precedes the brackets and put a circle above that column. This whole negated proposition, we see, is to be joined as a Conjunction with $-M$; so we work out the Table Value for $-M$ and put a circle above that column. The Conjunction to be worked out now includes $-[(D \vee M) \supset I]$ and $-M$, so we put a 3 in each of the circles above the Table Values given, work out the Table Value for this Conjunction and put an empty circle above the Conjunction symbol.

Now, of course, we have to think of using this full proposition as the antecedent of an Implication that has $(D \cdot -I)$ as its consequent. We need to find the Table Value for $(D \cdot -I)$, then, and we proceed to do this beginning with the simplest parts first. The Table Value for D may be copied from the column under D to the far left and the Table Value for $-I$ may be written as the Negation of the column to the left under I. Circles are put above each of these new Table Values and the *next higher number* is written in each of these circles to show the comparison of these two parts of a Conjunction. Note here that the last number used was 3 (the circle above the Conjunction in the antecedent was left blank). So our next higher number is 4, which should then be entered above the columns for D and for $-I$. The comparison of these latter as a Conjunction gives a column that tells us the Table Value of the consequent. A circle is drawn above this column and the number 5 is entered in that circle and in the one over the Conjunction in the antecedent. These two columns are compared as an Implication, a circle is drawn over this last Table Value, and the number 6 is entered into that circle to show—by the fact that 6 is the largest number present—that this is the Table Value of the total proposition, or argument. The Table Value is a column of *T*'s, so the proposition is a Tautology, which means that the argument is valid.

It may be noted that the Table Value of any proposition is indicated by the largest number that appears over that proposition. The numbers need not appear in left-to-right sequence, but the largest number will be found over the Table Value of the complete proposition.

The argument, we might say, has been examined from the inside out. The simplest parts of each proposition were examined first to find their Table Value. Then those values were used to find the Table Value of the proposition as a whole. From there we went to a combination of all the conditional clauses and propositions (the premises) into a complex Conjunction that then became the antecedent of the Major Implication—the antecedent of the argument.

The Major Implication is the one on which the validity of the entire argument depends. There may be one or many Implications within the premises or the conclusion of the argument (along with Conjunctions, Disjunctions, and Equivalences), but the Major Implication is the one that says, "If such and such conditions are true, then this conclusion must follow." The preceding conditions may involve propositions like Either George or Harry was there, It is not the case that Pete or Mike was there, If George was there, then Pete was there. And these conditions then, are considered together (joined as the Conjuncts of a complex Conjunction) as the antecedent of an Implication that has as its conclusion, say, George was not there. The argument is an Implication composed of a series of complex statements; and we use the Truth Table to find the Table Value of the antecedent of this Implication and the Table Value of the consequent of the Implication so that we can determine whether or not the Table Value of the argument as a whole is a column of *T*'s: the only condition that will produce for us what we call a valid argument. Such an argument that results in a column of *T*'s is called a Tautology.

There are two points that must be made and recognized here to reconcile our use of "Tautology" and "argument" with the rigorous definitions of these terms as they are used in the more systematic presentations of logic.

In the first place, a Tautology is not necessarily a Major Implication. Any logical statement that will produce a column of *T*'s on the Truth Table is considered a Tautology. Three examples of these other kinds of Tautologies are $p \vee -p$, $-(p \cdot -p)$, and $p \supset (p \vee q)$. Additional Tautologies will be given on pp. 76–81.

But more than that—to bring up the second point—the term Major Implication itself could be misleading when it is used to describe an argument. When we describe an argument as a Major Implication we are simply saying that the argument is sound or valid if there is no case wherein the antecedent is true and the consequent is false. The premises are presented as implying the conclusion and this is the argument we examine on the Truth Table. The Truth Table, then, tells us whether or not—for any truth values of the parts that make up the premises—the truth value of the Implication between the premises and the conclusion is always true. We see, that is, whether those premises do indeed always imply that conclusion. Any Implication *within* the premises may have *T* or *F* as its truth value in a valid argument, but the Major Implication, the Implication that is our argument, must always be true—a Tautology. (The distinction here is generally made as between a Logical Implication—Major Implication—and a Material Implication—the Implication as it was introduced on p. 63).

There are, of course, other possibilities for the outcome of our Truth Table analysis. Instead of a column of *T*'s, we could get a column of *F*'s for the Table Value, or even a column composed of both *T*'s and *F*'s. If we get a column of *F*'s, we say that the argument is a contradiction. That is, the premises of the argument not only do not imply the conclusion, they imply the direct opposite of the conclusion. By simply negating the entire argument we could get a list of *T*'s and thus make the argument into a Tautology.

A final Table Value composed of both *T*'s and *F*'s is an indication of neither a Tautology nor a contradiction and is of least interest to us as an argument. We say of such an argument that it is invalid and leave it marked as such.

Suppose, however, that we have a Major Implication with a conclusion q, and a Truth Table analysis produces a Table Value in which there is an intermixture of *T*'s and *F*'s. It is possible that a very simple change in the expression could produce a Tautology. It could be that by changing q to $-q$ the Table Value of the Major Implication would be made to come out all *T*'s. That is, an antecedent which does *not* imply q is true *may* imply q is false. For an illustration of this condition consider the expressions $[-(p \supset q) \vee -(p \vee q)] \supset q$ and $[-(p \supset q) \vee -(p \vee q)] \supset -q$. In the first case the Table Value is *TFTF;* and in the second case, wherein the conclusion is changed to $-q$, the Table Value is *TTTT*. This may be seen to be useful information to have available when a given set of statements is being examined simply to see what, if anything, such a set of statements, or premises, does actually imply.

There is one other possibility in the Truth Table analysis of an argument. There are occasions wherein the sentences or clauses that make up the antecedent of an argument produce, when taken together as a complex Conjunction, a column of *F*'s. That is, the antecedent is, in every case, false. Under these conditions, of course, the Major Implication will always be true. A false hypothesis produces a true Implication. If we haven't said anything true in the antecedent then anything may follow as a conclusion. This condition is defined as an argument with inconsistent premises.

Let us consider an example. Suppose we were given the following argument:

It is not true that she will either be homecoming queen or she will not take her medicine. If she has a cold, she will not be homecoming queen. She will not take her medicine and she has a cold. Therefore, she will be homecoming queen.

$$[-(Q \vee -M) \cdot (C \supset -Q) \cdot (-M \cdot C)] \supset Q$$

Q	M	C	④	①	②	①	⑥	③	④	③	⑦	⑤	⑥	⑤	⑧	⑦
T	T	T	F	T	T	F	F	T	F	F	F	F	F	T	T	T
T	T	F	F	T	T	F	F	F	T	F	F	F	F	F	T	T
T	F	T	F	T	T	T	F	T	F	F	F	T	T	T	T	T
T	F	F	F	T	T	T	F	F	T	F	F	T	F	F	T	T
F	T	T	T	F	F	F	T	T	T	T	F	F	F	T	T	F
F	T	F	T	F	F	F	T	F	T	T	F	F	F	F	T	F
F	F	T	F	F	T	T	F	T	T	T	F	T	T	T	T	F
F	F	F	F	F	T	T	F	F	T	T	F	T	F	F	T	F

This argument is symbolized and worked out on the Truth Table above. It does come out as a tautology, which would seem to indicate that the argument was valid. But notice the Table Value of the antecedent of the Major Implication—the column that appears under the first ⑦ to the left. The Table Value of this antecedent is a column of *F*'s. If the consequent of this Major Implication were $-Q$, i.e., "She will *not* be homecoming queen," the argument would still be a tautology. The premises of the antecedent are actually contradicting one another, and therefore will always be false, and the Major Implication will always be true.

The student must be aware that this kind of argument is possible and that he may get a neat column of *T*'s on the Truth Table even though the argument is quite invalid. It is, therefore, always wise to check the Table Value of the antecedent to be sure there is at least one *T*. If they are all *F*'s, the argument may immediately be labeled as "inconsistent premises" without going on to examine the Table Value of the conclusion.

2. A SET OF USEFUL TAUTOLOGIES. We have said that whenever the Table Value of a Major Implication consists of a column of *T*'s (no conditions of falsity whatever), the argument is called a Tautology. For example $[(p \supset q) \cdot p] \supset q$ was the first Tautology demonstrated.

There are a number of common—and rather simple—Tautologies that appear frequently in the kind of work we are doing here;

and, in preparation for the work coming up in the section on Logical Deduction, we will develop and examine in the following pages some of the most common Tautologies that emerge in an ordinary argument.

The Tautology mentioned above, $[(p \supset q) \cdot p] \supset q$, is one that has been known in one form or another for centuries. It has been given the name Modus Ponens in the past and that is the name we will use in this context. Modus Ponens refers to the process of affirming the antecedent in an Implication.

		①	②	①	③	②
p	q	$[(p \supset q)$	$\cdot$	$-q]$	$\supset$	$-p$
T	T	T	F	F	T	F
T	F	F	F	T	T	F
F	T	T	F	F	T	T
F	F	T	T	T	T	T

Another Tautology similar to Modus Ponens is that which is labeled Modus Tollens, which means denying the consequent. This Tautology may be demonstrated *as* a Tautology just as we did with Modus Ponens—through the use of the Truth Tables: We first symbolize the argument $[(p \supset q) \cdot -q] \supset -p$; then we check it for validity as we see done with the Truth Table on the left above.

Another commonly used Tautology may be illustrated by the following argument:

> **He will either get a haircut or he will buy sandals. He will not buy sandals. Therefore, he will get a haircut.**

Symbolizing that argument, we have: $[(H \vee S) \cdot -S] \supset H$.

		①	②	①	③	②
H	S	$[(H \vee S)$	$\cdot$	$-S]$	$\supset$	H
T	T	T	F	F	T	T
T	F	T	T	T	T	T
F	T	T	F	F	T	F
F	F	F	F	T	T	F

In checking its validity by the Truth Table on the left we see that the argument is indeed valid—it is a Tautology. If we substitute the letters p and q for H and S to give the statement more generality, we get the Tautology we will here label as Denial of a Disjunct: $[(p \vee q) \cdot -p] \supset q$.

Some of our Tautologies are so simple that Truth Table demonstrations hardly seem necessary. However, even in these it is best to *check* with the Truth Table if for no other purpose than just to be sure that the Truth Table procedure is showing validity in these simple cases wherein our intuition tells us validity is obvious.

One of the simplest arguments of the kind mentioned above is $(p \cdot q) \supset p$. For example, If it is cold and rainy, then it is cold. The Truth Table check for the validity of this argument is given to the right. This Tautology we will call Simplification, and we will indicate it with variables as we did before: $(p \cdot q) \supset p$.

		①	②	①
C	R	$(C \cdot R)$	$\supset$	C
T	T	T	T	T
T	F	F	T	T
F	T	F	T	F
F	F	F	T	F

Another Tautology we will find useful could be better named a rule of Deduction. But since we do not intend to discuss such rules until later in the book (see Chapter 4), we are introducing this argument simply as another Tautology. The name of the Tautology is Adjunction and it tells us no more than "if p is affirmed and q is affirmed, then we may affirm the Conjunction $p \cdot q$." In symbols it would be $[(p) \cdot (q)] \supset (p \cdot q)$.

The Truth Table demonstration of Adjunction plus the demonstration of the next three Tautologies will be left as an exercise for the reader.

Hypothetical Syllogism	$[(p \supset q) \cdot (q \supset r)] \supset (p \supset r)$
Absurdity	$[p \supset (q \cdot -q)] \supset -p$
Addition	$p \supset (p \vee q)$

It should be remembered that each of the above arguments is valid and must, therefore, result in a column of *T*'s for the Table Value of each Major Implication. The activity involved in proving these Tautologies will provide useful practice in the handling of Truth Tables. The practice then will lead to a greater adeptness in validating arguments plus a more vivid and profound understanding of this system of logic.

The last part of the list of Tautologies we are developing here will be devoted to Equivalences. An Equivalence is true, we have noted, if both parts of the Equivalence have the same truth value, that is, if both are true or both are false. And the Equivalence is false in the other two cases. The Equivalences to be considered in the work that follows may therefore be said to be clauses or sentences that are shown to have the same Table Values. Whenever the clause or sentence to the left of the Equivalence sign is true, then the one to the right is true—if the left is false, then the right is false. The clauses or sentences are *logically equivalent* to one another.

Another name for Equivalence is Double Implication. That is, it may be shown—by Truth Tables again, of course—that the two parts of an Equivalence logically *imply* one another: either part may be used as an antecedent of an Implication as the other is considered the consequent. (This fact is demonstrated as an Equivalence itself in the first part of Tautology Number 15, Biconditional Sentences, in the Table on p. 81.) In the work that follows this section—the Logical Deduction—we will use Equivalences simply as Double Implications: If either part of the Equivalence is affirmed, it will be considered that the other part has been implied as a Tautology.

To show by the Truth Table that two sentences or clauses are logically equivalent we must show that they both always have the same truth value. Suppose we take the Tautology, Double Negation: $p \equiv --p$. A Truth Table for one variable needs only two lines, of course, since the variable may have only two values: true or false. The identity of truth values is pointed out by the two columns labeled ③. The column of *T*'s under ④ shows the Table Value of the Equivalence, which identifies it as a Tautology.

	③	④	③	②	①
p	p	$\equiv$	$-$	$-$	p
T	*T*	*T*	*T*	*F*	*T*
F	*F*	*T*	*F*	*T*	*F*

Suppose the Equivalence, Double Negation, had been written as a Double Implication, thus: $(p \supset --p) \cdot (--p \supset p)$. The Truth Table examination of this is seen below. In this case Double Negation is written as a Conjunction of two Implications. The Table Value for the Conjunction is pointed out by the column labeled ⑧ and identifies the Conjunction as a Tautology. And, furthermore, each of the Implications is shown to be a Tautology by the two columns labeled ⑦. The Equivalence Tautology is seen then to be the Conjunction of two Tautologies of Implication formed by the reversal of the antecedent and the consequent.

	③	⑦	③	②	①	⑧	⑥	⑤	④	⑦	⑥
p	$(p$	$\supset$	$-$	$-$	$p)$	$\cdot$	$(-$	$-$	p	$\supset$	$p)$
T	*T*	*T*	*T*	*F*	*T*	*T*	*T*	*F*	*T*	*T*	*T*
F	*F*	*T*	*F*	*T*	*F*	*T*	*F*	*T*	*F*	*T*	*F*

It may be of some help at this point—considering what has just been demonstrated—to think of Equivalence not as an independently meaningful sign in its own right, but simply as a shorthand way of indicating the particular case wherein the antecedent and consequent of an Implication may be interchanged—where each part implies the other. In Chapter 4 Equivalence will be introduced in just this manner—that is, as a definition given in terms of Implication and Conjunction.

Another Tautology of Equivalence may be illustrated by the following argument: **Wealth implies happiness if and only if unhappiness implies poverty.** This argument is symbolized $(W \supset H) \equiv (-H \supset -W)$, and the Truth Table below reveals it as a Tautology. This Tautology we will call Contraposition, and it will be stated generally as $(p \supset q) \equiv (-q \supset -p)$.

		④	⑤	③	①	④	③	②
W	H	$(W \supset H)$	$\equiv$	$(-$	H	$\supset$	$-$	$W)$
T	T	T	T	F	T	T	F	T
T	F	F	T	T	F	F	F	T
F	T	T	T	F	T	T	T	F
F	F	T	T	T	F	T	T	F

The next Tautologies are De Morgan's Laws. These laws may be remembered from our discussion of sets. Just as for sets we said $(a \cap b)' = (a' \cup b')$, so now for our sentential logic we say $-(p \cdot q) \equiv (-p \vee -q)$. The fact that this is also a Tautology is demonstrated below.

		③	①	④	②	③	②
p	q	$-$	$(p \cdot q)$	$\equiv$	$(-p$	$\vee$	$-q)$
T	T	F	T	T	F	F	F
T	F	T	F	T	F	T	T
F	T	T	F	T	T	T	F
F	F	T	F	T	T	T	T

The second of De Morgan's Laws is $-(p \vee q) \equiv (-p \cdot -q)$, which may also be given Truth Table demonstration.

Five more Tautologies of Equivalence are:

Commutative Laws $\quad (p \cdot q) \equiv (q \cdot p)$

$(p \vee q) \equiv (q \vee p)$

Equivalence for Implication and Disjunction	$(p \supset q) \equiv (-p \vee q)$
Negation for Implication	$-(p \supset q) \equiv (p \cdot -q)$
Biconditional Sentences	$(p \equiv q) \equiv [(p \supset q) \cdot (q \supset p)]$
	$(p \equiv q) \equiv [(p \cdot q) \vee (-p \cdot -q)]$

Demonstrations of the Tautologies above will be left as an exercise for the student.

On pp. 80–81 all fifteen Tautologies mentioned in this section are collected in a single list. This list will be used as the main support of the material in the next section. It is suggested that the student memorize the list.

3. SUMMARY. This section on the use of Truth Tables has shown how an argument taken from ordinary language may be symbolized and examined for validity by means of a Truth Table. The sentential connectives have been used to bring together complicated sets of statements, and the Truth Table has been extended to handle three variables. For additional variables a rule was brought in from mathematics that tells us the number of lines on a Truth Table is a value equal to 2 raised to a power equal to the number of variables in the argument.

In the last part of this section we were engaged in developing fifteen common Tautologies, or valid argument forms, that will be used in the next section, Logical Deduction. These Tautologies are listed as Implications or Equivalences and their validity depends wholly upon Truth Table demonstration.

A TABLE OF SOME USEFUL TAUTOLOGIES

Simple Implication.

1. Modus Ponens (M.P.)	$[(p \supset q) \cdot p] \supset q$
2. Modus Tollens (M.T.)	$[(p \supset q) \cdot -q] \supset -p$
3. Denial of a Disjunct (D.D.)	$[(p \vee q) \cdot -p] \supset q$
4. Simplification (Simp.)	$(p \cdot q) \supset p$
5. Adjunction (Adj.)	$[(p) \cdot (q)] \supset (p \cdot q)$
6. Hypothetical Syllogism (H.S.)	$[(p \supset q) \cdot (q \supset r)] \supset (p \supset r)$
7. Absurdity (Abs.)	$[p \supset (q \cdot -q)] \supset -p$
8. Addition (Add.)	$p \supset (p \vee q)$

EQUIVALENCE OR DOUBLE IMPLICATION.

9. Double Negation (D.N.)	$p \equiv --p$
10. Contraposition (Contra.)	$(p \supset q) \equiv (-q \supset -p)$
11. De Morgan's Laws (D.M.)	$-(p \cdot q) \equiv (-p \vee -q)$ $-(p \vee q) \equiv (-p \cdot -q)$
12. Commutative Laws (Com.)	$(p \cdot q) \equiv (q \cdot p)$ $(p \vee q) \equiv (q \vee p)$
13. Equivalence for Implication and Disjunction (E.I.D.)	$(p \supset q) \equiv (-p \vee q)$
14. Negation for Implication (N.I.)	$-(p \supset q) \equiv (p \cdot -q)$
15. Biconditional Sentences (B.S.)	$(p \equiv q) \equiv [(p \supset q) \cdot (q \supset p)]$ $(p \equiv q) \equiv [(p \cdot q) \vee (-p \cdot -q)]$

LOGIC EXERCISES

Use Truth Tables to show whether the following are Tautologies, contradictions, or neither.

1. $-(-p \supset -q) \equiv (-p \cdot q)$
2. $(p \cdot -q) \supset -(-p \vee q)$
3. $[p \vee (-p \cdot q)] \vee [(-p \cdot -q)]$
4. $[-(-p \vee q) \supset r] \supset [r \vee -(p \cdot -q)]$
5. If not-q implies it is not the case that both p or not r, and if r, then p, then not p only if q.

Use Truth Tables to determine whether or not the following are valid arguments.

6. If Mark is hired, Jim will be advanced. Mark will be hired and Harry will be given a raise. Therefore, Jim will be advanced and Harry will be given a raise.
7. It is not the case that they will send the peaches and they will not send the apples. Either they will not send the grapes or they will send the peaches. They will send the peaches. Therefore, they will send the apples.
8. The soda machine is not working or you did not put in your dime or it is really a telephone booth. It is not the case both that it is not working and you did not put in your dime. If it is not a

telephone booth then it is working and you did put in your dime. It is either a telephone booth or it is not the case either that it is not working or that you did not put in your dime. Therefore it is really a telephone booth.

9. If we go to Wisconsin, we will visit the O'Briens. It is not the case that we will not go to Wisconsin or we will go to Nevada. If we do not visit the O'Briens, we will visit the Thomases. And we will either go to Nevada or we will not visit the Thomases. Therefore, we will visit the O'Briens.

Use a Truth Table for the following problem.

10. On the night of October 31, either Brian will be a prince or Lynn will be a queen or Cheryl will be a robber or Timmy will be a spook. But not all four. If Lynn is a queen, Cheryl will be a robber but Brian will not be a prince. If Timmy is a spook, Cheryl will not be a robber. If Lynn is not a queen, Timmy will be a spook and Brian will be a prince. If Brian is not a prince, Timmy will be a spook but Cheryl will not be a robber. Is there an arrangement that will solve the problem for the harried parents, or have the children fiendishly rigged up a set of inconsistent premises?

C. LOGICAL DEDUCTION

The arguments we have been analyzing on the Truth Tables have, fortunately enough, contained no more than four variables and have required, therefore, no more than sixteen lines. The addition of one more variable would have required thirty-two lines on a Truth Table, and six variables would require sixty-four lines to determine whether or not the argument was a Tautology.

It may be seen by this that it would be quite a bit to our advantage to work out a system whereby an argument may be investigated without the mechanical—but cumbersome—system of Truth Tables. By eliminating a little of the mechanical procedure and depending instead upon some additional activity of the mind, we may hope to make the process of argument-analysis briefer and somewhat more meaningful and practical.

We know now that a valid argument is simply one in which the premises that have been affirmed and accepted imply—in all cases of the truth or falsity of their parts—some conclusion given as the "therefore" sentence or clause in the argument.

1. EXAMINATION OF ARGUMENTS USING TAUTOLOGIES. On pp. 76–81 we developed a list of Tautologies said to be the ones most frequently used in arguments. We will in this section, then, go on to apply these Tautologies to our proofs. Rather than going through the demonstration of each Tautology again whenever that particular *argument form* appears, we will refer only to the Tautologies that have been proved and mention the fact that Truth Table proof has been given.

a. Simple Proofs. Suppose we are confronted with the following and asked to determine its validity:

> If pizza is served, we will quench our thirst with beer. Pizza is served. Therefore, we will quench our thirst with beer.

That argument may be generalized into $[(p \supset q) \cdot p] \supset q$, which, we may recognize, is essentially the Tautology (or argument form) called Modus Ponens. We know the argument is valid so all that is left for us now is to consider the manner in which this understanding may be presented.

The easiest system to be used in presenting any argument such as the one above—whatever its complexity and extension—is that system used in making proofs in plane geometry. We first simply write out on individual lines the premises that are given to us (in this case $p \supset q$ and p), and then make our deductions on the basis of information from the lines above, coupled with the Tautologies proved earlier on the Truth Tables.

The argument here then would be given as follows:

1. $p \supset q$	Premise
2. p	Premise
3. q	1, 2, M.P.

The premises and deduction are given to the left and the reasons are given to the right. In Step 3 q was our deduction and the reasons were given as Step 1, Step 2, and Modus Ponens.

Another argument form—Tautology—is that of Denial of a Disjunct.

Consider the following:

> Either the guests arrived late or Suzie is not mad. The guests did not arrive late. Therefore, Suzie is not mad.

This argument may be symbolized and presented as a proof in the following manner:

1. $L \vee -M$	Premise
2. $-L$	Premise
3. $-M$	1, 2, D.D.

Step 3 follows from Step 1 and Step 2 and Denial of a Disjunct.

Let us take an argument now and prove it as we did before—with a Truth Table—then prove it using the list of Tautologies.

Here is our argument:

> This is either a fire drill or a student's prank. If it is a student's prank, all men will be drafted. It is not a fire drill. Therefore, all men will be drafted.

Symbolized and entered on a Truth Table, the argument would appear as:

			①	②	①	③	②	④	③
F	S	D	$[(F \vee S)$	$\cdot$	$(S \supset D)$	$\cdot$	$-F]$	$\supset$	D
T	T	T	T	T	T	F	F	T	T
T	T	F	T	F	F	F	F	T	F
T	F	T	T	T	T	F	F	T	T
T	F	F	T	T	T	F	F	T	F
F	T	T	T	T	T	T	T	T	T
F	T	F	T	F	F	F	T	T	F
F	F	T	F	F	T	F	T	T	T
F	F	F	F	F	T	F	T	T	F

To test the same argument for validity using the Table of Tautologies we would proceed as follows:

Each sentence (or premise) of the argument is written on a separate line, given a number, and designated as a premise by the letters Pr. The conclusion we are seeking is noted on the far right.

1. $F \vee S$	Pr.	$/ \therefore D$
2. $S \supset D$	Pr.	
3. $-F$	Pr.	

In Step 4 we consider Steps 1 and 3 and use the third Tautology, Denial of a Disjunct, to get

4. S	1, 3, D.D.

In this step we took the Denial of a Disjunct, $[(p \vee q) \cdot -p] \supset q$, and compared it with Step 1, $F \vee S$, and Step 3, $-F$, and saw that these two premises would allow us to state q (or S) as having been *implied* by those premises. S is then stated as being true and our reasons for affirming it are given in the column on the right: Step 1, Step 3, and Denial of a Disjunct.

After having affirmed S in Step 4, we now consider Step 4 and the premise of Step 2 along with the first Tautology, Modus Ponens. In Modus Ponens we have $[(p \supset q) \cdot p] \supset q$. Using our present argument we would present it as $[(S \supset D) \cdot S] \supset D$. From Steps 2 and 4 and Modus Ponens we have Step 5:

5. D 2, 4, M.P.

The conclusion we wanted is achieved in two steps of a deductive proof rather than eight lines of Truth Table mechanics.

The approach we are using here we will call Logical Deduction to distinguish it from Truth Tables as a method of discovering the validity or invalidity of arguments.

We see by the above argument that we are using Logical Deduction here chiefly for the benefits it affords us in the saving of space and time. We could theoretically, at least, continue to use Truth Tables in any of the arguments that we meet in the future, no matter how long or complicated. But considerations of time and space would obviously make such action impractical.

b. Independence. It must also be noted at this point that we could go the other way in this matter. That is, where we have recognized that the Truth Table could be used to solve the most complicated arguments we find in Logical Deduction, it is also true that the system of Logical Deduction could be used to develop all but a basic four or five of the Tautologies we are using as fundamental building blocks in this system.

This leads us to an important point that must be mentioned before we continue any further in this work.

The point we wish to make here is expressed in the technical vocabulary when it is said that the Tautologies given in the list on pp. 80–81 are not independent. That is, we could take four or five of the Tautologies listed in the Table and prove all the remaining Tautologies by Logical Deduction rather than by the basically less rigorous system of Truth Tables. This will be demonstrated and elaborated upon in Chapter 4, where we will begin with the four postulates (assumptions) used by Russell and Whitehead in the book *Principia Mathematica.* These postulates, then, will be used to derive a list of theorems that will constitute the bulk of a system called the Propositional Calculus. At this point, however, we will use all fifteen of the Tautologies in our list as fundamental laws and thus avoid the more careful and rigorous development until the student has become a little more familiar with the terminology and procedures.

c. Translations from Ordinary Language. One should be careful to notice that, in Logical Deduction as well as in the Truth Table approach, we are demonstrating the validity of arguments only in the sense that the premises imply the conclusion under the rules and interpretations we have set forth for the use of sentential connectives. Many, perhaps most, arguments from ordinary language would be quite accurately interpreted by these connectives, and the question as to whether the premises support the given conclusion is answered in a way that stays very close to the original meaning of the problem. But there are subtleties and deviations and refinements in ordinary language that are intentionally avoided in the basic approach to logical analysis, and they can only be adequately handled by a more rigorous and complex system that we will aim *toward* in the development of this book. A logical system that would handle *all* the subtleties of ordinary language is perhaps impossible to conceive. As yet, at least, we have no such system available. But the student should find that even within the limited confines of the rules and procedures we have introduced here, a large amount of practical reasoning is clarified and given solid deductive support.

In the table of Tautologies we have listed a number of Implications that we have shown to be valid under the limitations we have set forth. Each of the first set of Tautologies says, "Given this specific set of conditions (in the antecedent), this particular consequent may be said to follow."

The Equivalences of the table are taken as Double Implications. Thus, not only does p imply $- -p$, but $- -p$ also implies p. If one is affirmed as a step in the proof then the other may be entered on the next step because the latter is immediately implied by the former.

It may be shown that there are numerous subtleties involved

in the meaning of Implication and Equivalence that have been overlooked.* But, as we say, the meanings that are retained for these symbols are still important enough and basic enough to give us a fairly powerful tool for use in handling ordinary arguments.

d. Additional Example. Let us go back now and take another example to be used in describing and clarifying the idea of Logical Deduction.

If a man has good schooling and reasonable opportunities he will not be a frustrated failure. Jim had reasonable opportunties and he is a frustrated failure. Therefore, he did not have good schooling.

Such an argument may be symbolized and set up for deductive proof as follows:

1. $(G \cdot R) \supset -F$	Pr.	$/\therefore -G$
2. $R \cdot F$	Pr.	
3. F	2, Simplification	
4. $--F$	3, Double Negation	
5. $-(G \cdot R)$	1, 4, Modus Tollens	
6. $-G \vee -R$	5, De Morgan's Laws	
7. R	2, Simplification	
8. $--R$	7, Double Negation	
9. $-G$	8, 6, Denial of Disjunct	

Steps 1 and 2 are the premises given. In Step 3 we used the Tautology $(p \cdot q) \supset p$; that is, if two statements are affirmed together as true, either one of them may be affirmed alone as being true.

[It may be noticed here that the order of appearance of the variables in the Tautology Simplification is not the same order as we see in Steps 2 and 3. The terms in the antecedent of $(R \cdot F) \supset F$ are reversed from those of $(p \cdot q) \supset p$. We could take care of this problem in the proof simply by using the Commutative Law—an Equivalence—on Step 2. For Step 3, then, we would have $F \cdot R$ and our reasons would be: 2, Commutativity. In making our first nod in the direction of brevity in our proofs, however, we will use this occasion to note that such a Tautology is available and may be mentioned if the question comes up, and

* For an involved and detailed discussion of the subject, read P. F. Strawson, *Introduction to Logical Theory* (London: Methuen and Co., 1960).

then we will go on to leave that particular step as assumed though not specifically stated in any of the following proofs that have need of it. The same may also be said about Disjunction when, for example, we used Denial of a Disjunct to get Step 9.]

Step 4 follows from Step 3 as one direction of the Double Implication or Equivalence. For Step 5, the $--F$ of Step 4 might be seen as $-(-F)$, and the comparison is then made between Step 1 and Modus Tollens. Setting up Modus Tollens over the argument given here, we have

$$[(p \supset q) \quad \cdot \quad -q] \quad \supset \ -p$$
$$[((G \cdot R) \supset -F) \cdot -(-F)] \supset -(G \cdot R)$$

The q of the Tautology is $-F$ of the argument we are examining; and p of the Tautology is $G \cdot R$ of our present argument. It may seem to be a little cumbersome to go through the procedure of writing $--F$ from F, because it is intuitively clear already that F denies $-F$. Our eventual goal, however, is the least possible dependence on intuition, and this is simply one step of our progression in this direction.

From Step 5 we use De Morgan's Law to get Step 6. From Step 2 and Simplification we get R in the same way we found F in Step 3. Then we use Double Negation to arrive at Step 8, which may, as in Step 4, be seen as $-(-R)$. For Step 9, then, we have *denied* the $-R$ (denied the Disjunct) of Step 6, which leaves us with the other Disjunct $-G$, and our proof is complete.

2. ARGUMENT FORM: IMPLICATION AND EQUIVALENCE. The procedure of Logical Deduction is seen to be simply an extension of the Truth Tables. Argument forms that have been shown to be valid on the tables are used in a deductive approach to avoid the necessity of going through the complete Truth Table analysis for every new argument.

The argument forms, or Tautologies, are Implications and Equivalences. We seek first to establish the antecedent of one of the Tautologies and, using that antecedent as our reason, we are then able to affirm in the next step the consequent of the given Tautology. By showing $(p \supset q) \cdot p$ we can then say that q has been implied and so put it down as the next step.

We have taken Equivalences to be used simply as Double Implications. That is, an Equivalence may be said to be an Implication read from left to right or from right to left. The affirmation of the expression on either side of the Equivalence sign implies the expression on the other side.

Equivalence Tautologies may be used in a way other than as Double Implications, however. Equivalences—but *not* Implications—may be said to be identities for our purposes here. That is, wherever we find an expression containing within it a smaller expression that is one part of an Equivalence, we may remove the latter and substitute the other part of the Equivalence in its place. For example, given the expression $(p \vee q) \supset -(r \cdot s)$ in one step of a proof, we may take out $-(r \cdot s)$ and substitute in its place $(-r \vee -s)$ by Tautology 11, De Morgan's Law. Also, we could substitute $--q$ for q in the given expression by Tautology 9, Double Negation. This is said to be the use of Logical Equivalence, where Equivalence means simply that the expressions on both sides of the Equivalence sign have the same Table Value on the Truth Tables.

The student should take special care to note that such substitution is *not possible* with Implications. We may *derive the next step* through a Tautology of Implication, but we cannot make substitutions for parts of an expression through this Tautology.

3. SPECIAL METHODS. We will continue with an examination of this system of Logical Deduction by investigating some of the special methods that are used to shorten and simplify the proof procedures.

a. Conditional Proofs. When we consider the most common meaning of Implication we find some hypothetical condition that, *if true,* leads to a certain conclusion. We do not say that the antecedent *is* true, but simply that *if* it is true then so-and-so will follow.

This understanding of Implication is an important preliminary to the understanding of a special kind of proof we will be using in Logical Deduction.

When a hypothetical statement—or Implication—is used in logic, we consider it to have truth value and *meaning* even though it does not describe the actual existence of a thing or circumstance. If we say, Men are muscular and hirsute, or, People are male or female, we are describing conditions that we mean to indicate actually exist. When, however, we say, If we go by air, we'll arrive two days earlier, or, If you drink that, you will be happy, then we are stating conditions that only *may* exist. But these statements would still be meaningful for us even though the conditions described in the antecedent did not now or never did exist.

In conditional proofs we play upon this use of Implication. We develop statements in our argument that are only hypothetical—only Implications—but that have clear and useful meanings in a logical discussion.

Take, to begin with, the statement, **There are no aviators present, or there is a baseball player present.** This is an affirmative statement—in the form of a Disjunction—of conditions that do exist. It may be symbolized $-A \vee B$. Suppose now we consider the possibility that a baseball player is not present. The premise $-A \vee B$ has been accepted and now we want to reason with the possibility that $-B$ is true. Setting up a deductive argument, we have:

1.	$-A \vee B$	Pr.
2.	$\quad\mid -B$	Hypothetical Premise (H. P.)
3.	$\quad\mid -A$	1, 2, Denial of Disjunct
4.	$-B \supset -A$	2–3, Conditional Proof (C. P.)

After affirming the given premise, we began in Step 2 a conditional proof. This is done by *hypothesizing* a condition that may or could exist in relationship to our given premise. The reason for Step 2, then, is given as Hypothetical Premise. From the hypothetical premise and the given premise and Denial of a Disjunct, $-A$ follows, as we see on the list of Tautologies.

We have now shown in a subordinate proof—which, in this case, is a very short, two-step proof—that $-B$ implies $-A$. This follows, we say, from the Steps 2 through 3 and conditional proof. Using a hypothetical premise, the given premise, and the rules of Logical Deduction, we have given to the right of the vertical line a conditional proof.

In Step 4, then, we enter this discovery as a legitimate, meaningful, and useful piece of information that may be considered as part of the major proof. "*If* no baseball player is present," we say, "then there are no aviators present." And this information is given to us by the premise of Step 1 and our rules of Logical Deduction.

The formal arrangement of the proof may make the procedure seem strange at first, but it may help to remember that all that is being done is the introduction of a hypothesis or supposition within the major proof to gain an Implication that may itself be enlightening or that may be used further on in the reasoning.

Let us consider the following argument and the proof given below:

If more work implies a higher salary, then the contract will be signed. There will either be no trainees or additional time will be allowed. It is not the case that there will be more work and no trainees. If we do not have higher salaries, then there will be no additional time allowed. Therefore, the contract will be signed.

1.	$(M \supset H) \supset C$	Pr. $/\therefore C$
2.	$-T \vee A$	Pr.
3.	$-(M \cdot -\mathrm{T})$	Pr.
4.	$-H \supset -A$	Pr.
5.	$\mid\ M$	H.P.
6.	$\mid\ -M \vee --T$	3, D.M.
7.	$\mid\ --M$	5, D.N.
8.	$\mid\ --T$	6, 7, D.D.
9.	$\mid\ A$	2, 8, D.D.
10.	$\mid\ --A$	9, D.N.
11.	$\mid\ --H$	4, 10, M.T.
12.	$\mid\ H$	11, D.N.
13.	$M \supset H$	5–12, C.P.
14.	C	1, 13, M.P.

Notice that the first premise of this proof tells us that we can affirm *C* as being true if we can show that *M* implies *H*. That is, the antecedent of the Implication that has *C* as a consequent is itself an Implication with *M* as an antecedent and *H* as a consequent.

Our procedure here, then, is to use a conditional proof. We say, "Suppose *M* to be true," and follow through with our deduction to discover *H* as a consequence of that supposition. When it has been shown that *H* follows from the assumption that *M* is true, we have the necessary conditions—as called for in the first premise—to state that *C* is true.

In making the conditional proof we used the premises that were originally given *plus* the hypothetical premise introduced in Step 5. Our hypothesis, *M*, is introduced as a statement that may be true with respect to the other statements given as premises. In working out our proof we are saying, "Taking *all* those premises as true as affirmed, what *could* we get if we supposed M to be true?"

Hypothesizing M has led us to H. M implies H, we may now say—and we *do* say that for Step 13, which is listed as part of the major proof. The next step refers back to Step 1 and Modus Ponens to give us C, our conclusion.

Any hypothetical premise may be introduced anywhere at all as the beginning of a conditional proof. It must always be remembered, however, that the premise that has been introduced will eventually come out as the antecedent of an Implication in the major proof. The chaos that we may seem to have been leading to with this unrestricted introduction of premises will be seen to be, in reality, a controlled set of conditions that will allow us no more uninhibited freedom than any of the other rules we use in the system of Logical Deduction.

b. Absurdity. The seventh Tautology gives us a procedure of proof that will be found to be quite useful in some cases where the problem can be particularly difficult.

The Law of Absurdity tells us that in the simpler cases of a two-valued logical system (wherein a statement may be considered as either true *or* false and must be one or the other),* one approach to a proof may be simply that of showing that a statement *cannot* be true and *must,* therefore, be false. A given statement is shown to lead to a contradiction—or absurdity—and is therefore denied as being true. The denial of the statement (or its negation), then, is affirmed as true.

The following exercise, using conditional proof and the Law of Absurdity, is an example of this procedure:

1.	$r \vee s$	Pr.	$/\therefore r$
2.	$s \supset t$	Pr.	
3.	$-s \vee -t$	Pr.	
4.	$\quad \mid -r$	H.P.	
5.	$\quad \mid s$	1, 4, D.D.	
6.	$\quad \mid t$	5, 2, M.P.	

* For logical systems that have more than two values see J. Rosser and A. R. Turquette, *Many-Valued Logic* (New York, Humanities Press, 1952).

7.	$\quad\vert\; --t$	6, D.N.
8.	$\quad\vert\; -s$	7, 3, D.D.
9.	$\quad\vert\; s \cdot -s$	5, 8, Adj.
10.	$-r \supset (s \cdot -s)$	4–9, C.P.
11.	$--r$	10, Absurdity (Abs.)
12.	r	11, D.N.

In order to prove that r was true, we hypothesized the negation of r. Then, through five more steps of the conditional proof we demonstrated that $-r$ led to an absurd statement, that is, s and $-s$ (which is something like "It is raining and it is not raining"). In Step 10 we expressed the conclusion of the conditional proof, $-r \supset (s \cdot -s)$, and in Step 11 we used the Law of Absurdity, which tells us that if p implies both q and $-q$, then p must be false. In our argument, if $-r$ is false, then $--r$, or r, must be true.

In summary, the proof by absurdity plays upon the important fact that we are considering meaningful statements in our system of Logical Deduction to have only two possible values. And if we are able to show that one value of a statement (either an affirmation or denial of the statement) leads to a contradiction, or absurdity, then we may say that the statement does have the opposite value.

The system of Logical Deduction, as it has been presented in this chapter, is essentially nothing more than an extension of the Truth Tables. Each step of the proof is supported by a Tautology that has been proved by the matrix system * we call Truth Tables. Two special kinds of deductive proof also derive from the Tautologies of the Truth Table. Conditional proof depends upon the meaning given to Implication as described in Truth Table symbols, and proof by absurdity depends upon the specific Tautology $[p \supset (q \cdot -q)] \supset -p$.

In a later chapter we will introduce a system called the Propositional Calculus (or the Calculus of Propositions) that will be developed in a much more rigorous style than Logical Deduction, although the procedures for making proofs will appear to be very

* A dictionary definition of "matrix" is "That within which something originates, takes form, or develops." A Truth Table, then, is a matrix for us because it is from the Truth Table that we learn the Table Value of a proposition and discover whether or not our arguments are valid.

much the same. In the Propositional Calculus the number of axioms—Tautologies, here—is reduced to the very minimum, and strict and exact rules are established to give the system a precision and exactitude that we are never quite able to achieve in Logical Deduction.

LOGIC EXERCISES

Prove by Logical Deduction using Tautologies:

1. If Communism is a success, then the Soviets will bury us. If it is not a success, the Soviets will be apprehensive. The Soviets will not bury us. Therefore, they will be apprehensive. (*C*, *B*, *A*)
2. If the Rio Grande Indians arrive, the meeting will come to a standstill. The Peruvians and the Quechuans will be there. Either the Rio Grande Indians will be there or the Quechuans will not. So it is clear that the Peruvians will be there and the meeting will be at a standstill. (*R*, *S*, *P*, *Q*)
3. This is either the name of something or the idea of something. If it is an idea then it is confusing. It is elementary and it is not confusing. Therefore, it is the name of something. (*N*, *I*, *C*, *E*)
4. If we go in the car, we will not take the animals. If we do not go by rail, we will not have enough space. We will either go by car or we will not go by rail. We will take the animals. Therefore (no matter what happens) we will not have enough space. (*C*, *A*, *R*, *E*)
5. If George is respected, then he is educated. He is admired and he is not denounced. He is either not educated or he is denounced. He is respected or he is admired. Therefore, he is not respected. (*R*, *E*, *A*, *D*)
6. The examination will be given and *A's* will be distributed. If performances are satisfactory, there will be no yellow slips. Either performances are satisfactory or no *A's* will be distributed. Therefore, no yellow slips will be distributed. (*E*, *A*, *S*, *Y*)
7. If the rains come, the shelter will be needed. It is not the case either that we will perish or the rains will not come. Either the shelter will not be needed or Tarzan will assist us. Therefore, we will not perish and Tarzan will assist us. (*R*, *S*, *P*, *T*)
8. We will either not pay taxes or a return must be filled out. We are overworked but we are not unorganized. If they send us a bill then we will have to get a loan and we will not enjoy the prospects. If we fill out a return and we are not unorganized then we

will be safe. If they do not send us a bill then we are unorganized. If we make a loan then we will pay our taxes. Therefore (we see with great relief) we will be safe. (*T*, *R*, *O*, *U*, *B*, *L*, *E*, *S*)

9. If he was Latin or Oriental, then he was a gentleman and he was not impertinent. It is not the case both that he was not impertinent and that he was corruptible. But he was Latin. Therefore, he was not corruptible. (*L*, *O*, *G*, *I*, *C*)

Use conditional proofs:

10. If you feed your pet armadillo too much, he will not ant-eat. He will either get chubby or he will no longer be tame. He will either be tame or he will not be fed too much. Therefore, if he is fed too much, then he will not ant-eat and he will be tame and chubby. (*F*, *A*, *C*, *T*)
11. If ours is a sun-centered solar system, then Oresme was prophetic. If Oresme was prophetic, he was not lazy-minded. Either the Aristotelian system is adequate or there is another reasonable explanation. Oresme was lazy-minded or the Aristotelian system is not adequate. Therefore, if there is no reasonable explanation, then ours is not a sun-centered solar system. (*S*, *O*, *L*, *A*, *R*)
12. If you do not have knowledge, you act automatically. Either your concepts are noetic or you do not think. You cannot both act automatically and have noetic concepts. Therefore, if you think, you have knowledge. (*K*, *A*, *N*, *T*)
13. If it is true that if one is not tolerant, he is not happy, then ideals are possible. A person is either not naive or he is overly kind to his fellows. It is not the case that one can be both not naive and not tolerant. If one is overly kind, then he is not happy. Therefore, ideals are possible. (*T*, *H*, *I*, *N*, *K*)

Prove by reductio ad absurdum: (Remember to look for cases of invalidity or contradiction).

14. The guests will leave if John sings or Mary plays the piano. If drinks are brought in or stories are told, then the guests will be entertained. If the party is not a happy one, then John will sing or stories will be told. If the guests are entertained or if they leave, then Mary will play the piano. Mary will not play the piano. Therefore, the party will be a happy one. (*L*, *J*, *M*, *D*, *S*, *E*, *H*)
15. If the lights go on and there is no action, then it is not the case that either a movie will be made or the producer will be happy. If a movie is not made, then Sandra the Starlet will never succeed.

It is not the case that either the lights will not go on or Sandra will not succeed. Therefore, the movie will be made and Sandra will succeed. (*L, A, M, P, S*)

16. Either the dog is in my bedroom or the room is not locked. If Mother is home then the dog is not in the bedroom. Therefore, if the door is locked, Mother is not home. (*D, L, M*)
17. Sanity will reign or operations will cease. If sanity reigns, we will not employ idiots. If operations cease the mob will rise. Therefore, either we will not employ idiots or the mob will rise. (*S, O, E, M*)
18. If Dorothy passed philosophy then she either flunked French or she lived on tranquilizers. She did not flunk French. Therefore, if she did not live on tranquilizers, then she either did not pass philosophy or she studied her assignments. (*P, F, T, S*)

Use any approach that is adequate to prove the following:

19. If it is not the case that if it is raining or snowing, then the lake is frozen and we will not camp, then we will stay home this weekend; or we will not be disappointed even though it snows. It does not snow. We will not stay home this weekend. The lake is not frozen. Therefore, it will not rain. (*R, S, F, C, H, D*) (How many lines would you need to work this out on a Truth Table?)
20. If it is a brown book, then if it is on metaphysics, then if it is not the case that it is trivial and platitudinous, then it is not true that if you are enlightened, you will consign it to the flames. Also, if it is not brown or it is not on metaphysics, it will be on the yellow shelves. You will consign it to the flames and it is not trivial. Therefore, it will be on the yellow shelves. (*B, M, T, P, E, C, Y*)
21. If it is true that if my friend gets a job, then if he pays his debts, then the moon is blue; then if he gets a job implies he pays his debts, then if he gets a job, then the moon is blue. (*J, D, B*)
22. If the police are there the function will be quiet. If a riot erupts the management will sue. Either the police will be there or a riot will erupt. Therefore, the function will be quiet or the management will sue. (*P, Q, R, S*)
23. If a man's ideas are criticized, then if he is healthy he will not avoid arguments. If he does not avoid arguments and takes notice of the points made, then he will not grow stale. If he is not educated, he will take notice of the points made but he will still grow stale. Therefore, if a man's ideas are criticized, then if he is healthy, he is educated. (*C, H, A, N, G, E*)

24. The method of substitution on Equivalences (described on p. 89) should be used for this problem. That is, given the expression $p \vee - - q$, q may be substituted directly for $- - q$, thereby making the expression $p \vee q$. The letters "I.S." (Identity Substitution) are used as a reason for this step.
If it is true that if peace and quiet are to prevail, then if reduction of armaments implies hope and not a solution, then there will either be tension but no war or it is not the case that there will either be confusion or no hope. There will be no reduction of armaments or there will be tension and hope. If there is hope there will be confusion. There will be no confusion or there will be no solution. Therefore, there will be no war. (*P, Q, R, H, S, T, W, C*)
25. If it is true that if he is happy and inebriated, then he is a caution; then if he is happy, if he is inebriated, he is a caution. (*H, I, C*)

4. EXISTENTIAL AND UNIVERSAL QUANTIFIERS. In the work we have been doing so far, we have concerned ourselves primarily with the handling of sentential connectives. It may have become more and more apparent as the arguments were analyzed that the phrases that were *joined* by these connectives were of no importance whatsoever in the logical function.

For example, consider an argument such as the following:

> If more work implies a higher salary, then the contract will be signed. There is not more work. Therefore, the contract will be signed.

Below is the symbolization and proof of this argument:

1.	$(M \supset H) \supset C$	Pr. $/ \therefore C$
2.	$-M$	Pr.
3.	$-M \vee H$	2, Add.
4.	$M \supset H$	3, E.I.D.
5.	C	1, 4, M.P.

But such an argument might also have been given as

> If the fact that Al is married implies he is happy, then his courtship was pleasant. It is not the case that he is married. Therefore, Al's courtship was pleasant.

Or it may stand for any number of other arguments that you wish to invent—limited only by your imagination.

This follows from the fact that we have been directing all of our attention to the connectives in the argument form rather than to the individual clauses that make up the bulk of the sentences or statements. We have not taken into account at all the differences between Universal and Particular propositions that were given careful treatment in the discussion of traditional logic. And we may say, therefore, that our treatment has definitely been a limited one in so far as we are unable as yet to deal with this obviously important area in the study of logic.

We need terms, phrases, and symbols that will enable us to differentiate between Universal and Particular statements, and we need a system of rules that will allow us to manipulate these terms or concepts with consistency and coherence.

The terms that have been developed for this purpose are called Existential and Universal Quantifiers. They are related to the Particular and Universal propositions of traditional logic in that they refer to *some* and *all* respectively, but there is an important difference between the ideas involved in each set of terms. The Universal proposition of traditional logic—as we have noted before—carries with it the assumption that there *are* members of the group to which it refers. It was not meant to be used, we might say, unless there *were* the kind of entities mentioned in the proposition. If All Martians are green were used in a syllogism, the question as to whether or not there were Martians would have to be decided in the affirmative before the argument would even be offered as a meaningful one.*

In modern logic, however, the Universal Quantifier is carefully defined in such a way that the question of existence is excluded from its meaning. The Universal Quantifier, written (x) and spoken, "For all x . . . ," means simply that we are to take a given quality or characteristic and consider every x that may *possibly* have such a quality; and the expression cannot be made meaningless by pointing out that there is nothing with these properties or nothing that we *know* as having these properties.

* P. F. Strawson contends in *Introduction to Logical Theory, op. cit.*, p. 177, that ". . . in order for any statement of one of the four forms [*A,E,I,O* propositions] to have a truth-value, to be true or false, it is necessary that the subject class should have members. . . . The adoption of this suggestion will save the rules of the traditional system from breakdown [from the standpoint of modern logic]."

Existence is not a controlling factor in our use of the Universal Quantifier, but it is very much our concern, obviously, in the case of the Existential Quantifier. The Existential Quantifier, written $(\exists x)$ and pronounced, "There exists an x . . . ," refers to one, some, many things in the universe that *do* exist and that *do* have the properties assigned to them in the part of the expression following the Quantifier. The Existential Quantifier is used to indicate *some* of a group or *part* of a group or *one* of a group, and so forth—but *always* to refer to an existent entity.

To get a better picture of the meaning of these Quantifiers, let us consider some phrases and the way they may be used to transmit information.

Suppose we say, **Khrushchev is a bartender.** The idea here is quite clear: There is a man we (apparently) know, and that man is a bartender: a case of clear communication through the use of a singular proposition. But suppose we wish to become more general—as indeed we do in mathematics and logic—so that our ideas will have wider application. Suppose we say, **x is a bartender,** then, to give us the generality of a variable used as the subject. This simple phrase we will call a formula. But what kind of information is communicated in this collection of symbols? By substituting a proper name for x we get as many singular propositions as we wish, but this still has not met our aim of providing ourselves with all the tools available to traditional logic. If, however, we precede the formula **x is a bartender** with a Universal Quantifier, we get, **For all x, x is a bartender,** meaning by this that everything is a bartender. It would be immediately clear, of course, that this statement was false and we would so label it.

If we said, **There exists an x, such that x is a bartender,** there is little question that this statement would be true. That is, there *are* bartenders. There is at least one thing in the universe such that it is a bartender.

x is a bartender is a generalization whose limited use would be in standing for any singular proposition. But for wider generalizations, in terms of *all* and *some,* it is necessary to introduce the formula with a Quantifier to give more extensive reference and usage to our method of symbolization. This is, to some logicians, an extremely interesting aspect of the use of quantifiers. Without any substitution on the variable we are still able to give the formula truth value by simply preceding it with an Existential or a Universal Quantifier.*

In using Existential and Universal Quantifiers, the variable x stands for an unfettered, unqualified, totally generalized item of the universe. It means anything that can be recognized as a unit or a specific and individual entity. The predicates of logic then are assigned to these individuals to allow us to indicate the unique aspect of the individual entities that we use (invent or recognize) in distinguishing between them.

Letting x be the variable on which unlimited substitution can be made, we assign predicates to this variable by placing a capital letter representing the predicate before the variable. The quality of being **happy** or being **green** or being **solvent** would be assigned to x, then, as Hx, Gx, and Sx, respectively.

Using the sentential connectives, relationships between the predicates can be noted. **Thing is happy and green** would be symbolized $Hx \cdot Gx$. **If thing is solvent then thing is green** would be $Sx \supset Gx$.

The Universal Quantifier may then be used to produce a logical sentence such as $(x)(Sx \supset Gx)$ or **For all x if x is solvent then x is green,** or **Anything that is solvent is green.** The use of the Existential Quantifier may give $(\exists x)(Sx \cdot Gx)$ or **There exists an x such that x is solvent and x is green,** or **There is something that is solvent and green.**

A few more examples of the use of the Quantifiers and predicates are:

All boys are mischievous.	$(x)(Bx \supset Mx)$
Some girls are not sweet.	$(\exists x)(Gx \cdot -Sx)$
No cigarettes are healthful.	$(x)(Cx \supset -Hx)$
Martians are green.	$(x)(Mx \supset Gx)$
Some women are fickle.	$(\exists x)(Wx \cdot Fx)$

One must be careful to avoid translating the last Particular proposition using an Implication in the formula. If we had used an Implication we would have symbolized it as $(\exists x)(Wx \supset Fx)$ which may be rendered $(\exists x)(-Wx \vee Fx)$, if we change the

* ". . . One of the profoundest facts of logic is that we do not have to replace variables by names in order to get true or false sentences [from such formulas as **x loved y** and $x + y = z + 2$]." Patrick Suppes, *Introduction to Logic* (Princeton: D. Van Nostrand, 1957), p. 47.

formula $Wx \supset Fx$ using the Tautology Equivalence for Implication and Disjunction given on p. 81. The truth of the latter sentence is dependent only upon the condition that there is something in the world which is not a woman. (A Disjunction is true if either one of the Disjuncts is true.) But this is *not* the idea that was originally meant to be expressed. Very rarely would one wish to affirm the existence of something in such a manner. Caution should be used to avoid such a mistake in the translation of Existential propositions.

For another problem in making translations, consider:

A few Russians are not Communists.

$$(\exists x)(Rx \cdot -Cx) \text{ or}$$
$$-(x)-(Rx \cdot -Cx)$$

The latter case is an illustration of the way in which a Universal Quantifier may be used in the place of an Existential Quantifier. But this fact calls for further elaboration.

5. TRANSLATIONS BETWEEN EXISTENTIAL AND UNIVERSAL QUANTIFIERS. If we will consider carefully what it is we are saying when we use Existential and Universal Quantifiers, we may see how translations can be made from one to the other while, at the same time, keeping the meaning of the proposition as it is given in ordinary language.

Let us start with a simple example. Consider Everything is material. Symbolizing with a Universal Quantifier, we get $(x)(Mx)$. Now, to say the same thing, to express the same proposition, using an Existential Quantifier we say, in effect, that there is not anything in the universe that is *not* material. Symbolically, $-(\exists x)-(Mx)$, which would be read, It is not the case that there exists an x such that x is not material.

For another example, suppose we wish to symbolize the proposition, There are some things that are not green. Using the language of Quantifiers this would be read, There exists an x such that x is not green, and would be symbolized $(\exists x)-(Gx)$. If we think of the same proposition in terms of Universal Quantifiers, we would restate it in the form, Not everything is green, or It is not the case that for all x, x is green. Using our symbols this would be $-(x)(Gx)$.

We see by these simple cases, then, that a proposition can be symbolized using either of the two Quantifiers without changing the meaning of the proposition as it appears in either form. But let us see how this would work with more complicated statements.

Suppose we are given the proposition, **All teachers are sympathetic.** This may be symbolized $(x)(Tx \supset Sx)$, or **For all x, if x is a teacher then x is sympathetic.** Now, to change this into an expression using Existential Quantifiers, we must first rephrase the proposition. We can say the same thing, produce the same meaning, by stating it as **There are no teachers that are not sympathetic,** or **It is not the case that there is something such that it is a teacher and it is not sympathetic.** In symbols: $-(\exists x)(Tx \cdot -Sx)$. As it now appears this Existential Quantification bears very little resemblance to the Universal Quantification given above of the same proposition. But let us take the formula alone $(Tx \cdot -Sx)$ and refer back to the Table of Tautologies on p. 81. The Tautology called "Negation for Implication" tells us that $-(p \supset q)$ is equivalent to (or, in one sense, may be substituted for) $(p \cdot -q)$. If we used that Tautology on $(Tx \cdot -Sx)$ we could get $-(Tx \supset Sx)$, or the negation of the formula as it was used with the Universal Quantifier. So the translation of $(x)(Tx \supset Sx)$ would be $-(\exists x)-(Tx \supset Sx)$.

For one more example, let us take **Some satellites are astronauts.** Using an Existential Quantifier, this would be given $(\exists x)(Sx \cdot Ax)$. If we thought of it in terms of Universal Quantifiers we might render it, **Not all satellites are not astronauts,** or **It is not true that all things are not both a satellite and an astronaut.** Symbolically, $-(x)-(Sx \cdot Ax)$. If it would make more sense, the latter expression could be rendered $-(x)(Sx \supset -Ax)$ through the use of Negation for Implication and Double Negation on the formula $-(Sx \cdot Ax)$. The latter Universal Quantification would be read, then, "**It is not true for all x that if x is a satellite then x is not an astronaut.**" (If the "all" of "for all *x*" is emphasized, i.e., "for *all x*," the meaning of this statement may become clearer.)

Let us now go on to an articulation of the rules of transformation that should be appearing in the examples we have given. Taking the four propositions from traditional logic, *A*, *E*, *I*, and *O*, we may express each of them using the Universal Quantifier as follows:

All A is B.	$(x)(Ax \supset Bx)$
No A is B.	$(x)(Ax \supset -Bx)$

Some *A* is *B*.	$-(x)(Ax \supset -Bx)$
Some *A* is not *B*.	$-(x)(Ax \supset Bx)$

The same propositions may be expressed using Existential Quantifiers:

All *A* is *B*.	$-(\exists x)(Ax \cdot -Bx)$
No *A* is *B*.	$-(\exists x)(Ax \cdot Bx)$
Some *A* is *B*.	$(\exists x)(Ax \cdot Bx)$
Some *A* is not *B*.	$(\exists x)(Ax \cdot -Bx)$

If, in the Universally Quantified propositions, the Implications are changed to Conjunctions, the Universal propositions may be shown to be equivalent to the Existential propositions in the following manner:*

$$(x)-(Ax \cdot -Bx) \equiv -(\exists x)(Ax \cdot -Bx)$$
$$(x)-(Ax \cdot Bx) \equiv -(\exists x)(Ax \cdot Bx)$$
$$-(x)-(Ax \cdot Bx) \equiv (\exists x)(Ax \cdot Bx)$$
$$-(x)-(Ax \cdot -Bx) \equiv (\exists x)(Ax \cdot -Bx)$$

In each case the formula remains the same on both sides of the equation and the signs preceding the Quantifier and the formula are exactly reversed.

When the above table is used to make a translation in a proof the reason for the step in which it occurs will be given as "Trans."

Consideration of the meanings of each of these sentences and the various ways in which they may be expressed will help to give a better understanding of the symbolism of modern logic *and* of the meaning of these four propositions that have been inherited from traditional logic.

SUMMARY. Modern logic, as opposed to traditional logic, treats Universal and Particular propositions with a concern for hypothetical or actual existence. The Universal Quantifier used in modern logic refers to all possible things that may have a given characteristic, but is pointedly and specifically defined in such a way as to exclude any reference to existence. The Existential Quantifier, on the other hand, *does* specifically refer to an existing entity.

* The change from Implication to Conjunction may be made as stated above by using the Tautology Negation for Implication: $-(p \supset q) \equiv (p \cdot -q)$. Then $Ax \supset Bx$ becomes, with Double Negation, $-(Ax \cdot -Bx)$: so $(x)(Ax \supset Bx)$ would be $(x)-(Ax \cdot -Bx)$. Using Existential Quantifiers it is $-(\exists x)(Ax \cdot -Bx)$.

An unquantified formula such as $x + 5 = 12$ (a phrase that is neither true nor false) is given a particular truth value through the use of an Existential or a Universal Quantifier. $(x)(x + 5 = 12)$ is false; $(\exists x)(x + 5 = 12)$ is true.

Predicates are used for descriptions in formulas. $Ax \cdot Bx$ means that a thing has the quality A (such as amber) and the quality B (such as breakable).

The Universal and Particular propositions of traditional logic may be expressed in modern logic through the use of *either* the Universal or the Existential Quantifier.

The next section will be concerned primarily with showing how the Existential and Universal Quantifiers may be used in the proofs of Logical Deduction, and how such devices serve to give the system greater application and flexibility.

6. LOGICAL DEDUCTION USING QUANTIFIERS. We noted on p. 97 that the propositions we have been using have been essentially unanalyzed; the propositions themselves carried no meaning for us in the development of our system of Logical Deduction. We were concerned only with the use of sentential connectives, and arguments such as the following could not be made the subject of our deductions:

> All men are mortal. Some octogenarians are men.
> Therefore, some octogenarians are mortal.

The problem in an example such as this, of course, comes from the fact that this argument does depend very specifically upon the meaning and analysis of the individual propositions that make it up. The subject and predicate of each statement are important in the consideration of the entire argument.

Whereas before we were considering entire propositions in relationship to one another through the sentential connectives, we have now made our analysis even more specific by breaking down the propositions themselves into their constituent parts—the subjects and predicates.

The argument above, which cannot be given meaningful and adequate translation using the limited system of symbolization we originally had available to us, *can* be symbolized by using the Quantifiers introduced in the last section.

$$(x)(Mx \supset Tx) \qquad \underline{/ \therefore (\exists x)(Ox \cdot Tx)}$$
$$(\exists x)(Ox \cdot Mx)$$

By considering both the subject and the predicate of each proposition as predicates and by referring—through the Quantifiers—to individual, unqualified elements of our universe,* we have a way to indicate all the atomic parts of a proposition. These elemental parts, then, can be brought together in different patterns of organization to represent most of the propositions we will be wanting to symbolize.

It may be well to mention again the fact that this method of symbolization gives us meaningful statements—statements that may be assigned the values of true or false—without sacrificing the generality that makes a formal system of mathematics or logic so useful. The abstract nature of the variable x is as useful to us in logic as a similar variable would be in algebra or the infinitesimal calculus.

Now that we have the Quantifiers, however, it will be necessary to consider the special ways in which they may be used in our proofs. An additional set of rules must be introduced to ensure the validity of the arguments in which these Quantifiers appear.

The rules that will be introduced here are similar to the ones found in the logical system identified as Predicate Calculus in other logic texts, although the work here, as we have said before, is still that of Logical Deduction, the extension of the Truth Tables.

a. Universal Quantifiers. Let us begin with the Universal Quantifier and re-examine its meanings as we discover the procedures for using it in Logical Deduction.

Once again, we will take a relatively simple argument with which to begin our description of the usage of Universal Quantifiers.

---

* In ordinary speech, when we consider a proposition such as All whales are mammals, we think rather loosely of the predicate, mammals, modifying the subject, whales. But in the language of Quantifiers, as in the language of sets, we are somewhat more cautious. It will be remembered that in the section on sets we spoke of "elements" that belonged to individual sets or that were shared in common by two or more sets. The proposition above, then, would be given as Any element of the set whales is also an element of the set mammals, thus indicating another set of elements described as the Intersection of the sets whales and mammals. We are doing much the same thing in the language of Quantifiers with our variable, x. Whales and mammals are no longer subject and predicate respectively, but each is a predicate modifying the unqualified element or variable, x.

All logicians are mathematicians. All Positivists are logicians. Therefore, all Positivists are mathematicians.

Symbolized and set up in the form of a proof, this would be:

1. $(x)(Lx \supset Mx)$ Pr. $\underline{/\therefore (x)(Px \supset Mx)}$
2. $(x)(Px \supset Lx)$ Pr.

In the generalized form shown above, the proposition would be difficult to manipulate in a standard deduction. Because of this, we approach it with a procedure that gives the idea of the proposition in specific terms without at the same time losing any of its generality.

Knowing that the proposition stands for any element in our universe ("For *all* x . . ."), we say that we are going to direct our attention—for the major part of the proof—to *one* of these elements chosen arbitrarily out of the entire number of elements available.

We will take $(x)(Lx \supset Mx)$ (which says that *any* x that has the property L will also have the property M) and choose an arbitrary element out of the universe to which we will assign the property L. By redirecting our thoughts, then, to some one element instead of to the collection of all elements, we have something specific to work with as we carry out our proof.

The rule that is introduced here to account for a step such as this is called Universal Specification, and it refers to nothing more than the simple act of specifying an arbitrary element out of the universe of all elements that may be considered to have a given property.

The next two steps in the proof begun above would be:

3. $La \supset Ma$ 1, U.S.
4. $Pa \supset La$ 2, U.S.

Here a replaces x to stand for the arbitrary element with which we are working. The letters U.S. indicate that we have Universally Specified—first, Step 1 and, second, Step 2.

Following through on the proof we would say $Pa \supset Ma$ for Step 5, giving the Tautology, Hypothetical Syllogism, for our reason and mentioning Steps 3 and 4 as referents.

We now have the sentential form we want in the conclusion, but again we need the Universal Quantifier if our proof is to be complete.

Checking back over the proof, we see that the element *a* that appears in the last step has been treated as a particular arbitrary element. No special characteristics have been introduced during the proof which would serve to qualify it in any way other than that in which it was first introduced. It was given to us as any element in the universe to which we may assign the predicate *L*. The premises told us what could be done with an element so modified, but nothing else was done throughout the proof to give the arbitrary element any more characteristics than would appear by the standard rules of our logic.

Therefore, *a* may be generalized. That is, we may now replace *a* with the variable *x* and turn our attention again to a consideration of all elements in the universe. The rule for this step is called Universal Generalization and is applied as follows:

6. $(x)(Px \supset Mx)$ 5. U.G.

The complete proof is given again below.

1.	$(x)(Lx \supset Mx)$	Pr.	$/\therefore (x)(Px \supset Mx)$
2.	$(x)(Px \supset Lx)$	Pr.	
3.	$La \supset Ma$	1, U.S.	
4.	$Pa \supset La$	2, U.S.	
5.	$Pa \supset Ma$	3, 4, H.S.	
6.	$(x)(Px \supset Mx)$	5, U.G.	

Looking back over the entire proof, we see that in order to work out a deduction we had to have some specific element in mind (even though we may admit that we could be in doubt about the very *existence* of such an element at all); and we use Universal Specification to make it clear that we are considering the various properties that may be assigned to this specific element. Then, at the conclusion of our proof, we make sure that we have done nothing that would add any special characteristics to our arbitrary element, and we Universally Generalize to get ourselves back to the most general kind of statement that can be affirmed in our logic.

b. Existential Quantifiers. The Existential Quantifier is handled in a somewhat similar fashion. There are, of course, restrictions and procedures that are unique to this Quantifier.

We will use the following example as an explanation of the use of the Existential Quantifier.

No rebel is a good security risk. There are rebels. Therefore, there are some who are not good security risks.

1. $(x)(Rx \supset -Sx)$ Pr. $/\therefore (\exists x)(-Sx)$
2. $(\exists x)(Rx)$ Pr.

An Existential Quantifier tells us that there is at least one thing in the universe that has the given property—in the above case, at least one individual. Once again, this Quantifier, like the Universal Quantifier, is expressing in general terms some information about an item or items seen within a universal scope. In making our proof we wish to deal with a specific item out of that universe. Hence, if (as we are told in Step 2) there *is* an x that has the property R, let us direct our attention to such an individual. Let us specify an individual that does have this property. We will say that α, the Greek letter alpha, will stand for the specified individual we will consider in our proof. Step 3 of the proof will be:

3. $R\alpha$ 2, E.S.

From Step 2 and Existential Specification, we have $R\alpha$.

Step 1 tells us that, of anything in the entire universe, if it has the property R then it will also have the property $-S$. In our first case of Universal Specification the instructions were to pick *any* arbitrary element to be considered in the proof. But in the present case, where we are considering a Universally Quantified statement in conjunction with an Existentially Quantified statement, there is some *existent* element now made available for use in our proof. We still may not have it directly in hand—we may not know exactly how many there are or where they are to be found—but the Existential Quantifier has told us of their, or its, existence, and in Step 3 we have specified one of these existing elements to be used in the proof.

Therefore, for our Universal Specification, instead of choosing any arbitrary element, we may now deal with the one element that has already been specified. Step 1 says, "For *all* x . . . ," so here we are taking a particular x we know to exist and applying the information from the Universal Quantifier to it.

For Step 4 we will have:

4. $R\alpha \supset -S\alpha$ 1, U.S.

Step 5 will follow as:

$$5.\ -S\alpha \qquad 3, 4, \text{M.P.}$$

And in Step 6 we will generalize again:

$$6.\ (\exists x)(-Sx) \qquad 5, \text{E.G.}$$

We were working with some particular, existent entity—as was indicated by the use of the Greek letter α. It is essential that we remember, then, to Generalize *Existentially* (Existential Generalization) and *not* Universally. Our preceding step did not concern an arbitrary element as in our proof with Universals. It was instead an element that had been clearly affirmed to exist. Our conclusion, then, must go from Step 5, which tells us a named individual has the property $-S$, to Step 6, wherein we say, "There is an individual with the property $-S$."

There are a number of cautions that must be taken in the use of the Existential Quantifier. As was just mentioned, if Specification is made from an Existential Quantifier in a proof, then a formula resulting from this proof must never be *Universally* Generalized. The procedure of using Greek letters for Existential Specification is introduced as an aid in remembering that the proof involves Specification from an Existential premise, and must therefore end with an *Existential* Generalization.

Also, in proofs that have both Universal and Existential statements for premises, Specification must always be done from the Existential premise first. It can be seen why this is necessary when one considers again what these specifications mean. In Universal Specification we are taking any arbitrary element out of our universe, and in Existential Specification we have selected one of the known existent elements in the universe. It is unreasonable to take our arbitrary element from Universal Specification and make it the particular element mentioned by the Existential Quantifier. But the particular element may easily be conceived to be one of those referred to by the Universal Quantifier.

Another mistake to avoid in specifying from Existential statements is that of using one letter to replace more than one variable. In traditional logic it is said that only one Particular proposition may appear in the premises. The case is similar for modern logic.

Suppose we consider an argument using two Existential premises:

Some boys are cheer leaders. Some girls are cheer leaders. Therefore, some boys are girls.

1.	$(\exists x)(Bx \cdot Cx)$	Pr.	$/\therefore(\exists x)(Bx \cdot Gx)$
2.	$(\exists x)(Gx \cdot Cx)$	Pr.	
3.	$B\alpha \cdot C\alpha$	1, E.S.	
4.	$G\alpha \cdot C\alpha$	2, E.S.	
5.	$B\alpha$	3, Simp.	
6.	$G\alpha$	4, Simp.	
7.	$B\alpha \cdot G\alpha$	5, 6, Adj.	
8.	$(\exists x)(Bx \cdot Gx)$	7, E.G.	

In the proof above, we used α to replace x in specifying Step 1, which was an acceptable procedure. But then we used α again in the specification of Step 2, and this was a mistake. We had already considered α to be the name of the entity, or *an* entity, mentioned in the description given in Step 1; so we would be going beyond the information given to suppose α was also the name of the entity mentioned in Step 2. Our rule to avoid this mistake will be: no letter may be used in Existential Specification that has already been used in the proof.

The reader may have noticed a similarity between the above example and an *III* syllogism from traditional logic. Rule 6 of the seven rules of syllogisms states, "No conclusion can be drawn from two Particular premises." We avoid this mistake in Quantifier logic by this rule that prevents us from using the same letter to refer to two or more Existential propositions. We *can*, of course, use the same letter in Universal Specifications, since Universal propositions are not limited to any specific elements. So any letter used for Existential Specification may also be used in a following Universal Specification thus:

Some boys are cheer leaders. All cheer leaders are agile. Therefore, some boys are agile.

1.	$(\exists x)(Bx \cdot Cx)$	Pr.	$/\therefore(\exists x)(Bx \cdot Ax)$
2.	$(x)(Cx \supset Ax)$	Pr.	
3.	$B\alpha \cdot C\alpha$	1, E.S.	
4.	$C\alpha \supset A\alpha$	2, U.S.	
5.	$C\alpha$	3, Simp.	
6.	$A\alpha$	4, 5, M.P.	
7.	$B\alpha$	3, Simp.	

8.	$B\alpha \cdot A\alpha$	6, 7, Adj.
9.	$(\exists x)(Bx \cdot Ax)$	8, E.G.

Specifications in our proofs should always be made from affirmative statements. If a statement appears with a negative sign in front of the Quantifier, then that statement should be made affirmative through the use of the other Quantifier following the procedure described on p. 103. A statement, for example, such as $-(x)(\mathrm{G}x \cdot -Hx)$ may be translated to $(\exists x)-(Gx \cdot -Hx)$.

Two proofs are given below to illustrate how these rules applying to Quantifiers are used in Deduction:

> It is not true that there is a person such that if it is not the case both that he is a sinner and that he is not perfect then he is not redeemable. No one is both redeemable and perfect. Therefore, no one is a sinner.

1.	$-(\exists x)[-(Sx \cdot -Px) \supset -Rx]$	Pr.	$/ \therefore (x)-(Sx)$
2.	$(x)-(Rx \cdot Px)$	Pr.	
3.	$(x)-[-(Sx \cdot -Px) \supset -Rx]$	1, Trans.	
4.	$-(Ra \cdot Pa)$	2, U.S.	
5.	$-[-(Sa \cdot -Pa) \supset -Ra]$	3, U.S.	
6.	$-(Sa \cdot -Pa) \cdot Ra$	5, N.I., D.N.	
7.	$-Ra \vee -Pa$	4, D.M.	
8.	Ra	6, Simp.	
9.	$-Pa$	7, 8, D.N., D.D.	
10.	$-(Sa \cdot -Pa)$	6, Simp.	
11.	$-Sa \vee Pa$	10, D.M., D.N.	
12.	$-Sa$	9, 11, D.D.	
13.	$(x)-(Sx)$	12, U.G.	

Another example, somewhat more complicated:

> *Universe: Animals in the Zoo.*
> It is not the case that some are not either alligators or not reptilian. They are either gawky and not unhappy or they are mean. If they are not unhappy, they are not alligators. Some of them are indolent and are not either mean or nasty. If they are not tame, they are reptilian. Therefore, some of the tame animals are not unhappy.

1.	$-(\exists x)-(Ax \vee -Rx)$	Pr.	$/ \therefore (\exists x)(Tx \cdot -Ux)$
2.	$(x)[(Gx \cdot -Ux) \vee Mx]$	Pr.	

3.	$(x)(-Ux \supset -Ax)$	Pr.
4.	$(\exists x)[Ix \cdot -(Mx \vee Nx)]$	Pr.
5.	$(x)(-Tx \supset Rx)$	Pr.
6.	$(x)(Ax \vee -Rx)$	1, Trans.
7.	$I\alpha \cdot -(M\alpha \vee N\alpha)$	4, E.S.
8.	$A\alpha \vee -R\alpha$	6, U.S.
9.	$(G\alpha \cdot -U\alpha) \vee M\alpha$	2, U.S.
10.	$-U\alpha \supset -A\alpha$	3, U.S.
11.	$-T\alpha \supset R\alpha$	5, U.S.
12.	$-(M\alpha \vee N\alpha)$	7, Simp.
13.	$-M\alpha \cdot -N\alpha$	12, D.M.
14.	$-M\alpha$	13, Simp.
15.	$G\alpha \cdot -U\alpha$	9, 14, D.D.
16.	$-U\alpha$	15, Simp.
17.	$-A\alpha$	10, 16, M.P.
18.	$-R\alpha$	8, 17, D.D.
19.	$--T\alpha$	11, 18, M.T.
20.	$T\alpha$	19, D.N.
21.	$T\alpha \cdot -U\alpha$	20, 16, Adj.
22.	$(\exists x)(Tx \cdot -Ux)$	21, E.G.

The examples above illustrate another point that may be made concerning the symbolization of arguments. Sometimes it is well to name the Universe of Discourse when such Universe is not immediately evident, just so that we may avoid the unnecessary use of one predicate throughout the proof. If, in the first proof, we had felt we must be careful to name all properties that could be considered, we might have also mentioned that x is human. Our premises then would have been

1. $-(\exists x)\{Hx \cdot [-(Sx \cdot -Px) \supset -Rx]\}$ Pr. $/ \therefore (x)(Hx \supset -Sx)$
2. $(x)[Hx \supset -(Rx \cdot Px)]$ Pr.

The procedure here, then, would involve a hypothetical proof wherein *Ha* is proposed as a hypothetical premise. The remaining steps would be essentially the same as given in the proof above.

The concern for mentioning all possible properties, however, could have been taken care of just as easily by defining the Universe of Discourse right at the beginning. If we had said our Universe was to be all humans the additional predicate *H* would have been unnecessary. The proof could then be given with all the detailed attention to all possible predicates, although the premises themselves contain only *S*, *P*, and *R*.

7. RELATIONSHIPS BETWEEN QUANTIFIERS AND TRADITIONAL PROPOSITIONS. There are some relationships between Logical Deduction, the concepts of sets, and syllogistic logic that may prove to be interesting at this stage of development. First, if we should take the syllogism *AAA*,1, we may express it simply as

All *B* is A. All C is *B*. ∴All C is A.

Using our set notation, this would be:

$$BA' = 0, CB' = 0, \therefore CA' = 0.$$

Then in terms of Quantifiers:

$$(x)(Bx \supset Ax). (x)(Cx \supset Bx). \therefore (x)(Cx \supset Ax).$$

The last representation may be translated into:

$$-(\exists x)(Bx \cdot -Ax). -(\exists x)(Cx \cdot -Bx). \therefore -(\exists x)(Cx \cdot -Ax).$$

The Intersection used in set notation unites *B* and not-*A* and relates them to the Empty Set. In like manner, Conjunction is used with the Existential Quantifier to unite *B* and not-*A*, and again to describe them in terms of nonexistence, no elements, or Empty Set.

Further relationships may be shown using other forms of the syllogism. Consider *AII*,1:

All *B* is C. Some *A* is *B*. ∴Some *A* is C.

In set terminology this would be

$$BC' = 0. AB \neq 0. \therefore AC \neq 0.$$

Using Quantifiers and the sentential connectives,

$$-(\exists x)(Bx \cdot -Cx). (\exists x)(Ax \cdot Bx). \therefore (\exists x)(Ax \cdot Cx).$$

The set symbols are generally analogous to the sentential connectives in the following relationships:

Union	$\cup$	....	Disjunction	$\vee$
Intersection	$\cap$	....	Conjunction	$\cdot$
Negation	a'	....	Negation	$-a$

Another notation used in discussions of sets is $\subset$, which stands for the Inclusion of one set within another. The expression $a \subset b$

means that every element that is in a is also in b. This symbol is sometimes introduced in a discussion of sets as a definition that may replace $A \cap B' = 0$. And here again we have a relationship between sets and the sentential connectives. In the latter case, we say that Implication $A \supset B$ may be given as $-(A \cdot -B)$. And when we use Quantifiers to express the Universal proposition, we have $(x)(Ax \supset Bx)$ or $-(\exists x)(Ax \cdot -Bx)$. The negation before the Existential Quantifier once more plays the role of 0, or the Empty Set in set notation. The Inclusion of one set within another, then, is seen to be related to the Implication of our sentential connectives.

The above relationships are not totally isomorphic—that is, all the functions in one may not be exactly duplicated in the other—but it can be shown that any valid argument determined in set concepts will be a Tautology of our Logical Deduction. This fact will be seen to be valuable after we have examined Switching Algebra and have shown the association of it with some of the material covered in the earlier portions of this book.

This work with Quantifiers has been no more than an introduction to the basic ideas. There is a great deal more to be done with Quantifiers and a number of additional rules that are needed for this further work. For example, we have not considered the use of two or more variables in a single proposition and the concomitant need for concern over free variables and constants used along with the variables. And it is in topics such as these that we find so much power and utility being added to the use of Quantifiers.

For those who are interested there are a number of good texts available for further study. The ones that have been used most frequently in preparation for this discussion (and that should, therefore, have more material in them that will be familiar to the student) are: Patrick Suppes, *Introduction to Logic, op. cit.;* Irving M. Copi, *Symbolic Logic* (New York: Macmillan Co., 1965); W. H. Halberstadt, *An Introduction to Modern Logic* (New York: Harper and Bros., 1960); and Benson Mates, *Elementary Logic* (New York: Oxford University Press, 1965).

LOGIC EXERCISES

Symbolize the following first by using Existential Quantifiers, then by using Universal Quantifiers:

1. Some animals are brown.
2. Golems are rude.
3. There is no such thing as a Platonic Form.
4. Gremlins don't exist.
5. The owl is nocturnal.
6. There are black swans.
7. Vipers are not lovable.
8. One kind of cetacean is the grampus.
9. Logical Positivists are cows.
10. Not all Democrats are horse thieves; but all horse thieves are Democrats.

Check the following for validity, using Quantifiers and Logical Deduction:

11. All apteryxes are birds. There are some things that are not birds. Hence, there are some things that are not apteryxes.
12. There are some people who are not sincere although they are polite. Anyone who is polite is elegant. And anyone who is not kind is not elegant. Therefore, there are some kind people who are not sincere.
13. Anything that is material and organic is real. Everything is either not organic or it is ephemeral. Everything is either not ephemeral or not real. Therefore, anything that is organic is ephemeral and not material.
14. If the fact that something is junk implies it is not expendable, then it is trash. It is not the case that there is anything that is expendable and not either not salable or not adaptable. There is something that is not either not mendable or not salable. Anything that is not adaptable is not junk. Therefore, there is some trash that is mendable.

    [Consider $p \vee (q \vee r) \equiv (p \vee q) \vee r$ a Tautology for this problem.]
15. If a man is a liar or he is offensive then he is not a gentleman. It is not the case that there exists a man who is idealistic and who is not courteous. There are men who are liars and are not courteous. If a man is a saint then he is either idealistic or a gentleman. Therefore, there are men who are not saints.

4

Derivation of Deductive Systems

In Chapter 1 we spoke of axiomatizing a system of logic or mathematics. It was indicated how one could begin with a basic set of unproved axioms or assumptions and build on these to construct a complete deductive system.

Our intention in this chapter is to axiomatize the two systems that we have been working with since the beginning of the text. The material on sets will be our background for the section here called Class Calculus or Boolean Algebra, and Truth Tables and Logical Deduction will support our work in the Calculus of Propositions.

We have so far depended too much on intuitive understandings, on explanations of our terms by reference to ordinary language and common experience, and on diagrams for the defense of proofs and the meaning of our terms. All of our understanding of sets was based upon the Venn Diagram and the areas of a Venn Diagram to which we let our symbols refer. And our complete system of Logical Deduction was founded on our work with Truth Tables, wherein we used the Truth Table as a convenient way of expressing a common meaning that we give to sentential connectives used in ordinary language.

It may be remembered that we used Tautologies all the way through the Truth Table logic. We began by associating the meanings we give to sentential connectives with a column of values on the Truth Table. Then we developed a set of tautologous statements out of these ordinary-language meanings and used those statements as the basis for our system of Logical Deduction.

Now we mean to begin with assumptions in the Propositional Calculus that have no necessary relationship to word meanings or Tautologies at all. But if we do show our assumptions to be Tautologies (if we interpret our assumptions in such a manner) after the Calculus is developed, then—if our rules of procedure are established to produce only Tautologies—we may say that in the Propositional Calculus we have axiomatized the system of Truth Table logic.

In Logical Deduction we were still too close to the experiences of ordinary language and diagrams and common usage to consider the deductions we performed as part of any rigorous deductive system. Even our preliminary list of Tautologies, as was pointed out on p. 85, was not independent. That is, we could have begun with only a fraction of the ones we used and developed the others out of these basic few.

It is hoped, however, that the student has learned in the foregoing chapters something of the process of deduction, that he has gained some experience in the manipulation of logical symbols, and that he has become aware of some of the advantages that may be gained from a much more rigorous system of logic. If these purposes have been accomplished, then the work in this chapter will be considerably easier than it would be for the student who came to it without any familiarity at all with the terms, symbols, and procedures.

A. AXIOMATIZATION OF ARITHMETIC

Before we begin the development of the two Calculuses, let us examine briefly some simple examples of deductive systems using symbols and ideas with which we have been familiar since the beginning of our school career.

1. DECIMAL NUMBER SYSTEM. Arithmetic and the decimal number system are common tools for the handling of problems of counting in our society. Most of us learn the rules and procedures intuitively and as a series of individual and separate rules of operation that have very little relationship to one another. For example, in counting we start at 0 or 1 and go up to 100 or 1000, mentioning numbers that we take to be totally independent of one another. For example, "5," "6," and "7" have only a vague similarity in appearance for us to "15," "16," and "17." But when we stop to give it consideration we may realize that what we call our decimal number system—the one we have been taught to use for counting—is composed essentially of a series of ten symbols and a few simple rules of combination. Our ten symbols are "0," "1," "2," "3," "4," "5," "6," "7," "8," "9," and these are all and the only ones that we have available. The rules that we use for the simplest function of counting are: (1) Apply each symbol, in the order given above, to each successive item or group being counted (generally beginning with the symbol "1"), and (2) in cases where there are more items than symbols, repeat the sequence but keep track of the number of times the sequence has been used by marking the symbol indicating that number to the left of each symbol used again.

Thus, if I am counting cars on the highway and go through 7, 8, and 9, I begin again at the beginning of the list of symbols with 0 and put 1 to the left of 0 to indicate that I have gone through the sequence once. Then when I have finished the series the second time I put 2 to the left of the symbols used again. After having gone through the symbols nine times, I put 10 to the left and go on like this as long as there are cars to count or I have the inclination to count them.

With a few more simple rules and a brief set of assumptions—or axioms—we can develop the whole system of ordinary arithmetic. As an example as to how this can be done, let us give the minimum set of symbols, rules, and assumptions it would take to prove that $2+2=4$.*

Our symbols will be: 1,2,3,4, +, =, ( ).

Our rules will be:

1. Quantities may be substituted for their equals.
2. A definition may be susbtituted for that which is defined.

Our definitions will be:

1. 2 means $1+1$.
2. 3 means $2+1$.
3. 4 means $3+1$.

Our assumptions will be:

1. A quantity is equal to itself.
2. The Associative Law. $a+(b+c)=(a+b)+c$, wherein any symbol 1,2,3,4 may be substituted for a or b or c.

The proof of $2+2=4$, then, is as follows:

1. $(1+1)+(1+1)=(1+1)+(1+1)$ Assumption 1.
2. $2+2 = 2+(1+1)$ Definition substitution 2 for $(1+1)$.
3. $2+2 = (2+1)+1$ Associative Law.

* The idea for this approach was taken from *Introduction to Logic* (New York: St. Martin's Press, 1964), by Nicholas Rescher.

4. $2+2 = 3+1$ Def. sub. 3 for $(2+1)$.
5. $2+2 = 4$ Def. sub. 4 for $(3+1)$.

This, of course, is a long process to go through for the proof of the simple statement $2+2=4$. But the importance of this procedure for the logician and theoretician is that once the basic symbols, rules, definitions, and assumptions have been given, the rest of the system can be developed using very little more than these few basic preliminary statements. Additional definitions and symbols may be brought in, but it will all still be, quite obviously, one system founded on one set of basic statements. It will be unified, coherent, and interrelated rather than, as a strictly intuitive approach would give us, a number of separate, unrelated, and independent rules of operation.

If we were to go on with the development of the arithmetic of decimal numbers, we would need a little more than we have here, of course. For instance, we would need the definition of all numbers through 9, we would need another assumption, the Commutative Law $a+b=b+a$, and we would need the introduction of a multiplication table–which could be derived from assumptions and definitions–and the Distributive law $a\times(b+c) = (a\times b)+(a\times c)$. This may seem to be a lot when we first see it like this, but if one would stop to consider the number of rules we use and assumptions we make in the simplest sort of multiplication and division problems, he would find a much greater number of unexplained rules of procedure than are offered here. Furthermore, as was noted above, these rules would have little or no relationship to one another and would seem then to have simply been invented to handle the problem of the moment (*ad hoc*, to use the legal terminology).

2. BINARY NUMBER SYSTEM. Other systems of counting may be used than that of the decimal system. One that has become very important for us in this age of computers is the binary system. Here, instead of using ten symbols we use only two: "0" and "1." But the counting procedure remains the same: If we start with "0," then the process of counting one object will have used up all our symbols. So we begin with "0" again but put a "1" to the left of the "0" to indicate we have used all the symbols once. Two, then, is 10. One more would be three, or 11. And, again, we have used all the symbols so we put 10, or two, to the left of our symbol "0" and begin again with four, 100.

Below is a list of binary numbers listed to the left of the decimal numbers up to the number thirty-two.

0	0						
1	1	1001	9	10001	17	11001	25
10	2	1010	10	10010	18	11010	26
11	3	1011	11	10011	19	11011	27
100	4	1100	12	10100	20	11100	28
101	5	1101	13	10101	21	11101	29
110	6	1110	14	10110	22	11110	30
111	7	1111	15	10111	23	11111	31
1000	8	10000	16	11000	24	100000	32

Definitions in this system are quite simple. We may say, "$0+0=0$," "$1+0=1$," and "$1+1=10$," and from there proceed to prove additions as we did in the decimal system with even less trouble.

In adding, say, $7+14$, or $111+1110$, we could set it up as we do a decimal addition:

$$\begin{array}{r} 1110 \\ +\ \underline{111} \end{array}$$

Then, starting from the right, we have $1+0=1$ in the first column; so we would put a "1" down in the first column of the sum. Adding $1+1$ in the second column gives 10, which we would take care of by putting a "0" in the second column of the sum and a "1" in the third column of the problem. $1+1+1=10+1=11$, gives us 1 for the third column of the sum and 1 to be added into the fourth column of the problem. $1+1=10$ in the fourth column gives 0 for the fourth column of the sum and 1 for the fifth column of the problem.

Collecting these numbers for the total answer, the sum, we have 10101, which we may check on the binary number table given above to confirm the addition with our familiar decimal system: $7+14=21$.

Of course, such a system is much too laborious to be used for everyday calculations. But the utility of the binary number system comes in its adaptability to the electronic computer, wherein an open switch could stand for 0 and a closed switch for 1. Electric impulses traveling at the speed of 186,000 miles per second would reduce the time for computations such as we have just made to negligible fractions of a second.

3. **MODULO SYSTEM.** A third system that may be con-

structed in a manner similar to the constructions of the decimal and binary systems is a modulo system. The main difference between the modulo system and the other two is that in the decimal and binary systems we have been discussing what are called infinite fields—there is no theoretical limitation to the numbers that may be introduced. A modulo system, on the other hand, is finite—or limited to a given set of numbers.

In the infinite fields we keep track of the number of times we have used our symbols. In a finite field, however, we simply use the symbols over and over in a given sequence without indicating in any way whatsoever the number of times the symbols have been used.

On the right is given the addition table for the finite field called Modulo 5. (There are *five* symbols used in its construction.)

+	0	1	2	3	4
0	0	1	2	3	4
1	1	2	3	4	0
2	2	3	4	0	1
3	3	4	0	1	2
4	4	0	1	2	3

Because of the fact that we do not use more than five symbols in this system and that we do not keep an account of the number of times we have used the symbols, when we add 1 to the fifth number, 4, we simply go back to the beginning and use "0" by itself again. $4+1$, then, is 0. $3+3=1$. $4+4=3$.

A multiplication table may be developed from the addition table we have given if we simply describe multiplication as the process of taking a given number a given number of times for the purpose of addition. If we take any number 0 times, of course, we get 0. If we take the number 2 one time—that is, 2 by itself, we have 2 alone; so we indicate this on our multiplication table: $1\times 2=2$. Also, if the number 1 is taken twice on the addition table we get 2, so $2\times 1=2$, verifying the commutativity of this multiplication. If 2 is taken 3 times, we have $2+2+2=4+2=1$, on the addition table. This is shown on the multiplication table as $3\times 2=1$. If 4 is taken 4 times, we get $4+4+4+4=3+4+4=2+4=1$. On the multiplication table it is $4\times 4=1$. Building in this manner, we eventually get a multiplication table that looks like the one on the right.

×	0	1	2	3	4
0	0	0	0	0	0
1	0	1	2	3	4
2	0	2	4	1	3
3	0	3	1	4	2
4	0	4	3	2	1

It is now possible to use these two tables—the addition table that was given and the multiplication table that was derived—to work problems in a special Mod 5 algebra.

Suppose we were asked to find the number such that if it were multiplied times 2 and the product were added to 3 the result would be 1. Using the letter "x" to stand for the unknown number, this problem could be symbolized $2x + 3 = 1$.

To solve this problem we first add 2 to both sides of the equation by an unstated assumption that could be verbalized as "Equal quantities may be added to equal quantities and the sums will be equal." We then have $2x + 3 + 2 = 1 + 2$, which according to the addition table is $2x + 0 = 3$. Then, since any number on the addition table added to 0 gives that number itself, we may substitute $2x$ for $2x + 0$ (substituting a quantity for its equal) to get $2x = 3$. The multiplication table, then, tells us that the number which, when multiplied by 2, will give 3 is 4. So we give 4 as the value of the unknown we had at the beginning. (We might have said, using ordinary algebraic notation, that $x = 3/2$, and then that the fraction $3/2 = 4$. As in any fraction of ordinary arithmetic, a fraction in Mod 5 is a division or a reverse multiplication.)

It is not immediately clear how the Mod 5 system can be put to any practical use. From our point of view here it may only appear to be a game that could have been invented and played by some imaginative mathematician with nothing else to do. It may, indeed, be true that numerous systems like this have been devised in this manner: certain rules are given, symbols are chosen, assumptions are made, and the system is then built up only for the purpose of getting as much out of it as possible while staying strictly within the limits imposed by the original presuppositions.

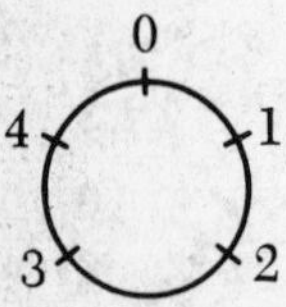

Actually the Mod 5 system does have possible practical application. For instance, if we wanted to know the *position* of a revolving wheel without caring at all how many times it has turned, then this system of mathematics would be useful to us. Suppose a wheel like the one on the left were needed in a telephone or electronics circuit. If one electrical impulse would turn the wheel one stop, then we could add groups of impulses, $2 + 4 + 3 + 4$, on our addition table and find the resultant position of the wheel after all pulses had come in—in this case, position 3. Or, if we knew that one given group of pulses came in twice and this was followed by a group of 3 to leave the wheel at the stop marked 1, then to find the number of pulses in the first two groups we would simply set up the equation $2x + 3 = 1$. Solving for x as we have already done, we see the number of pulses in each of the first two groups was 4.

4. SUMMARY. In the three mathematical systems given the briefest of treatments above, the student may see some of the approaches to axiomatizing a system. In the first case we went into a mathematical structure that has had a natural growth for centuries before our time and that is so familiar to us that analysis seems to be strangely artificial. But we did find—even here—that there are certain basic assumptions and rules that lie at the base of this system and that give it coherence and structural unity.

The system of binary numbers is a good example of a new system that may be derived by using the same rules as those discovered in the decimal arithmetic and simply changing the number of symbols available. Having discovered the rules and operational procedures of arithmetic in general, we could construct other systems using three symbols, eight symbols, twelve symbols, or any other number of symbols that we may find to be interesting. These other systems would be called "Base 3," "Base 8," "Base 12," and so on.

The Mod 5 system may also have been developed following the discovery of certain arithmetical rules in the "natural" systems. Here, of course, we simply varied one of the rules—the rule of keeping an account of the number of times we have used our symbols—and got another system that proves to be interesting and even useful in its own right.

The approach that has been used in the discussion of these systems of arithmetic is similar to the one that will be used in the development of two systems of logic in their axiomatized form.

B. PROPOSITIONAL CALCULUS

In our development of the Propositional Calculus, as in the development of any other complete deductive system, we must first describe the set of rules, symbols, and assumptions we are going to use and tell how the symbols may be brought together in a well-formed formula.

The system we are developing here will follow closely the one developed by Bertrand Russell and Alfred North Whitehead in their *Principia Mathematica.* This is a sytem that is in common usage in contemporary textbooks on logic and appears in various forms in modern courses in logic.*

1. PRELIMINARY STATEMENTS. The following presuppositions and rules of procedure must be stated in order to define the scope of our work and to indicate clearly the bases for all the deductions that will be made within the system.

a. Primitive Symbols. We must first describe our set of primitive symbols. That is, we must denote those symbols which are to be accepted as basic and undefined in this system.

The symbols to be used as variables will be $p, q, r, s, \ldots$. Symbols of operation will be $-$, $\vee$, and the grouping symbols ( ), [ ], { }. Further symbols of operation will be introduced and defined in terms of those primitives listed above.

b. Well-formed Formulas. A well-formed formula will be any variable, any variable preceded by the symbol $-$, or any pair of well-formed formulas connected by the symbol $\vee$ or by other symbols of operation introduced through definitions. A single variable will be called a simple well-formed formula; the others will be called complex well-formed formulas. "Well-formed formula" will be abbreviated wff. For example, p, q, and $-(p \supset -q)$ are wff's; $-pq$, $\equiv p$, and $\vee\, p \supset -$ are not wff's.

c. Definitions. Definition 1. The symbol $\supset$ will mean what is meant by the symbols $-$ and $\vee$ when the latter symbol connects two given wff's and the former precedes the first given wff. That is, if we indicate one simple or complex wff by P and another simple or complex wff by Q, then the wff $P \supset Q$ will mean $-P \vee Q$.

---

* It may be said here that the reader should feel free, as he goes through this section, to compare these systems with those of Logical Deduction and sets. For example, the theorems of Propositional Calculus may be tried out on Truth Tables, and Venn Diagrams may be used to compare statements in the language of sets to those made in the Class Calculus. The most important thing to remember in this regard is that the proofs of the theorems in either of these calculuses must always be given as totally complete within and dependent upon the individual system. One must be constantly on the alert to see that no defenses, no arguments, no support material is smuggled into the system unless clear and explicit acknowledgments and recognitions are made of the use of such material.

(Hereafter, definitions will be presented in this form: $P \supset Q = \text{def} -P \vee Q$. The meaning of this symbolic notation may be found by referring to the description of Definition 1 given above.)

Definition 2. $P \cdot Q = \text{def} -(-P \vee -Q)$
Definition 3. $P \equiv Q = \text{def} (P \supset Q) \cdot (Q \supset P)$

d. Rules of Operation. We shall use the following five rules of operation:

1. Substitutions may be made on *variables*. Any substitution made on any given variable must be made on that variable throughout the formula. For example, in subsituting r for p in the formula $(p \vee -q) \vee -p$, r must replace p in every instance, thus: $(r \vee -q) \vee -r$. It should be noted that this rule allows only for substitution on *simple* wff's. Substitution can *not* be made by this rule on the full formulas such as $-p$ or $(p \vee q)$, although substitutions can be made for the variables p and q that appear within these formulas or complex wff's.

2. Substitution may be made on definitions. Any wff may be replaced by another wff when the latter is given as a definition of the former or the latter is defined *by* the former. If we call that which is being defined the "definiendum" and that which defines the "definiens," then we may say that a definiens may replace its definiendum or a definiendum may replace its definiens. To illustrate by an example, whenever we see a wff (simple or complex) preceded by the sign "$-$" and conjoined to another wff by the sign "$\vee$," we may remove both these signs and conjoin the two wff's by the sign "$\supset$." The reverse procedure may be followed in substituting "$-$" and "$\vee$" for "$\supset$." This kind of substitution does not have to be made throughout the formula. For example, given the formula $-(-p \vee q) \vee (-q \vee p)$ a definitional substitution may be made to give $-(-p \vee q) \vee (q \supset p)$. Another definitional substitution possible on the given formula is $(-p \vee q) \supset (-q \vee p)$.

3. The rule of Implication will be used as follows: Given any wff of the form $p \supset q$ and another wff p, we may affirm as a derivation the wff q. This rule, also called "the rule of Modus Ponens," could be stated without the use of Definition 1: Given $-p \vee q$ and $- -p$, then q may be affirmed as a derived formula. The formulas $-p \vee q$ and $- -p$ may appear as assumptions or

as derived theorems in the system. (Assumptions and theorems are discussed below.)

4. A proof in our system will consist of a series of wff's. Each wff is accompanied by a statement to the right which is given as the *reason* for that particular wff.

5. Adjunction: Any two statements given as wff's on individual lines of a proof may be brought together as a single statement joined by the symbol "·".

e. Assumptions. The *assumptions* in this system are taken directly from *Principia Mathematica* with the exception of one assumption listed in the *Principia* which has since been shown to be unnecessary. These assumptions may be given with or without the use of the symbol introduced by Definition 1. That symbol will be used here for simplification of presentation.

Assumption 1. $(p \vee p) \supset p$
Assumption 2. $q \supset (p \vee q)$
Assumption 3. $(p \vee q) \supset (q \vee p)$
Assumption 4. $(q \supset r) \supset [(p \vee q) \supset (p \vee r)]$

2. THEOREMS. The bulk of the system will be found in the set of theorems that may be derived from the assumptions, rules of operation, definitions, and so on listed above. A theorem is the conclusion of a derivation in a proof. The first theorem we derive must begin with one of the above assumptions. The derivation of subsequent theorems, however, may use any one of the four assumptions *plus* any theorem that has already been derived. As theorems are accumulated, more complex theorems may be proved. The number of theorems that can be proved in this system is infinite. If we were given the task of adapting the system to some particular area of experience (e.g., writing legal contracts, programming a computer, making market determinations for a large industry), we could then have some idea of the kinds of theorems we might wish to prove and we could see a direction in which we would want to go in further development of the system. As it is, however, we will simply be considering the system in abstract, so to speak, and we will present a few theorems, therefore, as an example of what might be done with such a calculus.

We spoke at the beginning of this chapter of differences between the intuitive system of Truth Table logic and the more rigorous Propositional Calculus. Another difference between these two systems is that in the intuitive system the deductions are used more for the purpose of *verification* of arguments as Tautologies, and in the axiomatized system deductions are used to generate theorems from assumptions given and theorems already proved. In Logical Deduction we looked at our work from the point of view of analyzing arguments given to us in a finished form to determine their validity or invalidity. In the Propositional Calculus we see our task to be that of building up a set of theorems with proofs that are generated in a step-by-step process.

The following theorems are offered as examples of the theorems that may be developed in Propositional Calculus and as a basic set that may be used in the proofs of additional theorems within the system.

Theorem 1. $\underline{/q \supset (p \supset q).}$ (The theorem to be proved will always be indicated in this manner.)

1) $q \supset (p \vee q)$ Assumption 2
2) $q \supset (-p \vee q)$ 1, Substituting $-p$ for p
3) $q \supset (p \supset q)$ 2, Substituting definition $P \supset Q$

Hereafter, "Assumption 2" will be abbreviated A2. Substitutions will be indicated "$-p/p$," which may be read, "Substituting $-p$ for p." Substitutions on definitions will be abbreviated as "Def. $P \supset Q$."

In the reason for Step 2 we were required to refer to Step 1 to indicate the formula in which the substitution was made. This explains the "1" listed as one of the reasons for Step 2, and the "2" listed as a reason for Step 3.

Theorem 2. $\underline{/(q \supset r) \supset [(p \supset q) \supset (p \supset r)].}$

1) $(q \supset r) \supset [(p \vee q) \supset (p \vee r)]$ A4
2) $(q \supset r) \supset [(-p \vee q) \supset (-p \vee r)]$ 1, $-p/p$
3) $(q \supset r) \supset [(p \supset q) \supset (p \supset r)]$ 2, Def. $P \supset Q$

Theorem 2 will be quite useful to us in later work. The student may find it helpful to study the theorem carefully and to attempt to interpret it in terms of ordinary language.

Theorem 3. $\underline{/(p \supset -p) \supset -p.}$

1) $(p \vee p) \supset p$ A1

2)	$(-p \vee -p) \supset -p$	1, $-p/p$
3)	$(p \supset -p) \supset -p$	2, Def. $P \supset Q$

Theorem 4. $\underline{/(p \supset -q) \supset (q \supset -p)}$.

This theorem should be proved as an exercise.

Theorem 5. $\underline{/p \supset p.}$

1)	$(q \supset r) \supset [(p \supset q) \supset (p \supset r)]$	Th. 2
2)	$[(p \vee p) \supset p] \supset$ $\{[p \supset (p \vee p)] \supset (p \supset p)\}$	1, $(p \vee p)/q$, p/r
3)	$(p \vee p) \supset p$	A1
4)	$[p \supset (p \vee p)] \supset (p \supset p)$	2, 3, Implication
5)	$q \supset (p \vee q)$	A2
6)	$p \supset (p \vee p)$	5, p/q
7)	$p \supset p$	4, 6, Imp.

Let us examine some questions that arise in the proof of Theorem 5. This is the first use of Theorem 2, which may be used frequently in the proofs of subsequent theorems. The later proofs will follow, essentially, the same steps that were taken in the proof of Theorem 5.

Theorem 2 is related to the Tautology Hypothetical Syllogism. When we have one wff implying a second, and the second wff implying a third, we may, by Theorem 2, show that the first wff implies the third. Through the use of the rule of Implication the affirmation of an antecedent, as in Step 3, produces one consequent which is then the affirmation of a second antecedent which in turn produces the consequent we were looking for.

[Important: For this explanation, of course, we are interpreting the symbol "$\supset$" to mean Implication as it was used in Truth Table logic. This is a procedure used only to help the student in setting up his proofs. The use of the idea of Implication is what may be called a heuristic procedure that may suggest a path for us to take but is not to be thought of as part of the finished abstract reasoning that makes up the rigorous deductive system. The pedagogy involved here follows to some extent the thesis of George Polya as he expressed it in his excellent text, *How To Solve It* (Garden City: Doubleday Anchor Books, 1957).]

In Theorem 5 we are confronted with the apparently simple problem of showing that p implies itself. We cannot leave this statement with the comment, "It's obvious," because it has *not obviously* been said before anywhere in the system; and unless we *interpret* the symbol to mean "implies," it is not even necessarily true.

This brings us back to the question as to how we have used Theorem 2 in the proof of Theorem 5. In using Theorem 2 we must be able to show that p implies some given wff, which wff then is seen to imply p. We must find some middle term, so to speak. In Assumption 1 we have $(p \vee p) \supset p$, which gives us the second Implication we need. And to get the first Implication we can take Assumption 2 and substitute p for q to get $p \supset (p \vee p)$. Now we have them both: $p \supset (p \vee p)$ and $(p \vee p) \supset p$. Theorem 2 tells us that if q (some wff appearing as the middle term, which is $p \vee p$ here) implies a given conclusion r (in this case p), then if $p \supset q$ [i.e., $p \supset (p \vee p)$], then p implies r (or, $p \supset p$).

Once we have seen the theorem from a distance in this way it is an easy task to set down the formulas with their reasons, make the substitutions called for in the explanation above and proceed with the seven steps of the proof as shown.

Theorem 6. $\underline{/(q \vee p) \supset (p \vee q).}$

1)	$(p \vee q) \supset (q \vee p)$	A3
2)	$(r \vee s) \supset (s \vee r)$	1, r/p, s/q
3)	$(q \vee p) \supset (p \vee q)$	2, q/r, p/s

In proving this theorem one's first inclination is most likely to treat it simply as a matter of substituting p for q and q for p in Assumption 3. But according to the rule of substitution on variables, we must always substitute for *all occurrences* of a given variable and this would mean substituting p for q in every case to give $(p \vee p) \supset (p \vee p)$. The substitution of q for p, then, would give only $(q \vee q) \supset (q \vee q)$. Such a problem can be avoided by the simple device of first substituting r for p and s for q in one step and substituting q for r and p for s in the step following. For our convenience in the following proofs, however, we will consider *simultaneous substitution* (of p for q and q for p) as a legitimate logical move.

Theorem 7. $\underline{/-p \vee p.}$

This theorem may be proved in two steps using Theorem 5.

Theorem 8. $\underline{/p \vee -p.}$

The proof here may be given using Assumption 3, Theorem 7, and the rule of Implication.

Theorem 9. $\underline{/p \supset --p.}$

1)	$p \vee -p$	Th. 8
2)	$-p \vee --p$	1, $-p/p$
3)	$p \supset --p$	2, Def. $P \supset Q$

Theorem 10. $\underline{/p \vee ---p.}$

1)	$(q \supset r) \supset [(p \vee q) \supset (p \vee r)]$	A4
2)	$(-p \supset ---p) \supset$ $[(p \vee -p) \supset (p \vee ---p)]$	1, $-p/q$, $---p/r$
3)	$p \supset --p$	Th. 9
4)	$-p \supset ---p$	3, $-p/p$
5)	$(p \vee -p) \supset (p \vee ---p)$	2, 4, Imp.
6)	$p \vee -p$	Th. 8
7)	$p \vee ---p$	5, 6, Imp.

Theorem 11. $\underline{/--p \supset p.}$

1)	$(p \vee q) \supset (q \vee p)$	A3
2)	$(p \vee ---p) \supset (---p \vee p)$	1, $---p/q$
3)	$p \vee ---p$	Th. 10
4)	$---p \vee p$	2, 3, Imp.
5)	$--p \supset p$	4, Def. $P \supset Q$

In going from Step 4 to Step 5 our use of Def. $P \supset Q$ required that we see $---p \vee p$ as $-(--p) \vee p$. When we group the symbols of the first wff in this manner we may recognize the whole formula to be like $-P \vee Q$ of the Definition.

Theorem 12. $\underline{/p \equiv --p.}$

1)	$p \supset --p$	Th. 9
2)	$--p \supset p$	Th. 11
3)	$(p \supset --p) \cdot (--p \supset p)$	1, 2, Rule 5
4)	$p \equiv --p$	3, Def. $P \equiv Q$

Theorem 13. $\underline{/-(p \cdot q) \supset (-p \vee -q).}$

1)	$--p \supset p$	Th. 11
2)	$--(-p \vee -q) \supset (-p \vee -q)$	1, $(-p \vee -q)/p$
3)	$-(p \cdot q) \supset (-p \vee -q)$	2, Def. $P \cdot Q$

Theorem 14. $\underline{/(-p \vee -q) \supset -(p \cdot q).}$

The proof is left to the student.

Theorem 15. $/-(p \cdot q) \equiv (-p \vee -q).$

The proof is left to the student.

Theorem 16. $/(p \supset q) \supset (-q \supset -p).$

Here is a proof in which we may again use Theorem 2 and an interpretation into Truth Table language to help in finding the solution. We are attempting to prove $(p \supset q) \supset (-q \supset -p)$, which may be considered as the $p \supset r$ of Theorem 2: $(q \supset r) \supset [(p \supset q) \supset (p \supset r)]$. This would mean, of course, that we will substitute $p \supset q$ for p and $-q \supset -p$ for r. The only question remaining concerns the middle term q: We need some wff that *implies* r and is implied *by* p.

Theorem 4 tells us $(p \supset -q) \supset (q \supset -p)$. If we substitute $-q/q$ in Theorem 4, we get $(p \supset --q) \supset (-q \supset -p)$, which could now be substituted for $q \supset r$ in Theorem 2 using $p \supset --q$ as the middle term q. But this would mean that we would also have to show that $(p \supset q) \supset (p \supset --q)$. This latter can be done with *another* use of Theorem 2. We know that $q \supset --q$ (by substituting q for p in Theorem 9), so we can say that if q implies $--q$, then if p implies q then p implies $--q$. Substituting in Theorem 2: $(q \supset --q) \supset [(p \supset q) \supset (p \supset --q)]$. $q \supset --q$, therefore $(p \supset q) \supset (p \supset --q)$.

After having taken care of that little digression, we go back to the first part of the proof. All we needed, we said, was to show that $(p \supset q) \supset (p \supset --q)$, and we would then be able to use $(p \supset --q)$ as the middle term. We have that formula now so let us consolidate all we have into a formal presentation of the proof. (The order of presentation is rearranged for convenience and clarity.)

Theorem 16. $/(p \supset q) \supset (-q \supset -p).$

1) $(p \supset -q) \supset (q \supset -p)$	Th. 4
2) $(p \supset --q) \supset (-q \supset -p)$	1, $-q/q$
3) $(q \supset r) \supset [(p \supset q) \supset (p \supset r)]$	Th. 2
4) $(q \supset --q) \supset [(p \supset q) \supset (p \supset --q)]$	3, $--q/r$
5) $p \supset --p$	Th. 9
6) $q \supset --q$	5, q/p
7) $(p \supset q) \supset (p \supset --q)$	4, 6, Imp.
8) $[(p \supset --q) \supset (-q \supset -p)] \supset$	3, $(p \supset --q)/q$,

$\{[(p \supset q) \supset (p \supset --q)] \supset [(p \supset q) \supset (-q \supset -p)]\}$ $\quad (-q \supset -p)/r, \; (p \supset q)/p$

9) $[(p \supset q) \supset (p \supset --q)] \supset [(p \supset q) \supset (-q \supset -p)]$ $\quad$ 8, 2, Imp.

10) $(p \supset q) \supset (-q \supset -p)$ $\quad$ 9, 7, Imp.

Again in this proof we have used the procedure of *interpreting* our symbols into the language of Truth Tables to help us find the solution of the proof. It should be clearly recognized, however, that the finished proof—as it is seen in Steps 1 through 10—has *no dependence whatsoever* on the *interpretations* we gave in setting it up.

Theorem 17. $/(-q \supset -p) \supset (p \supset q)$

The proof is left to the student.

Theorem 18. $/(-p \supset q) \supset (-q \supset p)$.

The proof is left to the student.

Theorem 19. $/-p \supset (p \supset q)$.

In developing the proof for this theorem let us see first if we can make it appear like one of the assumptions or one of the other theorems that have already been proved. This may then suggest to us a procedure for setting up the proof that is not immediately clear as it now stands.

We have shown that $q \supset (p \supset q)$ in the proof of Theorem 1, but the appearance of the variables is in the wrong order and they have the wrong values, here.

However, if we changed Theorem 19 into $-p \supset (-p \vee q)$ by Definition $P \supset Q$, then we may recognize a similarity between this and Assumption 2: $q \supset (p \vee q)$. That is, if $(p \vee q)$ in Assumption 2 were changed to $(q \vee p)$—as Assumption 3 suggests is possible—we would have $q \supset (q \vee p)$; and by substituting $-p$ for q and q for p, we would have $-p \supset (-p \vee q)$ as called for in the first sentence of this paragraph.

The formal presentation of this proof will be left as an exercise for the student.

Theorem 20. $/(p \supset -q) \vee -(q \supset -p)$.

This proof is left to be done by the dedicated student.

Listed below are the four assumptions given at the beginning of this work and the twenty theorems that have been shown to be implied by those assumptions.

ASSUMPTIONS.

1. $(p \vee p) \supset p$
2. $q \supset (p \vee q)$
3. $(p \vee q) \supset (q \vee p)$
4. $(q \supset r) \supset [(p \vee q) \supset (p \vee r)]$

THEOREMS.

1. $q \supset (p \supset q)$
2. $(q \supset r) \supset [(p \supset q) \supset (p \supset r)]$
3. $(p \supset -p) \supset -p$
4. $(p \supset -q) \supset (q \supset -p)$
5. $p \supset p$
6. $(q \vee p) \supset (p \vee q)$
7. $-p \vee p$
8. $p \vee -p$
9. $p \supset --p$
10. $p \vee ---p$
11. $--p \supset p$
12. $p \equiv --p$
13. $-(p \cdot q) \supset (-p \vee -q)$
14. $(-p \vee -q) \supset -(p \cdot q)$
15. $-(p \cdot q) \equiv (-p \vee -q)$
16. $(p \supset q) \supset (-q \supset -p)$
17. $(-q \supset -p) \supset (p \supset q)$
18. $(-p \supset q) \supset (-q \supset p)$
19. $-p \supset (p \supset q)$
20. $(p \supset -q) \vee -(q \supset -p)$

This point has already been mentioned but is worth repeating: If our connecting symbols are interpreted in the language of Tautologies from the Truth Tables, the theorems of Propositional Calculus are then seen to be definable in terms of our common understandings. (Perhaps this should be qualified to "common Truth-Table understandings," which however, are certainly *related* to common-sense understandings, as we showed in the beginning of Chapter 3.)

Examples of the above claim may be taken as: Theorem 3, that can be interpreted as saying, "If a statement implies its own contradiction then the statement must be false;" Theorem 9 is the statement of Double Negation; and Theorem 15 is one of the Tautologies we knew as De Morgan's Laws.

APPENDIX ON POLISH NOTATION.

There are other kinds of notation used in the development of systems like the Propositional Calculus presented here. One of the most interesting of these is that called the Polish Notation, an approach used by the Polish logician Jan Lukasiewicz.

The procedure used in Polish Notation is that of writing the connective symbols *before* the well-formed formulas they connect. That is, the connective symbols that join any simple or complex wff's or any combinations of simple or complex wff's is placed before the two wff's it is meant to join. $p \supset q$, then, would be indicated $\supset pq$. $(p \vee q) \supset (q \vee p)$ would be shown as $\supset \vee pq \vee qp$, because the sign $\supset$ is meant to join the wff's $(p \vee q)$ and $(q \vee p)$, the first $\vee$ joins p and q, and the second $\vee$ joins *q and p.*

A negative sign would, of course, precede any simple or complex wff. Thus $-p$ would remain just as it is, but $-(p \vee -q)$ would be $-\vee p-q$. The $\vee p-q$ is a complex wff so the first sign, $-$, extends over the whole expression, whereas q is a simple wff modified by the second sign, $-$.

The advantage to this system is in its elimination of the need for grouping symbols. If any connective (except Negation) may refer to two and only two wff's, then all one need do in translating from Polish to conventional notation is assign the connective symbol to the first two wff's that follow it. In translating from conventional to Polish notation one simply places the connective before instead of between the wff's involved.

The system is often further simplified by using capital letters to stand for the connectives rather than symbols such as those that have been used here. The symbol for Implication, $\supset$, is replaced by *C;* the symbol for Disjunction, $\vee$ (Inclusive Disjunction, sometimes called "Alternation"), is given as *A*, Conjunction, $\cdot$, is *K*, and Equivalence, $\equiv$, is *E*. The four binary connectives, then, are *C*, *A*, *K*, and *E*. (In the "WFF'N Proof" game invented by Layman E. Allen,* they are called, appropriately enough, the "Cake Letters.") The symbol for Negation in this system is *N*. The lower-case letters continue to stand for variables.

Translating $p \supset q$ into this notation, we have *Cpq*. $-p \vee (q \supset -r)$ becomes *ANpCqNr*. And $\{p \supset [-(q \vee -r) \equiv (-q \cdot r)]\} \vee (-s \cdot t)$ is *ACpENAqNrKNqrKNst*.

3. SUMMARY. In Section B we have shown how a logic of propositions may be set up in axiomatic form and how theorems may be derived within the system.

The entire Calculus was based upon the presuppositions that were made in the beginning. No necessary references to Tautologies or Truth Table logic were made, although it was found that such an interpretation could be drawn if we wanted to use the system to give full rigorous support to the Truth Table logic.

* Layman E. Allen, *WFF 'N Proof, the Game of Modern Logic.*

It was also shown that the derivation of a theorem could be made somewhat easier by interpreting symbols in the language of Truth Table Tautologies. The student is left with the warning, however, that he should not take these interpretations as having been used as anything more than aids to the discovery of the procedures of a proof. In a rigorous deductive system there should be nothing in the finished proof that refers to any rules, understandings, assumptions, or definitions outside the well-established limits of the system.

In Section C we will develop the Class Calculus, which has a number of similarities to the Propositional Calculus. But as the Propositional Calculus has appeared to be closely related to Truth Table logic, so the Class Calculus will be seen to be related to the material on sets that was introduced in Chapter 2.

Additional theorems to prove for exercise.

21. $-(p \cdot -p)$
22. $[(p \vee q) \vee r] \supset [(p \vee q) \vee (q \vee r)]$
23. $p \supset (p \vee q)$
24. $-(p \cdot q) \supset -(q \cdot p)$
25. $[-(p \vee q) \supset -p] \cdot [-(p \vee q) \supset -q]$
26. $-p \supset -(p \cdot q)$
27. $(p \supset q) \supset -(p \cdot -q)$
28. $(-p \vee -q) \supset --(-q \vee -p)$
29. $(p \supset q) \equiv -(p \cdot -q)$
30. $(-p \cdot -q) \supset -(p \vee q)$

POLISH NOTATION.

Translate from Polish Notation to standard symbols:

1. *KCpNqNApq.*
2. *ApKrEsCtu.*
3. *ECpNNpNANqNq.*
4. *CCNqqq.*
5. *CCCKpNqKNrsKANpNrsq.*

Translate from standard symbols to Polish Notation:

6. $[(p \supset q) \supset r] \equiv [p \supset (q \supset r)]$
7. $[(p \vee q) \vee r] \supset [(p \vee q) \vee (q \vee r)]$
8. $[(p \supset --q) \supset (-q \supset -p)] \supset \{[(p \supset q) \supset (p \supset --q)] \supset [(p \supset q) \supset (-q \supset -p)]\}$
9. $[-c \cdot -(h \supset b)] \vee -[-g \cdot -p]$
10. $-[p \cdot -(-q \vee -r)]$

C. CLASS CALCULUS

The axiomatic system developed here is, in theoretical language, a type of Boolean Algebra.*

If we were to attempt to give the most rigorous development possible, this system should be constructed without any reference at all to experience and intuition. However, such a procedure would be less meaningful and useful to us in the context of this book than one in which we make a slight compromise by constructing a *kind* of Boolean Algebra—the Class Calculus. That is, we will here consider our symbols as referring to classes and our operations as referring to operations on classes rather than attempting to keep the symbols and operational functions totally abstract.

We will, in following this procedure, be doing very little in the way of withdrawing from a pure axiomatic system or the maximum limits of generalization. In the algebra of sets (Class Calculus) we have a system that could be used to describe any kind of Boolean Algebra simply by choosing the proper universal set. If, after we have constructed the Class Calculus, we should define our universe as the set of real numbers, or a set of propositions, or a set of switches in an electrical network, we would have the complete Boolean Algebra needed to manipulate the elements of these sets or classes. The Class Calculus, then, may be taken as a generalized Boolean Algebra that should satisfy all the demands we have for an axiomatized system in our further work.†

1. PRELIMINARY STATEMENTS. Here again, as in the Propositional Calculus, we will state the presuppositions and rules of procedure that will be examined and elaborated upon in order to bring out their full implications. These implications, or theorems, then, will be the bulk of the system of Class Calculus

---

* The elements of this algebra were given by George Boole in his *An Investigation of the Laws of Thought* (London, 1854). An elaboration and modification of the system was given in a three-volume work by E. Schröder published 1890–1905.

† I am particularly indebted to the text *Fundamentals of Symbolic Logic* by Ambrose and Lazerowitz, *op. cit.*, and the text *A Handbook of Logic* by J. G. Brennan, *op. cit.*, for the material in this section on Class Calculus. The influence of those texts may be seen throughout this one of mine, but this influence should be especially clear in the work immediately following.

as were the theorems of the Propositional Calculus the major part of that system.

a. Primitive Symbols. Our primitive symbols will consist of a set of variables *a, b, c, d,* . . . ; the operational symbol $+$ called "Union," the symbol of complementarity, $'$, and other operational symbols to be introduced by definition; and the grouping symbols ( ), [ ], { }.

Another basic symbol to be used is the identity symbol, $=$. This symbol is not, however, strictly speaking, a primitive, in that it may be said to be given definition by the rules for substitution on identities to be introduced shortly.

b. Well-formed Formulas. In this system we will call our variables *a, b, c,* etc. "class variables." An individual variable *a* will denote a simple class. The notion of a class will remain undefined. Any two classes joined by an operational symbol form a complex class. Any class followed by the symbol of complementarity is a complex class.

c. Definitions. Following are two definitions to be used within the system. Other definitions will be introduced later.

Definition 1. The symbol "$\times$" is called "Intersection," and defined as follows: $A \times B = \text{def } (A' + B')'$.

Definition 2. The symbol "$\subset$" is called "Inclusion" and defined as: $(A \subset B) = \text{def } [(A + B) = B]$.

d. Rules of Operation. Our rules of operation will include those rules stated for the derivation of proofs in the Propositional Calculus. Following is a restatement of some of those rules in the language of Class Calculus plus statements of additional rules.

1. Substitutions may be made on class variables, or simple classes. A substitution made on a class variable must be made on every occurrence of the class variable throughout the expression of which it is a part.
2. Substitutions may be made on definitions. Any complex class that appears as a definiendum may be substituted for another that appears as the respective definiens, or vice versa.
3. Substitutions may be made on identities in the following manner:

   (a) Any given class may be substituted for a second class if the given class is indicated to be identical to the second class by the fact that they are joined by the identity symbol. Such a substitution need not be made in every possible instance in a given expression. (Identity Substitution will be denoted "I.S.")

(b) Commutation of Identities. Two classes given as identical may be reversed in their order of appearance. For example, given $a + b = b$, these classes may be commuted to appear $b = a + b$. (Identity Commutation will be denoted "I.C.")

The identity symbol will also function as a grouping symbol in this system. It will be considered that the identity symbol stands as a relation between two classes that are grouped on either side of this symbol.

4. The rule of *reductio ad absurdum* will be used in making proofs within the system. Given any assumption, if that assumption should produce a contradiction when considered in a derivation that includes other assumptions or theorems within the system, then the given assumption will be said to have been proved false.

e. Assumptions or Postulates. We will use here—as is common practice in introductory presentations of the Class Calculus—one of the three sets of postulates originally proposed by E. V. Huntington.*

1. There are at least two nonidentical classes a and b.
2. There is a class 0 such that $a + 0 = a$. This class will be referred to as the Null Class, or the identity element for Union.
3. There is a class 1 such that $a \times 1 = a$. This will be referred to as the Universal Class, or the identity element for Intersection.
4. The Commutative Law for Union. $a + b = b + a$.
5. The Commutative Law for Intersection. $a \times b = b \times a$.
6. The Distributive Law for Union with respect to Intersection. $a + (b \times c) = (a + b) \times (a + c)$.
7. The Distributive Law for Intersection with respect to Union. $a \times (b + c) = (a \times b) + (a \times c)$.
8. For any given set a of the Class Calculus there is another set a' such that $a + a' = 1$ and $a \times a' = 0$. a' will be known as the complement of set a.

It may be of interest to note how a number of the assumptions

* "Sets of Independent Postulates for the Algebra of Logic," *Transactions of the American Mathematical Society,* Volume 5 (1904).

given above are applicable to our ordinary system of arithmetic. Assumptions 2 and 3 would be said to be introducing the additive and multiplicative identities in ordinary arithmetic. That is, given any number in our decimal system of arithmetic, we may add it to 0 and get the given number as the sum. 0, then, is the additive identity. The multiplicative identity in arithmetic is 1, by the fact that any number multiplied times 1 will produce as a product the given number itself.

Both Commutative Laws hold for ordinary arithmetic if we considered "$+$" to mean add and "$\times$" to mean multiply.

The Distributive Law for Intersection with respect to Union holds in ordinary arithmetic, also. But a simple calculation using numbers like 2, 3, 4, for a, b, c will show that the Distributive Law for Union with respect to Intersection does not hold in ordinary arithmetic. This, we see, is one place in which Boolean Algebra will clearly differ from the algebra we develop out of our decimal arithmetic.

2. THEOREMS. These Huntington Postulates will now be used for the construction of theorems in the Class Calculus. As in the Propositional Calculus, the student may expect to see some theorems that fit well with his intuitive understanding, some theorems that are not at all intuitively evident, and some that are intuitively so obvious that proof would seem unnecessary to anyone ignorant of the meaning of an axiomatic system. But, as before, the first theorems will be proved by direct reference to our basic assumptions, and the proofs of later theorems will use the assumptions *plus* earlier theorems, thereby giving *all* the theorems complete validity so far as proof is concerned. And all, and whatever, truth that rests in the assumptions and methods of logical procedure may then be said to rest also in the theorems.

Theorem 1. The Null Class, 0, is unique.

In Assumption 2 we say there is a class, 0, such that $a + 0 = a$. By the proof of Theorem 1 we mean to show that there is no *more* than one class that meets that description.

We will use the rule of *reductio ad absurdum* by first supposing there is such another class and then showing that this supposition leads to a contradiction.

Suppose there is another class 0_x such that $a + 0_x = a$, and 0_x is not identical to 0:

1) $a + 0 = a$	A2
2) $a + 0_x = a$	Hypothesis
3) $0_x + 0 = 0_x$	1, $0_x/a$
4) $0 + 0_x = 0$	2, $0/a$
5) $a + b = b + a$	A4
6) $0 + 0_x = 0_x + 0$	5, $0/a$, $0_x/b$
7) $0_x + 0 = 0$	4, 6, I.S.
8) $0_x = 0_x + 0$	3, I.C.
9) $0_x = 0$	7, 8, I.S.
10) 0 is unique	The proposal that there is a second, nonidentical Null Class leads to a contradiction.

Theorem. 2. The Universal Class, 1, is unique.

(Notice the similarity between this proof and that of Theorem 1.)

Suppose there is another class, 1_x, such that $a \times 1_x = a$, and 1_x is not identical to 1:

1) $a \times 1 = a$	A3
2) $a \times 1_x = a$	Hypothesis
3) $1_x \times 1 = 1_x$	1, $1_x/a$
4) $1 \times 1_x = 1$	2, $1/a$
5) $a \times b = b \times a$	A5
6) $1 \times 1_x = 1_x \times 1$	5, $1/a$, $1_x/b$
7) $1_x \times 1 = 1$	4, 6, I.S.
8) $1_x = 1_x \times 1$	3, I.C.
9) $1_x = 1$	7, 8, I.S.
10) 1 is unique	The proposal that there is a second, nonidentical Universal Class leads to a contradiction.

Theorem 3. $/a \times a = a$.

1) $a \times 1 = a$	A3
2) $a \times (a + a') = a$	1, A8, I.S.
3) $a \times (b + c) = (a \times b) + (a \times c)$	A7
4) $a \times (a + a') = (a \times a) + (a \times a')$	3, a/b, a'/c
5) $(a \times a) + (a \times a') = a$	2, 4, I.S.
6) $(a \times a) + 0 = a$	5, A8, I.S.
7) $a + 0 = a$	A2
8) $(a \times a) + 0 = (a \times a)$	7, $(a \times a)/a$
9) $a \times a = a$	6, 8, I.S.

Theorem 4. $/a + a = a.$

The proof for this theorem will follow, essentially, the same procedure as that given for Theorem 3. The student should work this proof as an exercise.

Theorem 5. $/a + 1 = 1.$

1)	$a + a' = 1$	A8
2)	$a \times 1 = a$	A3
3)	$a' \times 1 = a'$	2, a'/a
4)	$a + (a' \times 1) = 1$	1, 3, I.S.
5)	$a + (b \times c) = (a + b) \times (a + c)$	A6
6)	$a + (a' \times 1) = (a + a') \times (a + 1)$	5, a'/b, $1/c$
7)	$(a + a') \times (a + 1) = 1$	4, 6, I.S.
8)	$1 \times (a + 1) = 1$	7, A8, I.S.
9)	$a \times b = b \times a$	A5
10)	$a \times 1 = 1 \times a$	9, $1/b$
11)	$1 \times a = a$	2, 10, I.S.
12)	$1 \times (a + 1) = a + 1$	11, $(a + 1)/a$
13)	$a + 1 = 1$	8, 12, I.S.

It may have been noticed in the above proof that we used a number of steps to arrive at some statements of class relationship that will necessarily be repeated many times in future proofs. For example, we used three steps, 5, 6, and 7, to replace $a + (a' \times 1)$ with $(a + a') \times (a + 1)$; and we used another three steps, 2, 9, and 10, to commute $a \times 1$ to $1 \times a$. Therefore, for the purpose of simplifying the presentations in the proofs of theorems to follow, we will skip such steps as those mentioned and will simply indicate by reference to the relevant assumptions the steps we have left out.

The student must be cautious if he intends to follow such a procedure in his own proofs. It must be perfectly clear at all times that the missing steps may be supplied only from within the limits of the system of Class Calculus. Care must be taken to see that such a procedure of simplification does not allow the subtle introduction of any assumptions that have not been specifically mentioned within the system.

Theorem 6. The student is asked here to state the theorem that would most naturally follow Theorem 5 (considering the relationships between Theorem 1 and Theorem 2, and between Theorem 3 and Theorem 4).

Theorem 6 should then be proved as an exercise. (Theorem 6 is listed in the summary of theorems on p. 151.)

Theorem 7. $/a = a.$

The proof of this theorem is left to the student.

Theorem 8. $/1 = 0'.$

1) $a + 0 = a$	A2
2) $0' + 0 = 0'$	1, $0'/a$
3) $a' + a = 1$	A8, A4, I.S.
4) $0' + 0 = 1$	3, $0/a$
5) $1 = 0'$	2, 4, I.S.

Theorem 9. $/0 = 1'.$

A somewhat-less-than-meaty problem for the enlightened student.

Theorem 10. $/(a+b) \times (c+d) = [(a \times c) + (b \times c)] + [(a \times d) + (b \times d)]$

1) $a \times (b+c) = (a \times b) + (a \times c)$	A7
2) $(a+b) \times (c+d) = [(a+b) \times c] + [(a+b) \times d]$	1, $(a+b)/a, c/b, d/c$
3) $(a+b) \times (c+d) = [c \times (a+b)] + [d \times (a+b)]$	2, A5
4) $c \times (a+b) = (c \times a) + (c \times b)$	1, $c/a, a/b, b/c$
5) $c \times (a+b) = (a \times c) + (b \times c)$	4, A5
6) $d \times (a+b) = (a \times d) + (b \times d)$	1, $d/a, a/b, b/c$, A5
7) $(a+b) \times (c+d) = [(a \times c) + (b \times c)] + [(a \times d) + (b \times d)]$	3, 5, 6, I.S.

The brackets, [ ], will be left as they are for this proof; but after our proof of the Associative Law, Theorem 18, it should be plain to see how the arrangement of these brackets becomes arbitrary. (See how the theorem is stated on p. 151.)

Theorem 11. $/a = (a \times b) + (a \times b').$

1) $a \times 1 = a$	A3
2) $a \times (b + b') = a$	1, A8, b/a, I.S.
3) $a = (a \times b) + (a \times b')$	2, I.C., A7

In the following four theorems we will use the method of the Propositional Calculus to speak *about* classes. The symbols "$\supset$" and "$\equiv$" should not be considered here to be on the same level of meaning as the symbols "$+$" or "$\times$," or the one we have defined but not as yet used, "$\subset$," the symbol for Inclusion. (The definition for this latter symbol, it will be remembered, was given as $(A \subset B) = \text{def}\ [(A+B) = B]$.)

We are introducing these proofs here simply to give the student some idea of an important aspect of a more inclusive system that has not yet been described. This material is only a token of that which would be necessary for any further discussion of sets or classes.

The four theorems that follow, then, may be considered as a part of a more elaborate system of logic which we intend only to mention here.

Even considering the limited discussion we will give it, this more generalized system will require the use of two additional rules of operation. Those rules are as follows:

5. Rule of Conjunction. Any postulates and/or proved theorems may be joined as a Conjunction to produce an expression that is also a proved theorem. And, conversely, either Conjunct of a given Conjunction may be stated independently as a proved theorem.
6. Rule of Hypothetical Proof. Given some arbitrary expression H which, when used in a valid proof with any assumptions and/or proved theorems $A_1, A_2, A_3, \ldots, A_n$, leads to the derivation of an expression C, then $H \supset C$ may be given as a proved theorem.

Because of the fact that Inclusion will be the principal concern for us in the next four theorems (and because it has been given no meaningful treatment in the preceding pages), let us consider a brief intuitive description of Inclusion. Such a description may be given by referring to the individual *elements* of a set or class. When we say Set a is included in Set b ($a \subset b$), we mean that all the elements in a are also elements of b. We may mean by this that the elements of a are the *only* elements of b or we may mean simply that they are merely *among* the elements of b, which latter may number considerably more than are in a.

A less intuitive, but still revealing, description may be given using material from our earlier work. If we brought in the use of Quantifiers from Truth Table logic, we could define Inclusion as $A \subset B = \text{def } (x)[(x \in A) \supset (x \in B)]$. The symbol $\in$ would be read in this context as "is an element of."

Inclusion will be seen to be analogous to Implication in Truth Table logic; or, to put it another way, the symbol "$\subset$" of Class Calculus denotes a relationship that is analogous to the relationship denoted by "$\supset$" in Propositional Calculus.

Again, remember that the symbols from Propositional Calculus are used to talk *about* the expressions in Class Calculus—they are not themselves expressions in the Class Calculus. It may be said that we are putting one system to work to explain certain things about another system—just as we have been, throughout this book, using the system of ordinary language to discuss systems of logic and mathematics.

Theorem 12. $\underline{/0 \subset a.}$

1) $a + 0 = a$	A2
2) $0 + a = a$	1, A4
3) $0 \subset a$	2, def. $A \subset B$

This theorem, which may be taken to mean, "The Null Class is included in every class," may also be described as being analogous to the case of Implication in Truth Table logic wherein a false proposition is said to imply *any* proposition.

Theorem 13. $\underline{/\ a \subset 1.}$

To be proved as an exercise.

Theorem 14. $\underline{/[(a \subset b) \cdot (b \subset a)] \supset (a = b).}$

In the proof of this theorem we will use the two additional rules, Rules 5 and 6, that were introduced as being necessary for further work in the Class Calculus. In using Rule 6, the rule of Hypothetical Proof, we will hypothesize $(a \subset b) \cdot (b \subset a)$ and show how this hypothesis leads to, or implies, the conclusion $a = b$.

1) $(a \subset b) \cdot (b \subset a)$	Hypothesis
2) $a \subset b$	1, Rule 5
3) $a + b = b$	2, def. $A \subset B$
4) $b \subset a$	1, Rule 5
5) $b + a = a$	4, def. $A \subset B$
6) $a + b = a$	5, A4
7) $a = b$	3, 6, I.S.
8) $[(a \subset b) \cdot (b \subset a)] \supset (a = b)$	1–7, Rule 6

Theorem 15. $/(a \subset 0) \supset (a = 0)$.

The proof of this theorem is left as an exercise.

The following theorems are given with proofs that are, essentially, the presentations made by J. E. Whitesitt in his *Boolean Algebra and Its Applications, op. cit.* Most of the changes that have been made are modifications that are necessary to relate these proofs to the terminology and procedures we have been using. There are, however, a few additional steps and some revisions in presentation that have been introduced to intensify the rigor of the demonstrations.

Theorem 16. The Principle of Duality.

This theorem will serve to make our work considerably easier as we go through the proofs of further theorems and, later, when we speak of a practical system wherein the theorems are given empirical interpretation.

The Principle of Duality derives from the fact that the assumptions of the Class Calculus are symmetrical. That is, as may already have been noticed, in our list of assumptions (with the exception of number 1) there is always one assumption that is the direct repetition of another assumption under the following conditions: the sign $\times$ is used to replace the sign $+$, and $+$ is used to replace $\times$; and the identity elements, 0 and 1, are interchanged.

The Principle, as expressed in Whitesitt, is as follows:

"Every statement or algebraic identity deducible from the postulates of a Boolean Algebra remains valid if the operations (Union and Intersection), and the identity elements, 0 and 1, are interchanged throughout."

The proof, then, is contained in the expression of the postulates.

Each postulate is given as symmetrical, so that every operation has its direct counterpart and each identity element is used with one operation that is different from the operation used by the other identity element.

A warning must be given here about the use of the Principle of Duality. The Theorem tells us only of the *validity* of statements whose signs have been interchanged. It does not say that the two statements are identical. This is a common error made by students in using the Theorem. If we have proved, for example, that $a \times 0 = 0$, then we may say that $a + 1 = 1$ follows from the Principle of Duality. But $a + 1 = 1$ is *another* theorem that we now know to be valid; it is not another expression of the same proposition as $a \times 0 = 0$ and cannot therefore be substituted for the latter expression.

Whenever we make a change from one expression to another by the Principle of Duality we will describe this operation as affirming or taking the dual of the given theorem, and give as our reason: Theorem 16.

The theorem below is one needed in the work to follow.

Theorem 17. $a + (a \times b) = a; a \times (a + b) = a.$

1. $a \times 1 = a$	A3
2. $b + 1 = 1$	Th. 5, b/a
3. $a \times (b + 1) = a$	1, 2, I.S.
4. $a \times (b + 1) = (a \times b) + (a \times 1)$	A7, $1/c$
5. $(a \times b) + (a \times 1) = a$	3, 4, I.S.
6. $(a \times b) + a = a$	5, 1, I.S.
7. $(a \times b) + a = a + (a \times b)$	A4, $a \times b/a, a/b$
8. $a + (a \times b) = a$	6, 7, I.S.

The second part of the theorem, $a \times (a + b) = a$, follows from the Principle of Duality.

Theorem 18. $a \times (b \times c) = (a \times b) \times c;$
$a + (b + c) = (a + b) + c.$

This theorem, the Associative Law, is another theorem that is important in the development of our Calculus of Classes. The Associative Law, as can be seen above, expresses a rather uncomplicated idea; the proof, however, is *not* so uncomplicated. So, in order to show that our intuition contains no hidden errors or oversights—to show that what seems to be valid actually does follow from the rules of our system—we must go through the extended deductions given below.

The proof will be given in five parts; A, B, C, D, and E. A and B are worked independently to arrive at two separate equations. These equations are brought together as an intersection in C, and each side of the new equation is simplified in D. The final step is E, wherein both sides of the new equation, in their simplified form, are again set equal to one another to finish the proof of the Associative Law, Theorem 18.

A.	1. $a + (a \times b) = a$	Th. 17
	2. $a + [a \times (b \times c)] = a$	1, $b \times c/b$
	3. $a + [a \times (b \times c)] = a \times (a + c)$	Th. 17, c/b, I.S.
	4. $a + [a \times (b \times c)] = [a + (a \times b)] \times (a + c)$	3, Th. 17, I.S.
	5. $a + (b \times c) = (a + b) \times (a + c)$	A6
	6. $a + [(a \times b) \times c] = [a + (a \times b)] \times (a + c)$	5, $a \times b/b$
	7. $a + [a \times (b \times c)] = a + [(a \times b) \times c]$	4, 6, I.S.
B.	1. $a + (b \times c) = (a + b) \times (a + c)$	A6
	2. $a' + [a \times (b \times c)] = [a' + a] \times [a' + (b \times c)]$	1, a'/a, a/b, $b \times c/c$
	3. $a' + [a \times (b \times c)] = 1 \times [a' + (b \times c)]$	2, A8, I.S.
	4. $1 \times a = a$	A3, I.C.
	5. $1 \times [a' + (b \times c)] = [a' + (b \times c)]$	4, $a' + (b \times c)/a$
	6. $1 \times [a' + (b \times c)] = (a' + b) \times (a' + c)$	5, A6, a'/a, I.S.
	7. $1 \times [a' + (b \times c)] = [1 \times (a' + b)] \times (a' + c)$	6, A3, $a' + b/a$, I.S., I.C.
	8. $1 \times [a' + (b \times c)] = [(a' + a) \times (a' + b)] \times (a' + c)$	7, A8, I.S.
	9. $1 \times [a' + (b \times c)] = [a' + (a \times b)] \times (a' + c)$	8, A6, a'/a, a/b, b/c, I.S.
	10. $1 \times [a' + (b \times c)] = a' + [(a \times b) \times c]$	9, A6, a'/a, $a \times b/b$, I.S.
	11. $a' + [a \times (b \times c)] = a' + [(a \times b) \times c]$	3, 10, I.S.

C.

Taking the equation developed in A, $a + [a \times (b \times c)] = a + [(a \times b) \times c]$, we will call the left side θ and the right side ϕ giving, then, $\theta = \phi$. (This is done simply as a matter of convenience; the full statements could be written out without changing any of the steps of the proof.)

For the equation developed in B, $a' + [a \times (b \times c)] = a' + [(a \times b) \times c]$, we will call the left side β and the right side γ; then $\beta = \gamma$. Continuing the proof:

1. $\theta = \phi$	From A
2. $\beta = \gamma$	From B
3. $a = a$	Th. 7
4. $\theta \times \beta = \theta \times \beta$	3, $\theta \times \beta / a$
5. $\theta \times \beta = \phi \times \gamma$	4, ϕ/θ, γ/β, I.S.

D.

We will now proceed to simplify each side of the equation developed in Step 5 of Section C. Taking the left side first:

1. $\theta \times \beta$	Given
2. $\{a + [a \times (b \times c)]\} \times \{a' + [a \times (b \times c)]\}$	1, I.S.
3. $\{[a \times (b \times c)] + a\} \times \{[a \times (b \times c)] + a'\}$	2, I.C.
4. $a + (b \times c) = (a + b) \times (a + c)$	A6
5. $\{[a \times (b \times c)] + (a \times a')\} = \{[a \times (b \times c)] + a\} \times \{[a \times (b \times c)] + a'\}$	4, $a \times (b \times c)/a$, a/b, a'/c
6. $[a \times (b \times c)] + (a \times a')$	3, 5, I.S.
7. $[a \times (b \times c)] + 0$	6, A8, I.S.
8. $a \times (b \times c)$	7, A2, $a \times (b \times c)/a$, I.S.

$\phi \times \gamma$ is $\{a + [(a \times b) \times c]\} \times \{a' + [(a \times b) \times c]\}$ which may be reduced to $(a \times b) \times c$ following essentially the same steps as those given in the proof in D above.

E.

Substituting to show the results of the reduction of both sides of the equation $\theta \times \beta = \phi \times \gamma$, we have:

$$a \times (b \times c) = (a \times b) \times c.$$

From the above theorem and the Principle of Duality, we have:

$$a+(b+c)=(a+b)+c.$$

Theorem 19. a' is a unique class.

There is one and only one complement of any given class in our Calculus of Classes. For the proof, consider the class, a, and the class, a', as introduced in Assumption 8; and suppose there is another class x such that $a+x=1$ and $a\times x=0$. (This would give us, then, a second complement for the class a.)

1. $a=a\times 1$	A3, I.C.
2. $x=x\times 1$	1, x/a
3. $x=x\times(a+a')$	2, A8, I.S.
4. $x=(x\times a)+(x\times a')$	3, A7
5. $x=(a\times x)+(a'\times x)$	4, A5
6. $a\times x=0$	Supposition
7. $x=0+(a'\times x)$	5, 6, I.S.
8. $x=(a'\times a)+(a'\times x)$	7, A8, I.S.
9. $x=a'\times(a+x)$	8, A7
10. $a+x=1$	Supposition
11. $x=a'\times 1$	9, 10, I.S.
12. $x=a'$	11, A3

Any other class taken to be the complement of a will prove to be identical to a'. a' is unique by *reductio ad absurdum*.

Theorem 20. $\underline{/a=a''.}$

1. $a=(a\times b)+(a\times b')$	Th. 11
2. $a=(a+b)\times(a+b')$	1, Th. 16
3. $a=(a+a')\times(a+a'')$	2, a'/b
4. $a+a'=1$	A8
5. $a'+a''=1$	4, a'/a
6. $a'+a''=a+a'$	5, 4, I.S.
7. $a=(a'+a'')\times(a+a'')$	3, 6, I.S.
8. $a=(a''+a')\times(a''+a)$	7, A4
9. $a=a''+(a'\times a)$	8, A6
10. $a=a''+0$	9, A5, A8
11. $a=a''$	10, A2

Theorem 21. $\underline{/(a\times b)'=a'+b'.}$

1. $a=a$	Th. 7

2. $(a'+b')''=(a'+b')''$	1, $(a'+b')''/a$
3. $(a\times b)'=(a'+b')''$	2, def. $(a\times b)$
4. $a=a''$	Th. 20
5. $(a'+b')=(a'+b')''$	4, $(a'+b')/a$
6. $(a\times b)'=a'+b'$	3, 5, I.S.

Theorem 22. $\underline{/(a+b)'=a'\times b'}$.

1. $a=a$	Th. 7
2. $a'\times b'=a'\times b'$	1, $(a'\times b')/a$
3. $(a''+b'')'=a'\times b'$	2, def. $(a\times b)$
4. $a=a''$	Th. 20
5. $b=b''$	4, b/a
6. $(a+b)'=a'\times b'$	3, 4, 5, I.S.

The student may note the similarity between Theorems 21 and 22 and the De Morgan Laws given in the Table of Tautologies on p. 81. The same general idea is expressed by Theorem 15 in the Propositional Calculus. The laws, as they were originally stated by Augustus De Morgan in his book *Formal Logic*, were given in terms of classes such as are formulated above. Historically, the analogy was made, then, from Class Calculus to Propositional Calculus. Our exchange of the order of their presentation is a result of the particular approach we have been using to the introductory material with which we are concerned.

We present a list of all the assumptions (Huntington Postulates) and all the theorems that have been proved up to this point in our development of the Class Calculus. These assumptions and theorems are brought together here to make them easily available for reference when they are needed for the work in Chapter 5.

It is suggested that the student memorize these assumptions and theorems.

ASSUMPTIONS

1. There are at least two classes: *a* and *b*.
2. $a+0=a$
3. $a\times 1=a$.
4. $a+b=b+a$
5. $a\times b=b\times a$
6. $a+(b\times c)=(a+b)\times(a+c)$.
7. $a\times(b+c)=(a\times b)+(a\times c)$.
8. $a+a'=1, a\times a'=0$

THEOREMS

1. 0 is unique.
2. 1 is unique.
3. $a \times a = a$.
4. $a + a = a$.
5. $a + 1 = 1$.
6. $a \times 0 = 0$.
7. $a = a$.
8. $1 = 0'$.
9. $0 = 1'$.
10. $(a + b) \times (c + d) = (a \times c) + (b \times c) + (a \times d) + (b \times d)$.
11. $a = (a \times b) + (a \times b')$.
12. $0 \subset a$.
13. $a \subset 1$.
14. $[(a \subset b) \cdot (b \subset a)] \supset (a = b)$.
15. $(a \subset 0) \supset (a = 0)$.
16. Principle of Duality.
17. $a + (a \times b) = a$.
    $a \times (a + b) = a$.
18. $a \times (b \times c) = (a \times b) \times c$.
    $a + (b + c) = (a + b) + c$.
19. a' is unique.
20. $a = a''$.
21. $(a \times b)' = a' + b'$.
22. $(a + b)' = a' \times b'$.

3. **CONCLUSION.** We have in the Calculus of Classes, as in the Calculus of Propositions, developed a number of theorems from a few fundamental postulates or axioms and a set of rules limiting and describing our procedures. We have, in both these systems, attempted to stay within the absolute limits prescribed by the rules and postulates, and everything that has been done in the development of the theorems has been meant, therefore, to be nothing more than just exactly what was implied by the original (preliminary) statements.

In following such a rigid procedure we clearly realize that we were not speaking of common sense or practical considerations. We did not mean to be speaking in those terms. We meant to be making theoretical considerations. That is, we wanted to know just what the results would be if we *did* take those rules and postulates for their exact literal meaning and carry them out to the inevitable conclusions that we have labeled "theorems." In thus so rigidly adhering to the limits of our presuppositions, we hope to have developed a system that may be quite impractical and theoretical but that will have all the errors removed from it that arise from careless reasoning or mistaken intuition. Blanché quotes J. Cavailles concerning this point: "When the reasoning is written down the visible structure of the argument will betray any improper steps." *

* Blanché, *op. cit.*, p. 52.

Our next step, now, is to consider the *use* of these systems in a truly practical sense. It is at this point—after we have limited ourselves to the most rigorous approach possible—that we begin to loosen up on our restrictions. We know we cannot get exact measurements and relationships; so we consider the applications to be "as close as possible," "within minimum limits of error," "according to the highest probability," and so forth.

We expect all of the postulates to have some kind of meaning in the area of experience where we intend to apply our logical system, and we expect also to be able to use the theorems we have developed in a meaningful way. If the system fails to explain the particular area of experience to which we have attempted to apply it, then we look around for *another* system that will prove to be more useful.

In the next chapter we will apply the system of Boolean Algebra, or Class Calculus, to switching networks. Beginning with an interpretation of the Huntington Postulates, we will then go on to discuss the switching hook-ups, bringing in all the theorems needed to give us the tools for handling this particular group of empirical facts.

5

The Algebra of Electrical Switches

The algebra of electrical switches, or Switching Algebra, will now be developed as a case of practical application of the Class Calculus or Boolean Algebra. As we said in introducing the Class Calculus, the principal concern there was, as in the Propositional Calculus, to give a theoretical development of a formal system that could then be used as a guide and a foundation for application in the world of experience.

In Switching Algebra it will readily be seen that a large part of the work will need constant reference to practical circumstances and empirical data to make it meaningful. We will, in fact, begin right away by associating each of the Huntington Postulates with a physical set-up of electrical switches, and the elements 1 and 0 with closed and open circuits.

It must be kept in mind here, then, that we are now fully involved in the application of some logical theory to practical considerations and that all the theoretical backing we have serves only as our foundation for reference, not as our current course of action.

A. ALGEBRAIC INTERPRETATION

The electrical circuit we will consider here is composed of a voltage source and any number of switches (at first, only two) arranged in series and/or parallel circuits.

A parallel circuit is one in which either of two switches may be on (or closed) for current to flow, or *both* may be on to allow current to flow. If we considered a light bulb to be hooked up with two switches in parallel, then the light would go on if switch *a* were closed or *b*

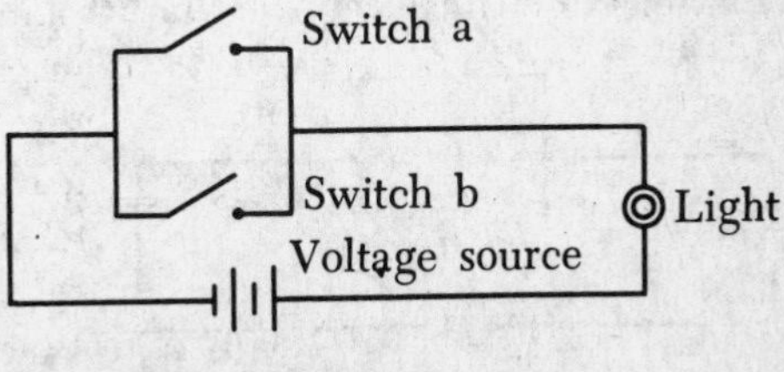

were closed or both *a* and *b* were closed. The diagram for this is shown on p. 153.

The light bulb is used simply to illuminate the idea of a parallel hook-up. [Neither the light nor the pun is needed in the general consideration of switching circuits, of course.]

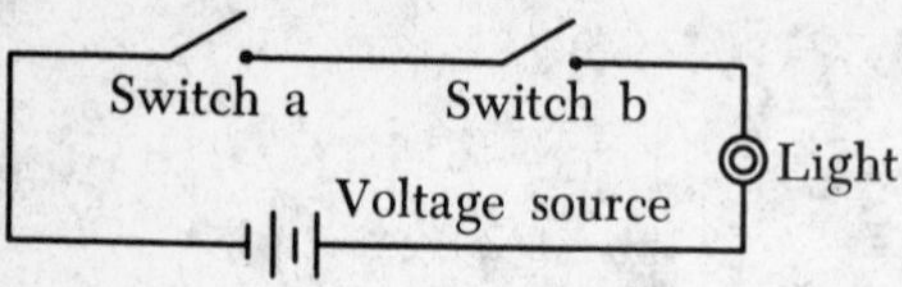

In a series switching hook-up, current will flow *if and only if* both switch *a and* switch *b* are closed. See the diagram at the left.

Here it may be seen that current will flow through the circuit and light the bulb only if both switches are on, or closed.

The section on well-formed formulas tells us that $a+b$ is a class. In the case of Switching Algebra, we will say that the algebraic expression, $a+b$, will stand for a parallel circuit. The relationship between the Union of two classes and the parallel circuit is a very close one. An element to be in the Union of two classes, *a* and *b*, must be *either* in *a* or in *b or* in both *a* and *b*. In a parallel circuit the switches that must be closed to allow current to flow are either *a* or *b* or both *a* and *b*.

The relationship between the series circuit and Intersection is no less complete. In the preliminary statements of Class Calculus we noted that $a \times b$ is a class. Here we say $a \times b$ is a series circuit. An element is in the class $a \times b$ if and only if it is in both *a* and *b*. Similarly, current flows through a series circuit if and only if both *a* and *b* are closed.

The identity elements for Union and Intersection are given special interpretation in the Switching Algebra. The expression $a+0=a$ tells us that we are introducing an element that, when combined with *a* in Union, will give *a* itself. In terms of switches we say we are introducing an element that can be placed in *parallel* with a given switch without making any change in the control the switch has over the circuit. This element connected

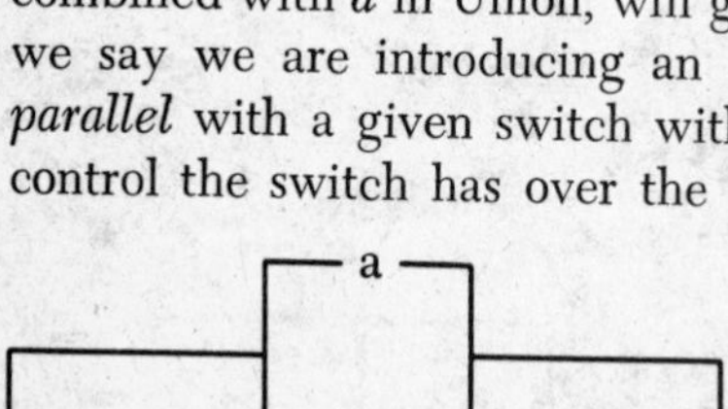

in parallel with switch *a* will, for all practical purposes, leave *a* as the factor that determines whether or not current will flow in the circuit. What kind of element would produce this characteristic? As we look at a circuit of this type we find that the element would be a switch that is constantly open. The identity element for a parallel circuit is an open switch that never allows current to flow. 0, for us, will then mean "open" or "no current flows."

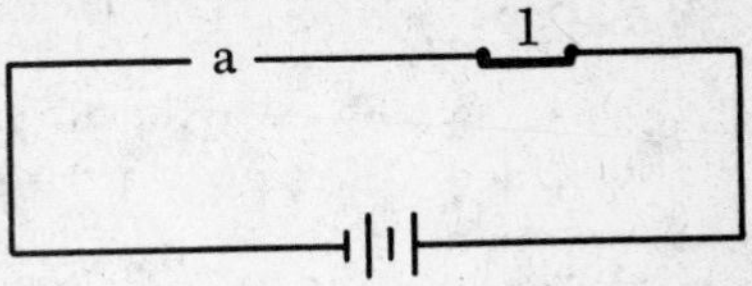

The expression $a \times 1 = a$ tells us we want an element that may be connected in *series* with a given switch without modifying the control the switch has in the circuit. If a is on, current will flow; if a is off, current will not flow—even though this new element is in the circuit as a series connection with a. The element we find to produce this characteristic is a switch that is always closed—or a closed junction. The identity element for a Series Circuit is a constantly closed switch. 1, for us then, will be used to mean "closed" or 'closed circuit" or "current flows."

It may be remembered that Huntington Postulate number 1 told us that there are at least two classes in our system that might be indicated by variables such as a, b, c, etc. In this work on the algebra of electrical switches we said the variables are to be considered switches. Now we will suppose that there *are* only two classes—the minimum allowed—that can be used to replace these variables. These will be, of course, the Null Class, 0, and the Universal Class, 1. Considering a simple variable (or switch) to stand for a simple wff and any combination of variables (or switches) to be a complex wff, we may say that any simple or complex wff represents *either* the Null Class *or* the Universal Class.

Speaking in this manner, then, if we substitute the Null Class, 0, for the switch (or variable) a we would mean that the switch was open; no current is flowing. When we substitute 1 for a we mean the switch is closed; current is flowing through the switch. The same might be said for a complex circuit of switches. If a circuit $a + b$ or $a \times b$ is shown to be equal to 0, the Null Class, then there is no current flowing. If such a circuit equals 1, then current is flowing through it.

These two terms, 0 and 1, will be used throughout this discussion to give information on current flow in a switching circuit. Whenever they are used they should be considered as referring to either the circuit itself or to some particular element in the circuit. If we say a given circuit, switch, or switch position has the value 0, current is not flowing through it. A circuit or switch that is assigned the value 1 *is* conducting current.

Assumptions 4 and 5 ($a+b=b+a$; $a\times b=b\times a$) tell us, in terms of switching circuits, simply that there is no difference in the conductivity of either a parallel or a series circuit if the positions of the switches are interchanged.

Assumptions 6 and 7 [$a+(b\times c)=(a+b)\times(a+c)$; $a\times(b+c)=(a\times b)+(a\times c)$] may be referred back to the demonstration given using Venn Diagram area numbers on p. 27. In the case of switches, Assumption 6 tells us that Switch *a* in parallel with two switches *b* and *c* will give the same circuit characteristics as the circuit *a* and *b* in parallel, coupled in series with the circuit *a* and *c* in parallel. That is, current flow will be determined by the same setting of switches in both circuits.

We may see this to be true by drawing the two circuits and examining their characteristics. The algebraic expression for the circuit is given beneath the diagram.*

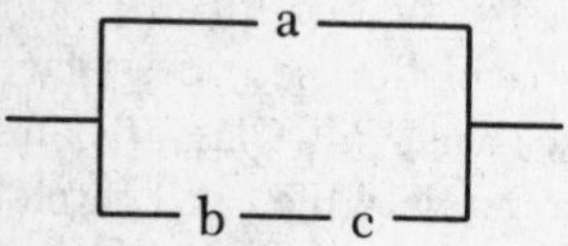

a + (b × c)

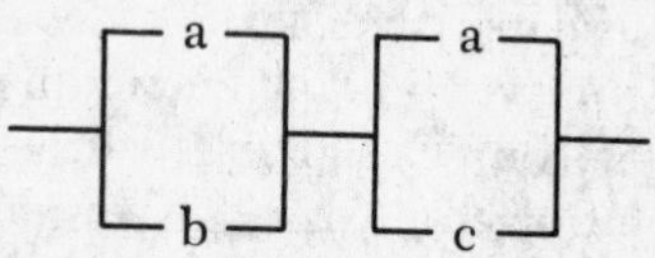

(a + b) × (a + c)

(From now on circuits will be diagrammed using letters alone to indicate switch positions at a given place in the circuit. Additional representations such as voltage source, lights, and switching bars will not be shown.)

If Switch *a* is open in either circuit, current may flow through Switch *b* and Switch *c*. If *a* and either *b* or *c* are open, however,

---

* In a schematic diagram it is often necessary to indicate the same switch (as, for example, Switch *a* above) in two or three or more different places in the circuit. We mean to say, simply, that the switch is—in terms of current flow in the circuit—in parallel with *b* and also in parallel with *c* and these two parallel circuits are in series with one another. Electrically, the switch is functioning in this way. Diagrammatically, it is necessary to produce it as given.

current will not flow in either circuit. Other arrangements of switch positions may be tried (as with a closed, b or c open, and so forth) to test the acceptability of this use of Assumption 6.

Assumption 7 tells us that a in series with b and c in parallel gives the same circuit characteristics as a in series with b and these in parallel with a in series with c. This equation should be examined in the same manner as the one above.

In Assumption 8 we introduce what we have heretofore called the complement of a class. In Switching Algebra we may interpret this postulate as to be introducing another kind of element into our circuitry. $a + a' = 1$ tells us that this additional element is one that will always allow current to flow when it is hooked in parallel with its complement. a combined as a sum with its complement will give 1, or current flow. In practical applications, one way we have of doing this is through the use of a single-pole, double-throw switch, that is, a switch that has three connections: one to receive current coming into the switch, and two to allow current to flow out. But the two outlets may be used only one at a time. If the selector is on one pole, then the other must necessarily be nonconducting. If the selector is on the other pole then the first must be nonconducting. If we label the poles a and a', then we may say that if $a = 1$ (current is flowing through a) then $a' = 0$ (a' must equal 0, current may *not* flow through the pole a'). One position precludes current flow through the other. According to Theorem 20: $a = a''$. The standard schematic diagram for such a switch is that given on the right.

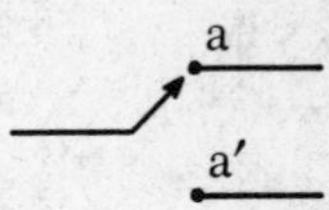

It is this switch, the single-pole, double-throw switch, that provides us with the requirements needed for a to have a complement.

As the Assumption says, if a and a' are in parallel—that is, if the hook-up is such that one will conduct when the other is off and vice versa—the circuit will always conduct. It will be, essentially, a constantly closed circuit. $a + a' = 1$.

If, on the other hand, the switch is wired so that both poles must conduct for the circuit to conduct, then it will be essentially a circuit that is always open. $a \times a' = 0$. As we have said, this kind of switch will conduct through only one pole at a time.

Assumption 1 may be interpreted as meaning that the only

circuits of interest to us in working out a Switching Algebra are those including two or more switches or switch positions.

We see here, then, that each of the abstract Huntington Postulates may be given a clear and precise meaning in terms of common experiences with switches in an electrical circuit. As original assumptions, the postulates were meant to refer only to the most abstract aspects of a generalized Class Calculus. And from that attempt at total objectivity a complete system of logic was developed in a sort of ivory-tower isolation from experience. The power of such a system can now be illustrated in the application we will give it to the handling of switching networks.

B. MATRICES

A useful method of indicating the circuit characteristics of switches connected in a parallel-series network is that of a circuit matrix, or the Truth Table that was used in the Propositional Logic.

Just as the Truth Table provided us with a tool for finding Table Values of propositions, so does the circuit matrix give us a way of expressing circuit characteristics of different switching hook-ups.

If, for example, we have two switches, *a* and *b*, hooked in parallel, we may show in the first two columns of our matrix all possible relationships between the two switches just as we show all possible combinations of *T* and *F* in the Truth Tables. Then we may mark down the results of each of these arrangements—each line of the matrix—for the specific parallel hook-up. The results, indicated in the third column, tell whether there is or is not current flowing through the system with this particular combination of switch positions. As we said in discussing Assumption 2, 0 stands for "no current flow," 1 means "current flow."

a	b	$a+b$
0	0	0
0	1	1
1	0	1
1	1	1

a	b	$a \times b$
0	0	0
0	1	0
1	0	0
1	1	1

With four possible combinations, the circuit expressed as $a+b$ is shown to conduct in every case except the one where both *a* and *b* are given the value 0. The circuit characteristic of $a+b$, then, is 0111.

The series hook-up can be analyzed in the same way. Two switches in series are symbolized $a \times b$. Setting up a matrix for this circuit gives us the circuit characteristic 0001. Both matrices are shown on p. 158.

The circuit characteristic of a series hook-up is seen to be 0001.

When we bring in the complement of a switch position—a', b', c', etc.—the description of our switches must be kept clearly in mind. The switches we are using are said to conduct on either one but not both of two possible poles. If it is not conducting on one pole then it *must* be conducting on the other. Therefore, if a given switch labeled, for example, as a is not conducting on the a-pole (plus pole, if that idea is more helpful), then it must be conducting on a' (or minus pole). If 0 appears under a (if a has the value 0), then we know that a is *not* conducting and a' *is* conducting. a' in that case, has the value 1.

The characteristics of more complicated circuits may be handled with these fundamental concepts. Suppose we are asked to find the circuit characteristic of $a' + b'$, using the circuit matrix.

The first step is to find the characteristic of each of the complements. This is done by referring first to a and exactly reversing that reading to give 1100, as listed beneath a'. Then, by reversing the characteristic for b, we get 1010 for b'.

		①	②	①
a	b	a'	$+$	b'
0	0	1	1	1
0	1	1	1	0
1	0	0	1	1
1	1	0	0	0

The next step is simply that of comparing a' and b' as two parts of a parallel circuit. From this comparison we see the circuit characteristic of $a' + b'$ is 1110.

Taking a more complicated example, consider $a' \times (a + b')$.

At this point let us, as we did in Chapter 2, substitute the common algebraic notation of multiplication for the Intersection, or series circuit, notation. For $a \times b$ we will say ab, dropping the sign $\times$. The above problem, then, will be symbolized $a'(a + b')$.

		②	③	①	②	①
a	b	a'		$(a$	$+$	$b')$
0	0	1	1	0	1	1
0	1	1	0	0	0	0
1	0	0	0	1	1	1
1	1	0	0	1	1	0

The characteristic of switch position a was originally established as 0011, which is repeated under a in the algebraic expression. The characteristic of b' is the opposite of that of b and this is noted under b' as 1010. Position a is then compared to position b' in terms of a parallel circuit and the characteristic 1011 is determined for $a + b'$.

The final step is that of comparing as a series circuit the characteristic of $a+b'$ with the characteristic of switch position a'. The characteristic of the entire circuit, $a'(a+b')$, is then found to be 1000.

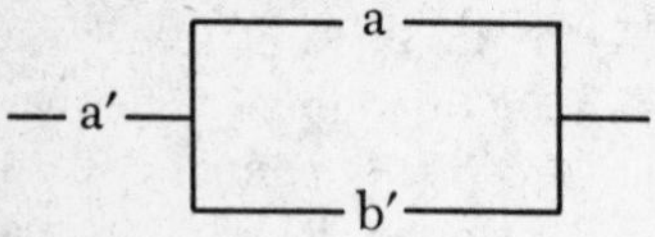

On the left is the diagram used to illustrate the last example.

The analysis of circuits containing three, four, or more switches would proceed in a similar fashion. Characteristics for circuits involving more than two variables (switches) will be seen to be similar to multivariable Table Values as determined by Truth Tables earlier in the text.

SUMMARY. The Huntington Postulates may be applied to series and parallel switching hook-ups in the following manner: First, a parallel circuit is represented by the algebraic expression $a+b$, and a series circuit is represented by $a \times b$. Second, the identity elements, 1 and 0, stand for a closed and an open circuit, respectively. (A corollary to this is the further understanding that current does or does not flow through a switch or circuit given the value 1 or 0, respectively.) Third, switches in series or parallel may be interchanged without changing the characteristic of the circuit. Fourth, the circuit represented by the algebraic equation $a+(b \times c)$ has the same characteristic as that represented by $(a+b) \times (a+c)$; and $a \times (b+c)$ the same as $(a \times b)+(a \times c)$. Fifth, each switch position will be known to have a complement designated by the prime sign, and these positions are incompatible with one another. Sixth, we will always be working with a minimum of two switches and/or switch positions in the Switching Algebra.

Switching matrices are used in Switching Algebra to help determine the circuit characteristics of particular switching hook-ups. The matrix analysis of any given circuit is analogous to the analysis of an argument by Truth Tables. The circuit characteristic is the counterpart of the Table Value in the earlier work.

The juxtaposition of letters will be used to indicate series connections; and single letters will be used to indicate switches in the diagrams.

These basic ideas and applications will now be used and elaborated upon in the development of a complete formal system to be used in the handling of switching networks. It will be found that this chapter dealing with practical applications *and* the previous ones dealing with theory and proofs will all be used as reference in the further activity of developing a circuit mathematics.

LOGIC EXERCISES

1. Draw circuits for the following algebraic expressions:

a) $a + bc$
b) $a' + b(a + c)$
c) $abc + a'b'c'$
d) $(ab + a'c)b'$
e) $ab[c(d + e) + c'(a + b')] + e'$
f) $a + [b + (c)]$

2. Give the algebraic expression for each of the following circuits:

a)

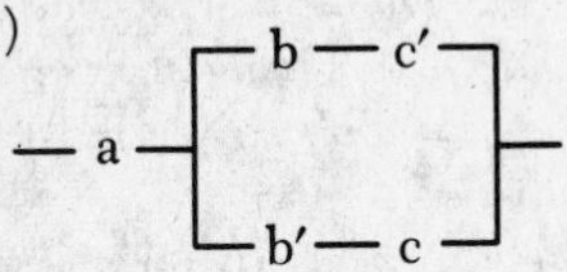

c)

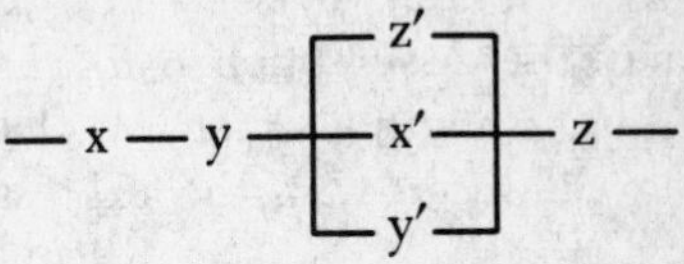

b)

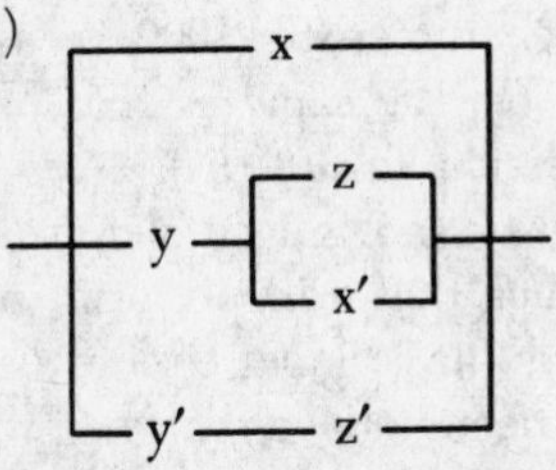

d)

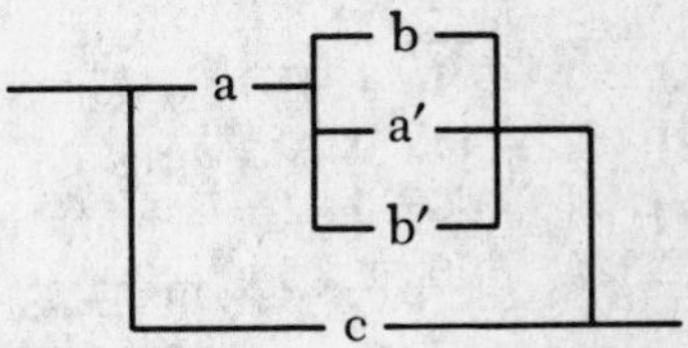

3. Determine the circuit characteristic on a circuit matrix for each of the circuits given in Exercise 2.
4. Can you see a way to simplify the following circuit?

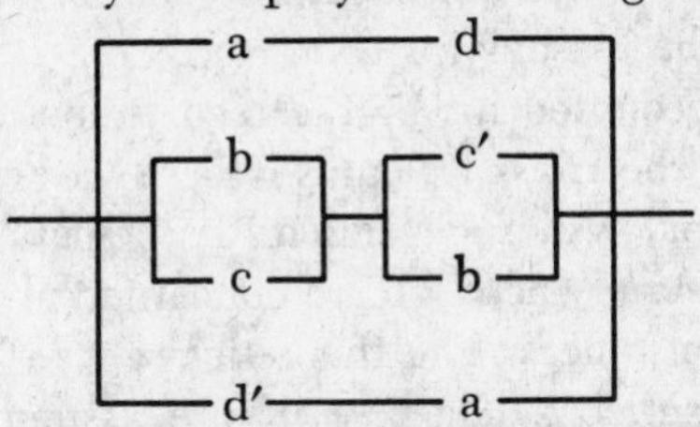

C. SIMPLIFICATION OF ALGEBRAIC EXPRESSIONS

The Huntington Postulates and the circuit matrices will now be used in the simplification of switching circuits, in the determination of characteristics of particular circuits, and even in the formulation of expressions related to given circuits.

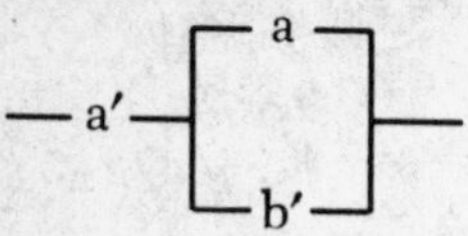

Let us begin with the operation of simplification. An example given in the last section involved a circuit that may be expressed as $a'(a+b')$. The characteristic of this circuit was shown to be 1000 and its schematic diagram was illustrated as it is given on the left.

Suppose we work with this expression $a'(a+b')$ using the postulates and theorems developed in the Class Calculus.

If a' is multiplied times $a+b'$ (that is, if we use Assumption 7 to distribute a' over a and b'), we will have $a'a+a'b'$. Then we may use Assumption 8 to change $a'a$ to 0, giving us $0+a'b'$. And Assumption 2 tells us that $0+a'b'=a'b'$; so we finish our simplification with the expression $a'b'$.

		①	②	①
a	b	a'		b'
0	0	1	1	1
0	1	1	0	0
1	0	0	0	1
1	1	0	0	0

Setting up the circuit matrix for $a'b'$ gives us the characteristic shown in the table on the left. The characteristic 1000 is, as we expected it to be, the same as that of the original expression $a'(a+b')$. And the schematic diagram shows a simpler arrangement of switches that will perform in the same manner as the original circuit.

It may have been noticed that the process of simplification was a much less rigorous procedure than was followed in the development of theorems of the Class Calculus. Nothing was done to make substitutions in the assumptions or to commute the terms when the meaning was obvious, or, in general, to give all the reasons for each step.

This may be accounted for by the recognition of our different purposes in, first, the Class Calculus, where we were developing an abstract, rational system of logic or mathematics, and, second, in Switching Algebra, where we are concerned about application in practical circumstances. The theoretical approach has already been given full support. The use of the assumptions and the theorems developed out of the assumptions is clear in our minds. Our major purpose now is that of modifying the expressions and adjusting them to the needs of our practical problems.

As a further example, let us take the circuit on p. 163 (top) and reduce it to the minimum number of switches in the simplest pattern of connections.

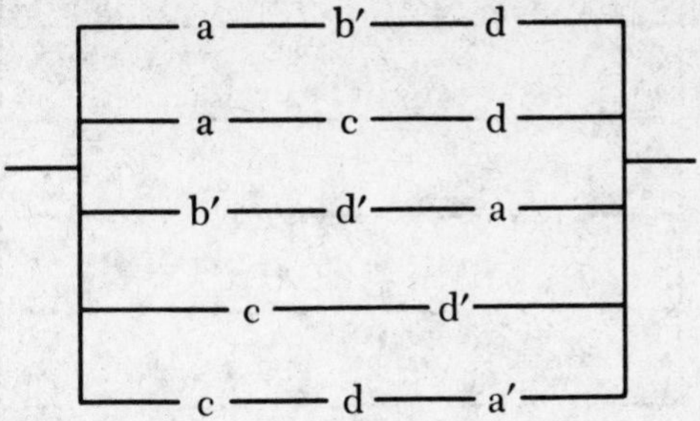

First we express the circuit algebraically:

$$ab'd + acd + b'd'a + cd' + cda'$$

Then we rearrange it, grouping terms for easier handling:

$$ab'd + ab'd' + acd + a'cd + cd'$$

Continuing with the simplification, we have:

$$ab'(d + d') + cd(a + a') + cd'$$
$$ab'(1) + cd(1) + cd'$$
$$ab' + cd + cd'$$
$$ab' + c(d + d')$$
$$ab' + c$$

The simplified circuit is schematized:

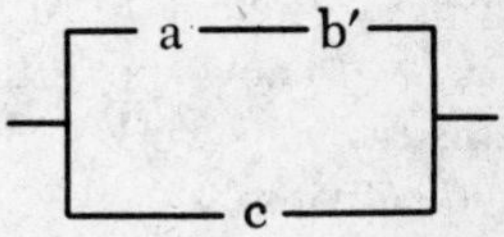

A number of steps were omitted in the simplification that would have to be given in the proof of a theorem. And no reasons were given for any of the steps. In subsequent problems even greater leaps will be taken from one step to the next. But it must always be clearly understood that anything we leave out for the purpose of convenience or speed may, whenever the occasion calls for it, be immediately produced to give theoretical support for this practical computation. If theoretical justification for any of the steps is not available, then we want to know why: what is wrong with our theory or with this particular application of our theory to experience?

Suppose now we take the circuit on p. 164 to illustrate a procedure used in the simplification of the more complex hook-ups.

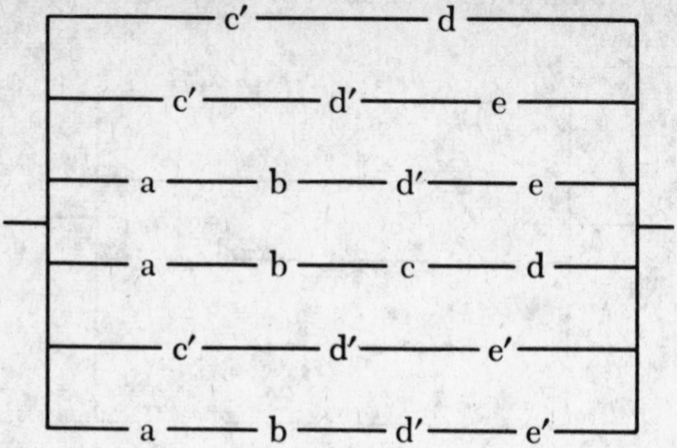

The expression for the given circuit is:

$$c'd + c'd'e + abd'e + abcd + c'd'e' + abd'e'$$

In this particular case we will divide the expression into two parts: (1) $c'd + abcd$ and (2) $c'd'e + c'd'e' + abd'e + abd'e'$.

Beginning with (1), we will use a method here that will serve to eliminate a number of steps in the problem. We know that if $c'd + abcd$ is valid, then, by the Principle of Duality $(c' + d)(a + b + c + d)$, or the dual, must be valid also. We do not mean we can *substitute* the latter for the former; we simply mean that we know the latter to be a valid expression. So, because in this case our work will be made easier, we will take the dual and indicate it as follows:

$$D(1)\ (c' + d)(a + b + c + d)$$

The $D(1)$ is written to the left as a reminder that we are working with the dual.

To go on; using Assumption 6 we can factor out the d. That is, Assumption 6 tells us that $a + (b \times c)$, or $a + bc$, is equal to $(a + b)(a + c)$. We could reverse this expression and say we were "factoring out" the a as we went from $(a + b)(a + c)$ to $a + bc$. In this problem we might rewrite the expression above as

$$D(1)\ (d + c')(d + a + b + c)$$

and then "factor out" the d to give

$$D(1)\ d + c'(a + b + c).$$

To go on:

$$D(1)\ d + ac' + bc'$$
$$D(1)\ d + c'(a + b)$$

And, taking the dual again (or "coming out of the dual"):

$$d(c' + ab).$$

For Part (2), we have:

$$c'd'e + c'd'e' + abd'e + abd'e'$$
$$c'd'(e + e') + abd'(e + e')$$
$$c'd' + abd'$$
$$d'(c' + ab)$$

Combining Part (1) with Part (2):

$$d(c' + ab) + d'(c' + ab)$$
$$(c' + ab)(d + d')$$
$$c' + ab$$

Our simplified circuit is $c' + ab$, which may be drawn as the diagram on the right.

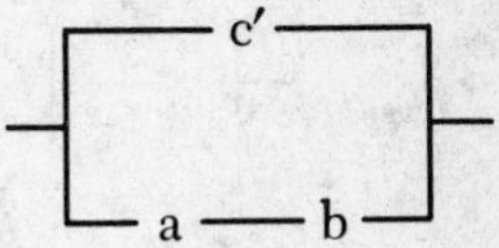

Further verification may be given of the equivalence of these two circuits by determining on a circuit matrix whether the circuit characteristic for each of them is the same.

LOGIC EXERCISES

Simplify the following circuits:

1.

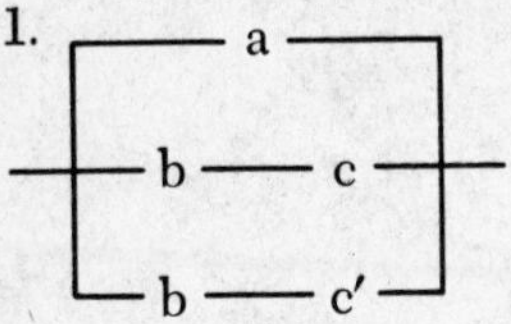

2.

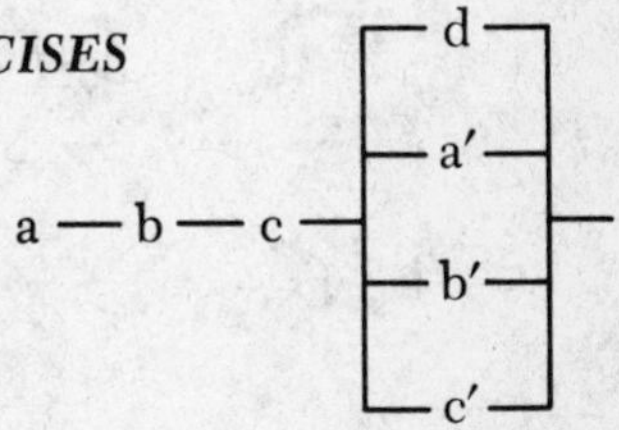

3.

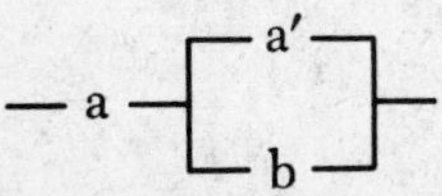

4.

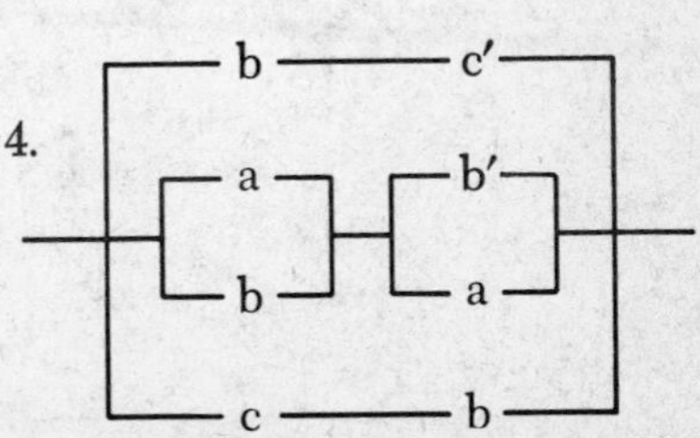

5.

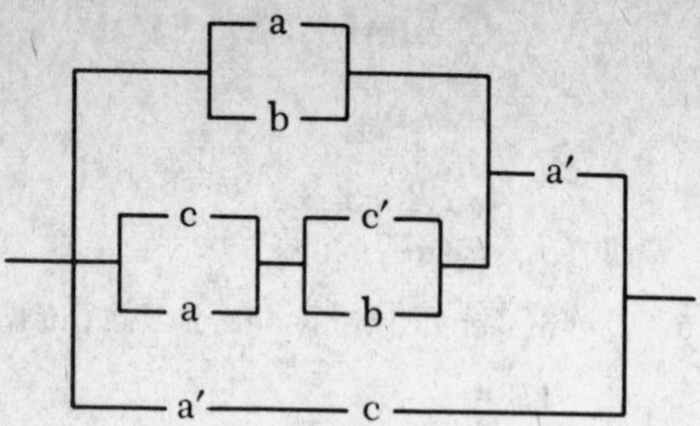

6.

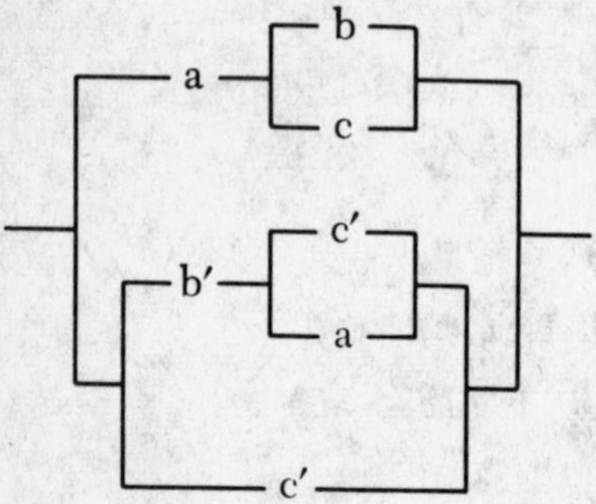

7.

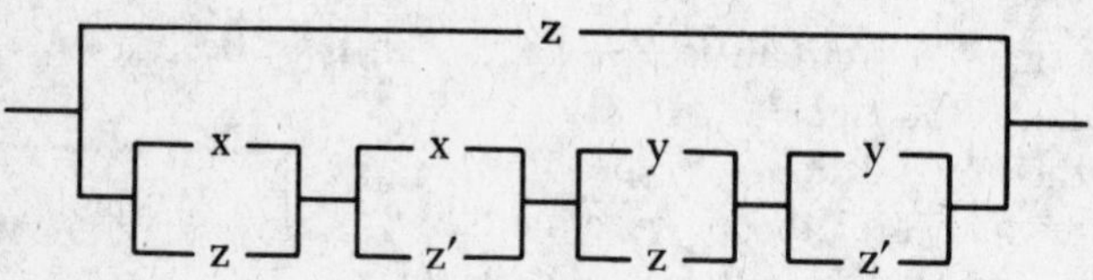

8.

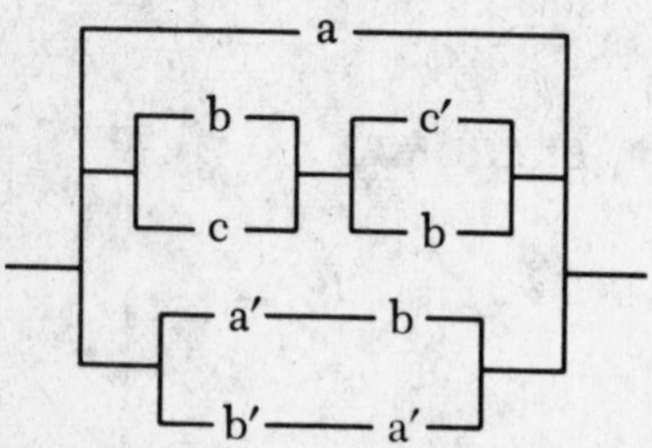

9.

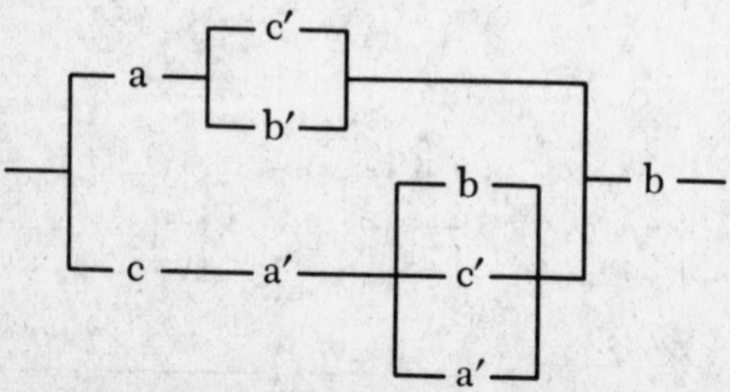

10.

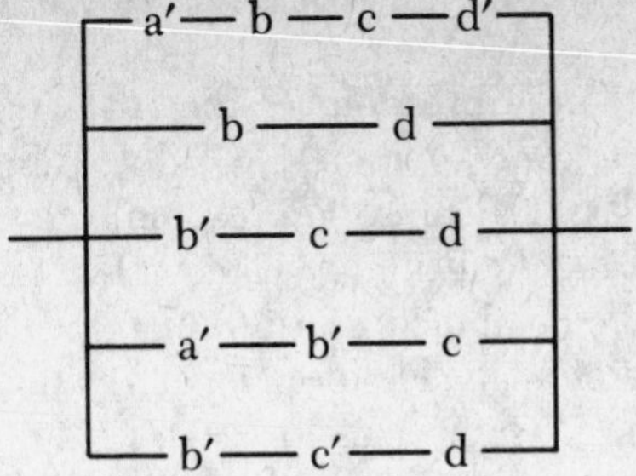

D. DETERMINATION OF THE ALGEBRAIC EXPRESSION FROM A GIVEN CHARACTERISTIC

We have seen how a circuit given as a schematic diagram may be expressed in symbols using the terms of Switching Algebra. And we have shown how, once the expression is given, we may use the circuit matrix to determine the circuit characteristic of the given arrangement of switches.

Now we shall go on to investigate the procedures for determining the circuit that would produce a given circuit characteristic. That is, we shall *begin* with a characteristic, say 1010, and work from there to determine what arrangement of switches is necessary to produce this given set of values.

1. DISJUNCTIVE NORMAL FORM. Let us first take another look at the way variables may be used in a function.

The expressions we have been using have contained any number of variables used in no specific pattern throughout the expression. There *are* patterns that are useful to us, however. The first such pattern we will consider is the *Disjunctive Normal Form.*

Any disjunctive expression in which every variable found in the expression is also found in each disjunct–or term–of the expression is called an expression in Disjunctive Normal Form, or DNF.

Expressions such as $ab' + a$ or $ab + b'c$ are not in DNF, but $ab' + ab$ or $xyz + x'yz'$ *are* expressions in DNF.

Notice that it makes no difference *how* the variable appears in the disjunct–either primed or unprimed–and it makes no difference as to how many variables there are. All that is required for DNF is that all variables (or switches) appear in all terms.

One reason for the utility of the DNF is the fact that it gives a standard way of expressing any of the given switching circuits.

Any of the algebraic expressions of the switching networks may be made into an expression in DNF by using the rules and postulates of Class Calculus. For example, let us change the expression $ab'+a$ into DNF. We know by Assumption 3 that the term a may be combined as a product with 1 without losing its identity. Therefore, we multiply $a(1)$; only we write 1 as $b+b'$, following Assumption 8. Then $a(b+b')=ab+ab'$. Putting our new expression for a back into the original expression gives us $ab'+ab+ab'$, or $ab'+ab$. ($ab'+ab'=ab'$ following Theorem 4: $a+a=a$.)

For another illustration, let us take the expression $x+y'$. To put this into DNF we follow the same procedure as above:

$$x(y+y')+y'(x+x')$$
$$xy+xy'+xy'+x'y'$$
$$xy+xy'+x'y'$$

In the last expression $xy+xy'+x'y'$ we may notice that all but one of the possible combinations of the two variables have been mentioned. The only one not listed is $x'y$.

If $x'y$ *were* in the expression, giving us four terms with all the variables in all possible combinations, the expression would be one in *Complete Disjunctive Normal Form*, or CDNF. (This expression in CDNF, however, would *not* be connected to the original expression $x+y'$—as $xy+xy'+x'y'$ was a translation of $x+y'$.)

Before we go any further let us consider what we have. An expression such as $x+y'$ gives us the function for some particular circuit. If we analyzed that expression using the circuit matrix we would find that it has the particular circuit characteristic 1011. It must be true, then, that the expanded version of $x+y'$ in DNF, i.e., $xy+xy'+x'y'$, must also have the characteristic 1011.

		①	②	①	③	②
x	y	xy	$+$	xy'	$+$	$x'y'$
0	0	0	0	0	1	1
0	1	0	0	0	0	0
1	0	0	1	1	1	0
1	1	1	1	0	1	0

On the matrix presented here we find this is indeed the case. (We may notice also, by the way, that the one line in which all values are 0 is that line on which the assignment of values to x and y was x' and y, or the missing term in the *Complete* Disjunctive Normal Form.)

Looking at the meaning of the circuit characteristic and using the illustration above, we may say that an expression in DNF will tell us all the combinations of switch positions where the circuit characteristic takes on the value 1, and that those terms from the CDNF that do not appear in our DNF expression are terms that take on the value 0 in the circuit characteristic. We may describe the same situation from another point of view by directing our attention to the circuit matrix first.

a	b	a + b
0	0	0
0	1	1
1	0	1
1	1	1

Any meaningful expression such as $a+b$, given on the matrix to the right, has a mixture of 0's and 1's in its characteristic. If we direct our attention only to the 1's, or the occasions in which current is flowing, we may use the left-hand columns wherein the original values have been assigned to say, "No current flows when $a=0$ and $b=0$. Current does flow when $a=0$ and $b=1$. Current does flow when $a=1$ and $b=0$. Current does flow when $a=1$ and $b=1$." Using our rules for making an algebraic expression, then, we will indicate the fact that *current flows* in this particular circuit when $a=0$ and $b=1$, *or* when $a=1$ and $b=0$, *or* when $a=1$ and $b=1$, by symbolizing it thus: $a'b+ab'+ab$. Each of the terms tells us the switch settings that will allow current to flow.

This expression may be simplified, then, as follows:

$$a'b+ab'+ab$$
$$a'b+a(b'+b)$$
$$a'b+a$$
$$(a'+a)(b+a)$$
$$a+b$$

The analysis of the circuit characteristic gave us the DNF, and the latter is simplified to give the original expression.

a	b	c	f
0	0	0	0
0	0	1	0
0	1	0	1
0	1	1	0
1	0	0	1
1	0	1	0
1	1	0	1
1	1	1	0

If, now, we are asked to *determine the expression* for the circuit that gives us a particular circuit characteristic (that is, we are told we want a circuit in which current will flow under such-and-such an arrangement of switches), we have the means of doing so.

As a further example, let us say we are asked to find a circuit with three switches in it that has the characteristic 00101010, as shown in the matrix. (The f at the top stands for the unknown function or expression.)

Using the switch values given opposite the 1's on the matrix, we find the expression in DNF is:

$$a'bc' + ab'c' + abc'$$

Our next move, then, is to simplify that expression:

$$a'bc' + ac'(b' + b)$$
$$a'bc' + ac'$$
$$c'(a'b + a)$$
$$c'(a' + a)(b + a)$$
$$c'(b + a)$$

And we have in $c'(b+a)$ the simplest expression of a switching network that will give us the characteristic requested.

2. CONJUNCTIVE NORMAL FORM. Another pattern that may be used for a standard algebraic expression of a circuit is that called the *Conjunctive Normal Form,* or CNF.

In the DNF every variable of the expression must appear in every disjunct. In CNF, then, as might be expected, every variable must appear in every conjunct—or factor, using a word from ordinary algebra.

Expressions such as $(a+b)(a'+b')$ and $(x+y+z)(x'+y+z)(x'+y'+z)$ *are* given in Conjunctive Normal Form; but $(a')(a+b)$ and $(x+y')(z+y)$ are *not* in CNF.

A *Complete Conjunctive Normal Form* is an expression in which all variables appear in all possible combinations.

Any expression may be changed to CNF through the use of Assumptions 2 and 8. The expression $a'(a+b)$, we said, is not in CNF. If we want to change it to CNF we add bb' (or 0) to a', which gives us $(a'+bb')(a+b)$. Then, applying Assumption 6 to $a'+bb'$, we have $(a'+b)(a'+b')(a+b)$, which *is* an expression in CNF.

The CNF may, as the DNF, be used in determining the expression that stands for a given circuit characteristic. A CNF expression, however, is developed from the switch positions appearing opposite the 0's of the characteristic, rather than from those opposite the 1's, as in the DNF .

Let us consider an expression from the point of view of the 0's in its circuit characteristic.

If we were asked to find the expression for a circuit that had the characteristic 01110101, we would set up a circuit matrix such as the one on the right and proceed as follows.

a	b	c	f
0	0	0	0
0	0	1	1
0	1	0	1
0	1	1	1
1	0	0	0
1	0	1	1
1	1	0	0
1	1	1	1

Our first look at the characteristic tells us that there are fewer 0's than 1's in this case. If we have a way to denote the circuit by referring to the 0's instead of to the 1's, we may develop an expression with fewer terms in it than are in the DNF that would, therefore, be easier to manage. The 0's tell us that current is *not* flowing. To get an expression that tells us when current *does* flow, we must first reverse each of the switch settings we see opposite the 0 and bring these together as a disjunction (giving, for example, in the first row $a+b+c$). We do this in every line that the 0 appears. These disjunctions, then, will themselves be brought together in a conjunction and the expression we have will be given in CNF. This CNF expression will have three factors—or conjuncts. (Each of the conjuncts is composed of three disjuncts, just as in a similar case the disjuncts of a DNF would each be composed of three conjuncts.)

An expression in CNF tells us again—just as one in DNF—the exact switch positions that will allow current to flow, but the CNF does so by a kind of elimination. Each of the switch positions we look at opposite the 0 of the characteristic is negated; so that we are, in effect, eliminating this particular set of switch positions from the expression. "Reverse either *a* or *b* or *c*," we say, "to allow current to flow." (In a disjunction this could be made true by reversing *a* and *b*, or *a* and *c*, or *a*, or *b*, . . . and so on.) Then, by making a conjunction of all those negating factors, we imply the positions opposite the 1's.

Going back to the example, we were given the characteristic 01110101. Let us look at the matrix again and write out the expression for the circuit in CNF.

$$(a+b+c)(a'+b+c)(a'+b'+c)$$

The value for each switch opposite each 0 in the Characteristic has been reversed.

Simplification of this expression may be made easier by working with the dual.

$$D\ abc + a'bc + a'b'c$$
$$D\ bc(a + a') + a'b'c$$
$$D\ c(b + a'b')$$
$$D\ c(b + a')(b + b')$$
$$D\ c(b + a')$$
$$c + ba' \text{ or } a'b + c$$

The expression for the circuit that will give the characteristic 01110101 is thus found to be $a'b + c$.

If we had used the 1's in this characteristic to find the DNF and then simplified that expression, we should have come to the same result:

$$a'b'c + a'bc' + a'bc + ab'c + abc$$
$$a'b'c + a'b(c' + c) + ac(b' + b)$$
$$a'(b'c + b) + ac$$
$$a'(b' + b)(b + c) + ac$$
$$a'b + a'c + ac$$
$$a'b + c(a' + a)$$
$$a'b + c$$

E. TRANSLATIONS BETWEEN THE NORMAL FORMS

The CNF may be obtained by taking what may be called two kinds of complements of the DNF, and the same thing may be done to obtain the DNF from the CNF.

The first kind of complement would be that for which the Complete Normal Form is given as the Universe. The Normal Form Complement of an expression in CNF would simply be the remaining factors of the Complete CNF that are not mentioned in the given expression in CNF. In the example above we were given the expression $(a + b + c)(a' + b + c)(a' + b' + c)$. The Normal Form Complement of that expession would be $(a + b + c')(a + b' + c)(a + b' + c')(a' + b + c')(a' + b' + c')$.

The second kind of complement we will use is one we will call here the De Morgan Complement. In Theorems 21 and 22 of the Class Calculus we proved that $(ab)' = a' + b'$ and $(a + b)' = a'b'$. These theorems were then described as being one way of stating De Morgan's Laws. So a De Morgan Complement will be described here as the complement taken through the use of Theorems 21 and 22. If our expression is in Conjunctive Normal

Form, taking the De Morgan Complement will produce an expression in Disjunctive Normal Form, and vice versa.

Let us at this point, then, take the De Morgan Complement of the expression above and simplify:

$$[(a+b+c')(a+b'+c)(a+b'+c')(a'+b+c')(a'+b'+c')]'$$

$$(a+b+c')'+(a+b'+c)'+(a+b'+c')'+(a'+b+c')'+(a'+b'+c')'$$

$$a'b'c+a'bc'+a'bc+ab'c+abc$$

The last line gives us an expression in DNF which, we see, is exactly the DNF expression of the original characteristic. (See matrix on p. 171.)

The same procedure may be followed in translating an expression in DNF to one in CNF. Suppose we take the expression $a'bc+ab'c+abc'$. We will write out the matrix for this expression so that we can check our work as we make an algebraic translation from DNF to CNF.

a	b	c	f
0	0	0	0
0	0	1	0
0	1	0	0
0	1	1	1
1	0	0	0
1	0	1	1
1	1	0	1
1	1	1	0

To begin with, we take the Normal Form Complement of the given expression to get $a'b'c'+a'b'c+a'bc'+ab'c'+abc$.

Then we take the De Morgan Complement and simplify:

$$[a'b'c'+a'b'c+a'bc'+ab'c'+abc]'$$

$$(a'b'c')'(a'b'c)'(a'bc')'(ab'c')'(abc)'$$

$$(a+b+c)(a+b+c')(a+b'+c)(a'+b+c)(a'+b'+c')$$

If we should go back to the matrix and write the expression out in CNF, we would have the same expression as that given above in our last line of the simplification, thereby checking the validity of our computation.

SUMMARY. In this chapter we have shown how the Class Calculus may be applied to the solution of problems in a network of electrical switches. Our examples have all been given in terms of simple mechanical switches, although in any modern computer these units would be small, electronic switches called "transistors," which allow for much greater speed and control than could ever be achieved with the simple mechanical device.

The interpretation of the assumptions of Class Calculus was

given in terms of switches and arrangements of switches in an electrical circuit. A procedure for describing current flow in a switch or circuit was introduced in the material on circuit characteristics and circuit matrices. A circuit characteristic tells whether or not current is flowing in a switching circuit for a given set-up of the switches: *a* on, *b* off, *c* on; *a* off, *b* off, *c* off; and so forth.

It was shown how complex circuits could be simplified through the use of the theorems and assumptions of the Class Calculus, and a procedure was introduced for determining the circuit that would produce a given circuit characteristic.

In describing the latter procedure it became necessary to introduce the ideas of Disjunctive Normal Form, Conjunctive Normal Form, and complete Disjunctive and Conjunctive Normal Form. We first discussed the use of Disjunctive Normal Form in the development of an expression to give a desired circuit characteristic. It was then shown how Conjunctive Normal Form could serve the same purpose, and the latter part of the chapter was devoted to an explanation of the procedures used to translate from Disjunctive to Conjunctive Normal Form and vice versa.

This work in Switching Algebra is not to be considered as anything more than a brief introduction to the algebra of electric and electronic circuits. For further information in this subject the student would need some background in electrical engineering plus more courses in mathematics than have been required for an understanding of the material in this book. For anyone interested in pursuing the subject of Switching Algebra, our first recommendation is the book by J. Eldon Whitesitt, *Boolean Algebra and Its Applications, op. cit.* Another book that covers essentially the same subject area is *Applied Boolean Algebra* (New York: Macmillan Co., 1960), by Franz E. Hohn.

EXERCISES

1. Change the following expressions to Disjunctive Normal Form:

a) $x+y'$	e) $x'(xy+zx'+y)$
b) $ab'+a$	f) $(a+b')(a'+c)(a+c')$
c) $x'+y+z'$	g) $(a+b+c'+d)(a+b')$
d) $abc'+ac+ba$	h) $x'+(x'+y)(y'+z)$

2. Simplify the expression given in Exercise 1-d and show its circuit characteristic on a matrix. Inspect this characteristic to see that the switch positions opposite the 1's are exactly those given in the DNF found in working 1-d.
3. Change the following to Conjunctive Normal Form:

a) $a'b$
b) $x(y+x)$
c) $xy'+xyz$
d) $ab'+ca'+b$
e) $a(b+c')+b'c'+a'bc$
f) $y'(x+z)+y(x'+z')+x'z+xz'$

4. Give an algebraic expression in its simplified form for each of the circuits whose characteristics are expressed below:

a) 00101010
b) 00001110
c) 01101111
d) 00111011

5. Consider a circuit through which current flows under the following conditions:

> Whenever switch a is 1 and c is 0 unless both switch a and switch b are 1. Current also flows if a is 0 and c is 0 but only if b is 1.

Sketch the circuit and use a circuit matrix to find the Disjunctive and Conjunctive Normal Forms.
Then use Boolean Algebra to translate from Disjunctive to Conjunctive Normal Form and compare with the statements derived from the circuit matrix.

6

Theory and Definitions

There were a few topics mentioned in the foregoing chapters that could not at the time be given any more than the most cursory treatment. The difference between the meanings of "truth" and "validity," for example, and the use of the words "sentence" or "statement" and "proposition" were subjects that could not be given any more than a brief discussion without going into an extensive digression that could serve more to confuse than to enlighten.

We have saved the more involved discussion of these matters for this last chapter so that we can give them more of the full treatment they deserve and, at the same time, consider them in relationship to one another as an aid in explanation. It is hoped, also, that the discussion of these topics will serve partially as a further elaboration and partially as a summary of the thesis expressed in the first chapter and referred to in various places throughout the book: Logic is an investigation of the abstract form of a rational argument; and the concern in logic is for the validity of the system built out of certain presuppositions and not for the empirical truth or falsity of the presuppositions themselves.

In making the latter statement we again used the words "truth" and "validity" without as yet having told exactly what it is we mean by them. Let us, then, get on with that task.

A. TRUTH AND VALIDITY

Ludwig Wittengenstein * said in the beginning of his influential work in philosophy, *Tractatus Logico-Philosophicus,* "The world is everything that is the case." From this he derived the definition of a true sentence as being a sentence that expresses something that is the case.

* A major philosopher of the 1920's and 1930's; student and protégé of Bertrand Russell. A figure who had a strong influence on, though he was not a member of, the Vienna Circle—the group that set the stage for the development of modern Logical Positivism.

An explanation such as this may appear to be meaningless or trivial to a reader looking for a definition of "true," but when one stops to think of it, a good definition must always give the simplest and most general explanation that can be given. An explanation such as this, then, will always appear more or less trivial. Whether the explanation is meaningless or not can be decided only after it has been used in the context of the discussion for which it was given.

If we take Wittgenstein's statement as basic for our discussion here then, "a true sentence" will mean for us a sentence that expresses a condition that actually exists: something about the world. Of course, the next question that comes up immediately is, "But how do we know what exists in the world?" That is an important question that cannot be ignored in a discussion such as this; but let us leave it for the moment and come back to it after we have paved the way for a more comprehensive answer.

A true sentence is one that expresses something that is the case in the world, we said. Next we must explain what we mean by "valid"—what is a valid expression? Let us begin this explanation by considering an example. Suppose we are given the following argument: All campers are honest; all Democrats are campers; therefore, all Democrats are honest.

Is this a valid argument? Yes, it is. We can see almost without analysis that it is a syllogism of Mood *AAA* and Figure 1, which is the first valid syllogism on our list of valid syllogisms.

The next question, of course, is, "Is it true?" Perhaps no one—certainly very few Republicans—would claim that the conclusion, All Democrats are honest, is true. We may become aware of how we got this questionable conclusion when we look again at our premises: All campers are honest, and All Democrats are campers. There is certainly nothing about either one of those premises that would make us defend them as sentences expressing conditions that actually and absolutely exist in the world.

So what did we mean when we said this argument was valid? We obviously meant only that if one says, All *x*'s are *y*, and all *z*'s are *x*'s, then, without considering what x, y, and z stand for, a *valid* argument will result if we present as our conclusion, All *z*'s are *y*. Validity is simply a matter of form. The only thing we are concerned about in determining validity in an argument is whether or not a correct form has been used.

Truth, in the way we have been describing it, is not a matter of concern in logical analysis. "Truth" used in this way is a word, not of logic, but of semantics. If I should say, "My friend George is in Chicago," then this statement is verified or falsified by any one of a number of different experimental tests devised to show how the words of my sentence refer to conditions that do or do not exist. 'Validity," on the other hand, is a word that refers only to a relationship between expressions. In a valid argument the conclusion is valid only because it is a part of a valid argument form. What the conclusion says—what conditions of the world it actually refers to—is not what we are considering when we describe it as valid.

B. SENTENCES, STATEMENTS, AND PROPOSITIONS

Another approach to the same problem may be made through a discussion of the meanings given by some logicians to the words "sentence," "statement," and "proposition."

On p. 37 the meaning of "proposition" was discussed briefly. In that chapter on Aristotelian logic a distinction was made between a proposition, such as one which gives the information that a certain dog is big, and a sentence which expresses this proposition through the use of English words, "The dog is big." or French words, "Le chien est grand."

For a further refinement on this way of speaking let us introduce the word "statement" to refer not to just any sentence but only to those sentences that may be given a truth value—that is, those that are either true or false. Then we may say that only statements express propositions, whereas sentences may be statements or they may be prayers—"Grant me the ease that is granted so free"—or poems—"The fog comes in on little cat feet"—or exclamations—"Great Scott! A test!"

We then say that propositions are true or false and statements are kinds of sentences that are used to express propositions.

We should not let ourselves be confused into thinking we now have some new kind of existence like "the world of propositions" that is distinct from a "world of statements" or a "world of sentences." A proposition is nothing more than what is *meant* by a statement, and any attempt to give it a separate reality decreases its utility in this assigned role.

In the arguments of logic we are looking for sentences that are Tautologies, contradictions, or neither. We want to find sentences that are always true or always false or identify them as being neither true nor false. It is raining or it is not raining is always true regardless of the conditions of the world. It is night and it is not night is a statement that is always false. The first is a Tautology because of its form; the second is a contradiction because of its form. Any statement-phrase could have been used to replace It is raining, on the one hand, or It is night on the other, and the first sentence would still be a Tautology and the second a contradiction.

We have a definition that says a statement is true or false by the fact that it expresses a true or false proposition. For example, we say, "Sea water is salty is true if and only if sea water is salty." This description appears to be rather trivial, of course, and it could hardly be defended as anything more. To say a statement is true if it expresses a true proposition certainly does not say much, but it must not be considered to be circular or redundant on that account. By making these distinctions and giving these definitions we have not made the search for truth any easier or even suggested new methods of procedure for finding the truth. All we have done is to give a definition of "truth" so that the word is a meaningful one in the language of our logic.

This clarification is some help to us in making the distinction between logic and the empirical sciences. When we say, "Sea water is salty is true if and only if sea water is salty," we, as logicians, are doing two things: we are describing what it is we mean by "true" and we are getting out from under the responsibility of actually having to determine the truth or falsity of any given proposition.

Determining whether or not sea water is salty may seem to be an easy task: simply walk down to the beach and take a sip. (Of course, if we defined "salty" as having such and such a proportion of salt to such and such a proportion of other chemicals and agents, then even that determination may be more difficult than we first thought.) But if the statement had been The moon is covered with a ten-foot layer of dust, it may be seen that we are given greater challenges in the determination of its truth or falsity.

Notice, however, in this last example, that we may use the

statement The moon is covered with a ten-foot layer of dust in a logic problem even though we do not know whether it *is* true or false. Consider the problem:

> If certain observations are correct, then the moon is covered with a ten-foot layer of dust. It is not true that there either is erosion or the satellite is not airless. Either there is no natural landing platform or the moon is not covered with dust. If there is no natural landing platform, then there is erosion. Therefore, the observations are not correct.

We may easily determine whether or not that argument is a Tautology using whatever method of the Truth Table logic suits us best, and we may produce, then, some information that could be found useful to the engineers and astronauts who have their hearts set on moon exploration. No empirical data are discovered here and no actual circumstances are changed; but we are saying that if we *assume* certain facts and conditions, when they are considered in relationship to one another in the special way mentioned above, then a given conclusion may certainly be drawn.

In their text, *Natural Deduction* (Belmont: Wadsworth Publishing Co., 1962), Anderson and Johnston state the point: "One reason why mathematical [logical] proofs can be rigorous is that the question of the truth or falsity of the assumptions on which they rest usually does not arise, and when it does arise it falls outside the scope of the axiom systems themselves." *

In analyzing the argument we are only seeking to determine whether or not the conclusion and that set of premises are tautologically true. We use the statement The moon is covered with a ten-foot layer of dust, and it is required that such a statement must be *either* true *or* false, but it does not matter to us *which* it is. This statement along with all the others in the argument must present a Tautology for us to consider the argument valid. On the Truth Table, given all possible assignments of truth and falsity to the collection of statements we call the argument, the total complex statement—the Major Implication—must always be true.

When the Major Implication is shown to be true on the Truth

* *Op. cit.*, p. 4.

Table, then, it is an indication of the *validity* of the argument form, or a Tautology composed of individual sentences that may be either true or false. This Tautology, of course, is always true—it expresses a true proposition—but we must remember its limitations. "The sentence 'It is raining or it is not raining,'" as Wittgenstein wrote, "is true, but it tells us nothing about the world." Knowledge about the world is knowledge that comes to us through the perceptions of our senses: experience, it may be said, or empirical data.

For a practical conclusion concerning the question, "Is the moon covered with a ten-foot layer of dust?" we may in the last analysis rely only on our senses and whatever extensions we have given to them (such as telescopes, television cameras, meters, and the like). These experiences can produce for us knowledge that we may use as premises in an argument, but we must always be careful to note that the truth or falsity of the argument with regard to its stating a fact about the world is always dependent upon the premises given: the convictions or assumptions arrived at through some type of sensory experience.

When our interests turn away from a consideration of logical form and toward the more empirical considerations of facts about the world, we are confronted first of all with the realization that the facts we know and work with are never the absolute truths and falsehoods that appear in our logic problems. We mentioned parenthetically that the attempt to designate one kind of water as salty may produce problems that would make such designation no easy task. We could also say that even if we were on the moon with a measuring stick it would be impossible to determine *absolutely* the height of a layer of dust—even if there were such a layer. No measurement taken by instruments that must ultimately be interpreted by our senses will ever have absolute precision. No matter how fine we make the measurement—with any instruments we have available—there is always a smaller *possible* measure. In fact, in the theory of Werner Heisenberg it is said that there is a certain refinement of measurement beyond which it is *theoretically* impossible to go—that there is a built-in uncertainty in all measurement.*

* Heisenberg's Uncertainty Principle is discussed in an article in *The World of Mathematics* (New York: Simon and Schuster, 1956), edited by James R. Newman, pp. 1047–1055.

Such a condition is generally no problem in practical circumstances, however. The engineer, the architect, the astronaut all are concerned with precision in measurement, of course. But they all also have "margins of error." These are margins that are specified to allow for deviation that cannot be controlled and that are insignificant in the applications. For the astronaut the measurement of a layer of dust may need to be taken only to the closest centimeter, or fraction of an inch, or maybe even only to the closest inch. The architect may worry about the weight of a steel beam only to the closest pound—or, perhaps, to the closest ounce. The physicist is concerned with measurements of electromagnetic waves to small fractions of a centimeter, but even with him there is an allowance—a tolerance—made in his measurements. "Plus or minus one-tenth of one per cent" may be his stated limits of precision. But the margin of error to be allowed is always there. It is, in fact, an important piece of data attached to any measurement reported or requested by the physicist, engineer, chemist, astronomer, or any other scientist who is putting his theory to work in the handling of complex empirical facts.

In logic and mathematics we say "true" and "false." We say, "$5 \times 7 = 35$," and "$7 + 5 = 12$," and those are exact statements when we use them in our theoretical system. But when we go to apply them to experience we say, "True, within a certain set of conditions," and, "$7 + 5 = 12$, for all practical purposes." We know there may be extenuating circumstances or unobserved errors or small deviations in measurement, but these are made insignificant in the situation wherein we are using the theoretical system. If they cannot be made insignificant, of course, then we cannot use this system in this particular area of experience.

The absolutes and certainties are in the realm of theory, and the approximations and minimized errors are in the realm of experience. A famous quotation from Albert Einstein goes, "In so far as the statements of geometry speak about reality, they are not certain; and in so far as they are certain, they do not speak about reality."

In the next section we will discuss another axiomatic system—probability mathematics. In this system of deduction the distinction between rigorous formality and empirical approximations is not always clear. We will here attempt to show how the mathematics of probability is an abstract, formal system just as is the mathematics of arithmetic, and the question of the meanings of "true" and "false" in probability are answered in essentially the same way they were in the work just presented.

C. PROBABILITY

Our daily lives are filled with judgments made and actions performed on the basis of probability estimates. Some things we are quite sure of—as our conviction that the Salk vaccine will prevent polio—and other things we only assume or suppose to be true—as our assumption that there is no animal life on Mars.

Most of us are so certain that the Salk vaccine will make us immune from polio that we are willing to take whatever trouble, expense, and risks are necessary to have the vaccination. We know there have been cases of polio that occurred in spite of the vaccination and we may even have heard of some cases wherein the vaccination itself is said to have been the cause of polio. But, as we would say, "for all practical purposes" the vaccination is a preventative; the risk is small and the trouble is well worth it.

The same may be said about driving an automobile along a busy freeway. No one expects to become involved in a serious highway collision although there are weekends during which more than five hundred people are killed in traffic accidents. But when we consider the vast number of cars on the highway and the long periods of time during which we ourselves have been able to avoid accidents, we develop a great deal of assurance that we can use our automobile to travel the freeway and reach our destination safe and sound.

How is truth involved in considerations such as these? May we say it is true that Salk vaccine will immunize against polio? Could one say it is true that he will travel from one town to another by automobile without getting involved in a traffic accident? Whether we admit the word "truth" or not, it is obvious by our actions that we consider those statements to be facts about the world. There is, as we must always admit, the possibility that our expectations will not be fulfilled but, we say, "More than likely—there is a high probability—that they will."

In these cases the intuitive use of the word "probable" is, essentially, a correct usage according to the mathematical definition of the word. But "probable," like many other words in our language, is not always used following a strict mathematical definition, and it is, in fact, used many times in direct contradiction to the definition.

Let us look at one procedure used in theoretical science for forming statements that refer, not to simple truth or falsity, but to various degrees of probability. This will be a brief examination of some aspects of mathematical probability.

A very readable and interesting discussion of this topic is given in the text *Introduction to Finite Mathematics,* by Kemeny, Snell, and Thompson, *op. cit.* The approach to probability in that work is through the use of subject matter that has been emphasized in this text. Illustrations involve the use of sets and Truth Tables and the terminology that has been introduced here for the discussion of these topics. A thorough introduction to probability is given in this manner with the minimum amount of strain to the student.

One of the most common uses of probability is that made by insurance companies in the development of their actuarial charts. This is the system of statistical probability that is the kind we were referring to in the discussion above of Salk vaccine and automobile accidents. In computing probabilities of this kind the procedure is essentially that of investigating statistics of deaths, accidents, illnesses, and so forth among given groups of people and, on the basis of these statistics, making predictions for similar groups in the future.

When all the cautions have been observed—those mentioned above and many others that become necessary in sophisticated cases of modern insurance calculations—the results achieved are extremely useful, most impressive, and, in some cases, almost unbelievable. Predictions can be made within fractions of a per cent concerning the number of deaths by auto accident, cases of illnesses and broken bones, births and marriages, and a number of other occurrences that are commonplace but difficult to predict by unaided common sense. An amazing amount of data can be predicted with astonishing accuracy if the group is large enough and past statistics are available for it.

An important thing about all of this is that the predictions can be made only for groups. Nothing can be said about any individual member of the group but only about how many members will meet with such and such circumstances. That John J., a particular policy holder, will meet with an automobile accident that places him in the hospital for six months is a prediction that cannot be made with statistical probability calculations. But it can be said, for example, that twenty to twenty-five people will meet with an accident of that nature, and this can be said with a high degree of dependability. In some cases by stretching the limits, let us say, to between fifteen and thirty people, the nature of the prediction can be called certain, "for all practical purposes."

Speaking of probability in this way, we must recognize that in considering large groups or large numbers of occurrences of some particular action, the certainty of the prediction is relative to the precision that is demanded by the prediction. The narrower the limits, as in the above example, the less positive is the prediction. The broader the limits the more positive is the prediction. This leads us to say that there are some predictions made on the basis of probability that are made as virtual certainties —at least as we use the word "certainty" in any empirical discourse.

Let us take another familiar example of the use of probabilities in our everyday life. Consider the tossing of a coin for heads and tails. Taking what we will call a "fair coin," that is, one that is perfectly balanced, we may say that it is equally as likely to fall heads as it is to fall tails. That is, for a well-balanced coin there is for each toss a 50% probability of getting heads and a 50% probability of getting tails.

H,H	H,T
T,H	T,T

Building from this, we can see that if we tossed the coin twice the possible outcomes would be Heads, Heads; Heads, Tails; Tails, Heads; or Tails, Tails. Let us put this on a matrix for easier reference. Each block of the diagram above shows how the two tosses *may have* resulted. We see by this table that the probability of getting two heads in a row is only 1 in 4, or ¼, or 25%. The same may be said for two tails in a row. But the probability of getting one head and one tail is 2 in 4, or 2/4, or 50%, because there are two ways that this latter event may occur whereas there is only one way that each of the other events may occur.

Tossing the coin three times would give any one of the possible results listed on the chart on p. 186. Here it may be seen that the probability of getting three heads in a row is only 1 in 8;

that of getting at least two heads in a row is 3 in 8, or 3/8; and that of getting at least one head is 7 in 8.

H,H,H	H,H,T	H,T,H	H,T,T
T,H,H	T,H,T	T,T,H	T,T,T

A common erroneous use of the word "probable" with respect to the tossing of coins appears when a coin has fallen, let us say, five times heads up. One is then inclined to say, "The coin will *probably* fall tails up at the next toss," or "The odds are in favor of tails next." But if we stop to consider we must realize that the fair coin we have chosen to toss must, on *every* toss, have a 50% probability of falling heads—nothing that happened previously can have anything to do with this *particular* toss. The coin knows nothing of the previous falls. It is not any more probable, then, that the coin will fall tails even if it has fallen heads 50 or 100 times previously.

What *could* be said about this case is that the probability of six heads in a row occurring in an experiment of six tosses is 1 in 64. But if we wished to extend the experiment, the probability of six heads in a row occurring in ten throws is approximately 1 in 25, and as the number of throws increases the probability becomes better and better.

Just as in statistical probability, wherein the predictions become more and more dependable as the number of elements in the group becomes larger, so is it true that as the number of tosses of a coin increases, the predictions get closer and closer to certainty.

The probability of getting at least one head in two tosses is 3 in 4, or 75%. The probability of getting one head in three tosses is 7 in 8, or 87.5%. And the probability in ten tosses is 1023 in 1024, or 99.9%.

Consider what our attitude would be toward an experiment—or a game—that was being carried out on the basis of tosses of a coin. When the coin falls as alternate heads and tails all seems to be going normally. When it falls with two or three tails in a row all we say is that the element of randomness is made clear and our inability to predict the next fall is confirmed. But if the coin falls four or five or six times tails up, the situation gets more and more unusual because the number of other possible combinations is so great. If the coin falls tails ten times in a row we would more than likely suspect something to be wrong: that we were being tricked, that the coin was off balance, or that something about the way it was being tossed was too precise and consistent to allow for random selection.

A deviation from the probable outcome to the extent of getting no heads in ten tosses would lead us to examine the conditions under which the tosses were made. Our conclusion would be that something went wrong. The obvious implication of such a conclusion is that the results of calculations made with probability mathematics are as dependable as the results of calculations made using any other mathematical system. If we add a column of figures and get a sum that cannot be reconciled with certain sensory data, then we begin to look for mistakes or inaccuracies in the data. Here, when the sequence becomes more and more mathematically improbable, we begin to look for errors having to do with observation and measurement.

Actually, it is true that the formal, mathematical presentation may only be a supplement to an intuitive conviction for most of us. In the case of the coin most people's assurance would be strengthened more by making the experiment than by making the calculations. They would have to sit for a while tossing a coin or be involved in a game or experiment of coin-tossing for an extended period of time to gain full assurance and confidence in the mathematical predictions.

Mathematical probability, however, opens new areas of discovery that would be unknown if we stuck to the simple, intuitive approach. Outcomes of high probability can be suggested that may then be found by experiment to carry what we would intuitively call "practical certainty."

A professional gambler—even if he knows nothing of probability mathematics—knows in some way or another that the probability of getting 7 in the roll of two dice is ⅙, or 17%; the probability of getting snake-eyes, or two 1's, is 3%; the probability of getting two numbers whose sum is greater than 7 is 42% (slightly less than 50–50; the odds are against it); and the probability of getting two numbers whose sum is greater than 6 is 58% (the odds are in favor of it).

It is unlikely, however, that anyone could make even a close intuitive estimate as to the probability of two people out of a group of 23 having the same birthday. That is, given 23 people selected at random, what is the probability that two of them will have been born on the same day of the year? It generally comes as a surprise to find that there is better than a 50% probability of such an occurrence. And if we increase the number of people in the group, the probability of two people having the same birthday increases at an amazing rate. With 25 people it is 57%; with 30 people it is 71%; and with 50 people it is 97%. In this latter case one might say that "for all practical purposes" it is certain that there will be at least two people born on the same day of the year.*

In the first example above, the professional gambler has learned the odds or probabilities intuitively. That is, his experiences have led him to cultivate certain habits and these habits have enabled him to be successful in what were for him an acceptable number of cases. There has been little computation involved in the gambler's discoveries, and none of the development of a systematic approach that could be called "mathematics." In the case of the birthdays, however, the very opposite is the case. The discovery of the probabilities in favor of a concurrent birthday is made through a sophisticated mathematical system. The results of computations in this system are given intuitive justification by experience only after the computation has described the conditions that must be arranged.

It is interesting to note that the mathematics of probability was given initial formulation under the impetus of a gambler's experiences. Blaise Pascal, a seventeenth-century philosopher and mathematician who gave us the first outline of a probability mathematics, is said to have developed his theory in order to answer certain questions put to him concerning gambling by his friend the Chevalier de Méré.

The experiences provoke the questions and give hints as to procedures for the development of an axiomatic system, but the system, once axiomatized, produces results that make new and more exciting and rewarding experiences possible.

---

* The mathematical proof of these probabilities is given in *Introduction to Finite Mathematics*, pp. 125–126. The student should find it relatively easy and quite interesting and enlightening to go through the preparatory work it takes to follow this proof.

What can be said about truth and falsity in the cases of extreme probability? We may say, for example that "for all practical purposes" an event is certain to occur. But for *theoretical* purposes what can we say? Obviously, for theoretical purposes we can say no more than, "There is such and such a probability that the event will occur." If we want a logical system to work with events that are given probability measurements we will have to leave our simple two-valued logic and go to one that deals not with statements that are simply true or false but with statements that have various degrees of probability.

But we still have the distinction we made before between mathematical and empirical knowledge, whether we are speaking of true-false or degrees of probability. Mathematical probability is indeed just that: a theory involving mathematical relationships. It becomes, as does any other meaningful theory, extremely useful when applied to the circumstances of our experiences, but the calculations in a mathematical system—even in probability mathematics—give precise figures of absolute character, and such precision is not what we deal with in the experiences we have or the experiments we perform.

It will be remembered that in the coin-tossing experiment we spoke of using a fair coin—a coin that was perfectly balanced so that its fall would be completely random. We realize, of course, that *perfect* balance is an ideal goal. A balance may be achieved that is so fine that the effect on the randomness of the coin's fall would not be discernible in the outcomes of a large number of tosses, but there is still that aspect of application of the theory which cannot always be completely ignored. Also in the case of birthdays, the selection of people in the group can never be absolutely random, although whatever deviation there is from such an ideal can be made insignificant in so far as the outcome of an experiment is concerned.

In the earlier examples we suggested that we could never tell *precisely* what the ratio of salt was to other elements in sea water. And we could never measure *exactly* the height of a layer of dust on the moon; or, to go further, we could not even get *absolute* measurements on a sand pile in our own back yard. But in most cases there are limits to the precision and exactitude we need. If I am building a table, I need measurements to fractions of an inch, but I do not need measurements to thousandths or millionths of an inch. In flying an airplane a pilot must know how many feet he is over the surface beneath him, but he does not need to know how many inches or centimeters he is over the surface.

In the case of probability, the coin must be balanced to a certain fine degree, but this balance does not have to be carried to an accuracy within fractions of a milligram. And the selection of participants in any experiment involving statistical probablity must be made as a random selection. But a perfectly random selection is beyond our capabilities; and furthermore such *perfect* randomness is not even necessary. The variations introduced by whatever we fail to achieve in absolute randomness have an insignificant effect on the calculations that are made to construct insurance tables or to make other practical statistical predictions.

The measurement limits do become barriers, of course. There are circumstances in which scientists *need* finer measurements than they can get. And there is always progression to ever finer measurements that can then be used in more profound calculations. But the question as to how far such measurement can ever go—whether or not there are actually theoretical limits to it and whether the observer himself, as it is said by some, will always be introducing an error that cannot be eliminated as he tries to see the outside world—these questions must be left to further developments and interpretations by such scientists as Werner Heisenberg and the followers of Albert Einstein.

When we indicated that a true statement is one that reports a fact about the world, we did not mean to say that we could *give* an unqualified and absolute fact about the world. We were only describing what it is we *mean* by "true" and "false." Now we see that the statements that we actually use are true only within certain limits, but we see in this no cause for despair. Just as long as we know the limits, the limited truths we get are all we need—as can well be illustrated by the three or four centuries of exceptional progress in the understanding of our physical world that has been made since the Scientific Revolution.

D. DEFINITIONS AND USE-MENTION

There is another kind of truth that must be considered in this last section in order to be sure it is not confused with the physical or empirical truth we have been discussing earlier. This is the kind of truth we get by definition. It is, essentially, a tautological truth that is all too often subtly concealed in our sentences. It is in the failure to recognize a definition that we may convince ourselves and others that we have said something absolute about the world when, as a matter of fact, we have only described something as being identical with itself.

Suppose we say, "No Californians live in Nevada." Then suppose we are challenged by someone who says, "I am a Californian. I was born and raised in San Francisco and I now live right here in Reno, Nevada." "But then," we say, "you are not a Californian. A Californian is someone who lives in California." What is the inevitable trend of this argument? It is obvious that such an argument will very soon have to come to focus on the meaning we are giving to "Californian." Our opponent will say "Californian" means someone who was born in California. We will say it means someone who is living in California. The truth or falsity of our original statement will, then, depend simply upon which definition is finally accepted.

It becomes evident by such problems as this that definitions are an important consideration for any argument. We must know how we are using our terms before any kind of meaningful discussion can take place.

But there are limits as to how far we can go with our definitions. We may use one word or series of words to define another, but then we need others yet to define the words used in our definition and words to define these latter words and so on.

It will be remembered that in the construction of the deductive systems we took certain symbols as primitive and then used those symbols to define others that were introduced later for convenience. And this is, essentially, what we must do in ordinary language. Some words must be taken as basic and these, then, may be used to define others. Exactly which words are basic in our ordinary language and how their meaning is achieved at all is a topic we will leave for other sources. It should be enough to point out here that the definitions we find in the dictionary are circular—that is, in looking up a given word we are referred to another which may itself refer us to another and so on until we come back to the original word again. This means that all one expects to get from a dictionary is reference *eventually* to some word whose meaning does not have to be given—a word that is a fundamental unit in one's vocabulary.

It is of some help in discussing definitions to make a clear distinction between the word being defined and whatever it is the word refers to. The Funny Old Man on a television program is asked to give a word that sounds like "cows." So he says, "Moo." (This is a children's program, you understand.) The straight man says, " 'Moo' doesn't sound like 'cows.' " "That's how cows sound to me," says the F.O.M.

To clarify this point—which is the last thing in the world the F.O.M. and his accomplice would like to do—all we need is the punctuation we have used in the presentation of the incident. When we want to talk about, or mention, the *word* "cows," we put it in quotes. If, on the other hand, we want to talk about the *animals*, cows, we use the word without quotes to refer directly to the animals themselves.

We say that to mention the animals, cows, we use the word "cows." If, to go further, we wanted to mention the word "cows" we would have to use the symbol " "cows" " for this purpose. As we said on p. 37, we may use words to mention an idea or, as we have illustrated here, we may use a symbol to mention a word. This is the distinction that is made between use and mention whenever we find it necessary to go to second and third levels of language usage. We may use our language to talk about things or propositions, but we need another language to talk about the primary language. And we may even need other languages above that, depending upon how complex is the nature of the idea we are attempting to articulate. These additional abstractions—the languages used to *speak* of language—are called metalanguages, and the construction of such metalanguages is an important part of the more advanced activities of symbolic logic.

In speaking of definitions we need only the basic idea of use-mention to carry us through our procedure of simplification. Let us look at a few more examples of words being used and mentioned in order to clarify this point. Consider the sentences:

1. **Man is a biped.**
2. **Man is a three-letter word.**
3. **Pittsburgh is bigger than Chicago.**
4. **Pittsburgh is farther south than Chicago.**
5. **The dodo is extinct.**
6. **The dodo is unnecessary.**

All the sentences in this list are either meaningful or they can be made meaningful through the use of quotes. The first is all right as it stands. The second needs quotes encompassing "man" to make it meaningful and true. The third cannot be true if it is referring to the populations or physical sizes of Pittsburgh and Chicago, but it is true of the *words* "Pittsburgh" and "Chicago." The fourth is meaningful and true. The fifth is meaningful and true, and the sixth can be made meaningful by putting quotes around "dodo," thereby giving a sentence in which an editor may be suggesting the removal of a word from a manuscript.

Now if we want to define a word like "salty," we can say, " 'Salty' means having the taste of salt." Or, we could say, " 'Salty' means having not less than 29.9% salt in suspension." The first definition is almost trivial and the second has such a precision that it would require us to make careful chemical analysis in order to determine whether or not a given substance is salty.

There is always truth, but there is also a kind of arbitrariness, about definitions. We introduce a definition to make our work a little easier—to make it possible to say in one word what would normally take many words. But we often fail to remember that what we are saying is not a statement about the world—or about whatever is the case. We must not begin to think of an arbitrarily assigned definition as being something that is inherently true and irrefutable about the nature of things.

As an example of the above, some extremist may say, "Nikolai is a Communist." When questioned about this the extremist says he did not mean that Nikolai was a registered member of the Communist party, or that he knowingly advocated the overthrow of the government, or that he functioned as a subversive in carrying out the explicit orders of the Communists, or any other generally accepted meaning of the word "Communist." He meant simply that Nikolai has expressed certain views that he, the extremist, has labeled as "Communist views" and therefore Nikolai must be labeled as "Communist." If it were not for the particularly bad connotation that has become attached to the word "Communist" in these times, such a definition given by the extremist would be harmless. The only one who would suffer at all would be the extremist himself, in that he would find it more difficult to communicate with and understand those who were being more careful about definitions and word usage.

The interesting thing about such an utterance is that the person who makes it is more than likely convinced that he is saying something that is true about certain circumstances of his political and social environment. The actual situation that he is concealing from himself and others is, of course, the fact that he is arbitrarily making a definition that he wishes to use as a replacement for the standard definition. In this case it is clear that he would also like to *retain* all the negative and evil connotations and implications associated with "Communist." Then as the word with his new definition is generously distributed among all of his political enemies, he hopes to gain some measure of success in destroying those adversaries.

A definition, being basically arbitrary in the first place, must be *given* stability and authority by those who use it in communication. We freely bow to the authority of the dictionary, for example, in order to gain the advantage of greater ease and precision in our conversation. There is no law that says we must accept dictionary meanings, but if someone refuses to accept the dictionary as a final arbiter in controversies over the meanings of words, then we see that further discussion of any subject matter that interests us is brought to a standstill.

It may, in fact it should, be pointed out that the dictionary is written by people who do little more than report the usage that is given to words in the conversations of people who speak the language. There can be no doubt that meanings come from general usage. But the task of those writing a dictionary is still not a simple one. In order to assign meanings to words there must be discovered a certain consistency about the way they are used. Some people whose lives are simple, narrow, and unencumbered with the complexities of a variegated environment may be able to express most of their ideas with words that mean many things in general and very little in particular. They do not investigate implications fully or refer to anything but the most superficial meanings with the words they use in ordinary conversation. But others who do carry out implications and who are concerned with the more profound meanings given to words must therefore be more careful in their usages. Those whose task it is to compile a dictionary, then, find this latter group—writers, editorialists, scientists, teachers, diplomats, linguists—to be a more reliable source for meanings that can actually be expressed and that will be found to be useful when introduced in most contexts of verbal communication.

The source for the dictionary writers is common usage, but not vulgar usage. For, although common usage does indeed provide the authority, if the writers went to vulgar usage they would not be able to get any kind of over-all precision to their definitions.

As we do accept a given source for word meanings, then, we find ourselves confronted with a kind of absolute truth. When we say, "A bachelor is an unmarried man," or "'Bachelor' means an unmarried man," then this cannot be disputed. Even if someone else says, "'Bachelor' means someone who has graduated from college," we may simply accept that as another definition and leave the determination of which definition is being used to an examination of the context in which the word is placed. But after we have accepted the dictionary as our source of definitions and when we see the definition clearly spelled out, then there should be no argument about the *meaning* of the word. The absolute nature of the definition is needed for refinements and precision in conversation, and that absolute must not be violated (without due cause and clear understanding among the communicants) even though we may recognize that, somewhere in the past, the definition has been more or less arbitrarily assigned in the first place.

E. CONCLUSION

In ending the discussion of definitions we come again to an expression of the idea that language—whether of logic or mathematics or ordinary conversation—requires an absolutism that we may never expect to find in the course of our experiences. A precise language, logic, or mathematics sets up kinds of ideals that are then used as guides in the performance of activities that are totally dependent upon sense experiences.

There is a metaphysical question involved here that has concerned philosophers ever since Plato in the fourth century B.C. Plato said that there is a world of ideals that has even more reality to it than the world we experience. It is, he said, the world of perfection and absolutes. It is the reality we must continually strive to achieve and according to which we must pattern our lives and our works in this lesser, imperfect world that we know of as our physical existence. We will never achieve the world of absolutes in this life, said Plato. Such success is possible only after our physical death. But we can learn a lot about the absolutes through the use of our intellects. Just as we use our sight to sense physical things, so may we use our intellect to sense or comprehend entities of the ideal world—the world of Forms.

The Platonistic philosophy of the reality of an abstract world has appeared in numerous forms throughout the development of Western intellectual culture and may be found as an aspect of some respected philosophies even today.

We do not here mean to maintain such a position, although we believe the emphasis laid by Platonism on the importance of abstraction and formal reasoning is an aid to the understanding of the differences between logical and mathematical absolutes on the one hand, and empirical or experimental facts on the other. We are not suggesting a World of Absolutes as opposed to a World of Experience. We are saying that there are two principal approaches used by man for understanding his environment and that these approaches are inextricably dependent upon one another. The systems we call absolute grow from the experiences of our world as Euclidean geometry grew from the experiences with physical shapes and figures and as the dictionary grows from common language usage. But it is also true that the experimental procedures we derive and invent owe a huge debt to the systems we have axiomatized and made absolute as these latter are brought to bear on the practical problems of our physical conditions. Neither approach is more important than the other—or more real or more productive—because neither approach is at all independent of the other.

Answers to Exercises

Answers to Exercises

Pages 32–35

1. A ——
   B ——
   C {Washington, Oregon, California, Hawaii, Alaska}
   D ——
   E {45, 54}
   F {1, 2, 3, 4, 5, 6, 7, 8, 9, 10, 11, 12, 13, 14, 15, 16, 17, 18, 19}

2. G $\{x \mid 2 \leqq x \leqq 16$, x is an integer$\}$
   H $\{x \mid$ x is a U.S. President between the years 1934 and 1961$\}$
   J $\{x \mid 1 < x < 9$, x is an even integer$\}$
   K $\{x \mid$ x is a natural satellite of the earth over 2000 miles in diameter$\}$
   L $\{x \mid$ x is a satellite$\}$

3. M {3, −3}
   N {2, 3, 4, 5}
   O ——
   P {Mercury, Venus, Earth, Mars, Jupiter, Saturn, Uranus, Neptune, Pluto}
   Q {4, −3}

4. (a) $R \cup S = \{1, 2, 3, 4, 5, 6, 7, 9\}$ $R \cap S = \{3, 5\}$
   (b) $T \cup X$ {Everyone who is a college student or is over 21 or is both}
   $T \cap X$ {College students over 21}
   $W \cap X$ {Football players over 21}
   $T \cup (W \cap X)$ {Anyone who is either a college student or a football player over 21 or both}

5. $(A \cap B) \cap C$ {Philosophy}
   $A \cup (B \cap C)$ {Math, Physics, Philosophy, German, French}
   $(A \cup B) \cap C$ {Philosophy, German, French}
   $A \cap (B \cap C)$ {Philosophy}
   $A \cup B \cup C$ {Math, Physics, Philosophy, German, English, Humanities, French, Latin, Eskimo}

6. $A \cup B$ {Ann, Bob, Charlie, Dianne, Elvis}
$A \cap B$ {Bob, Charlie}
$B \cap C$ 0
$A' \cup C$ {Ann, Dianne, Elvis}
$C' \cup B$ {Bob, Charlie, Elvis}
$C' \cap B$ {Bob, Charlie, Elvis}

7. $B \cup C$ {v, z, y}
$A \cap D$ {w, x}
$C' \cap A$ {w, x}
$B' \cap D$ {w, x, }
$A' \cup C'$ {v, w, x, z}

8. A: {6, 7} B: {2, 3, 4} C: {4} $1 = \{2, 3, 4, 5, 6, 7\}$
$A \cup B$ {2, 3, 4, 6, 7}
$A \cup B'$ {5, 6, 7}
$C \cup A'$ {2, 3, 4, 5}
$A \cap B$ 0
$(A \cup B) \cap C$ {4}
$(A \cup B) \cap C'$ {2, 3, 6, 7}
$B \cup C'$ $\{2, 3, 4, 5, 6, 7\} = 1$
$A' \cap B'$ {5}

9.

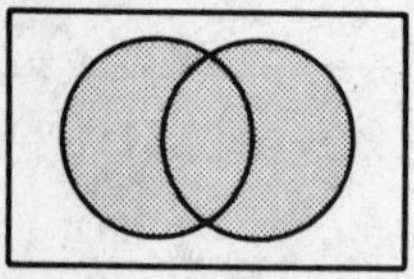

$a \cup b$

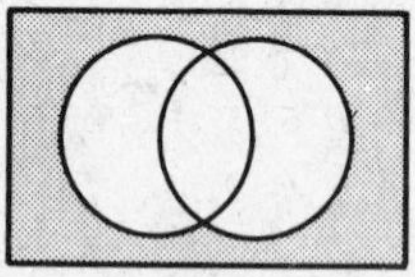

$a' \cap b'$

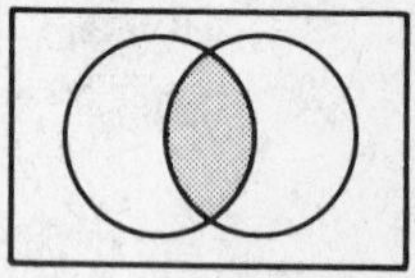

$a \cap b$

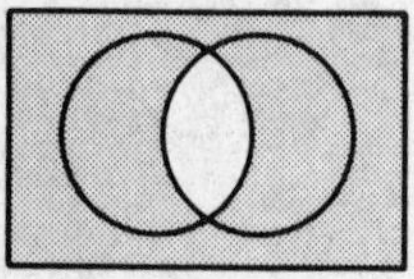

$(a \cap b)'$

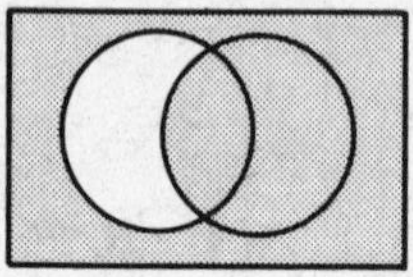

$a' \cup b$

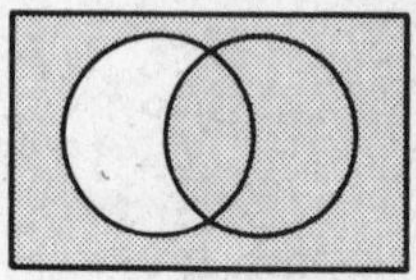

$(a \cap b) \cup a'$

10. a)

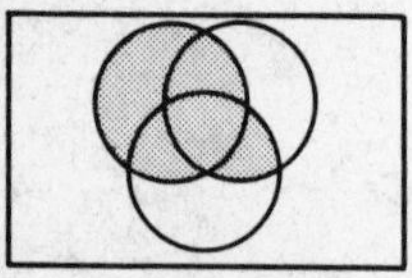

(1,4,5,6,7)

b)

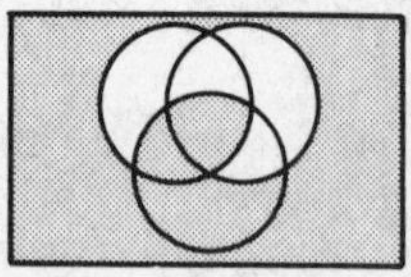

(3,6,7,8)

c)

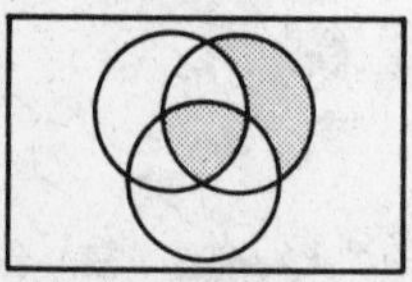

(2,7)

d)

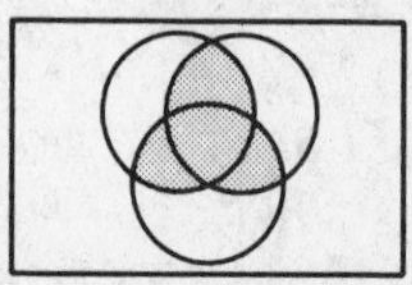

(4,5,6,7)

11.

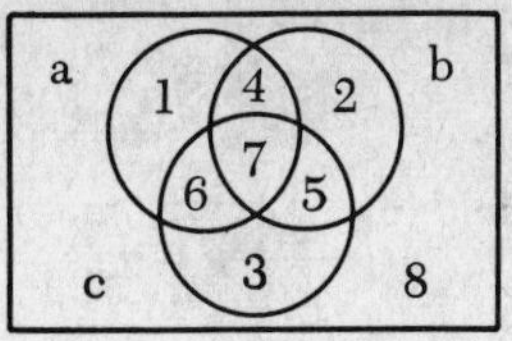

a) $a \cap (a \cup b) = (1, 4, 6, 7)$, $a = (1, 4, 6, 7)$ } Equal

b) $a' \cup b' = (1, 2, 3, 5, 6, 8)$, $(a \cap b)' = (1, 2, 3, 5, 6, 8)$ } Equal

c) $a \cup (a' \cap b) = (1, 2, 4, 5, 6, 7)$, $a \cup b = (1, 2, 4, 5, 6, 7)$ } Equal

d) $(a \cup b) \cap (a' \cup c) = (2, 5, 6, 7)$, $(a \cap c) \cup (a' \cap b) = (2, 5, 6, 7)$ } Equal

e) $(a' \cap b') \cup (a' \cap b) \cup (a \cap b')$
$= (1, 2, 3, 5, 6, 8)$
$1 = (1, 2, 3, 4, 5, 6, 7, 8)$ } Unequal

f) $(a \cap b)' = (1, 2, 3, 5, 6, 8)$, $a' \cap b' = (3, 8)$ } Unequal

12.

a)
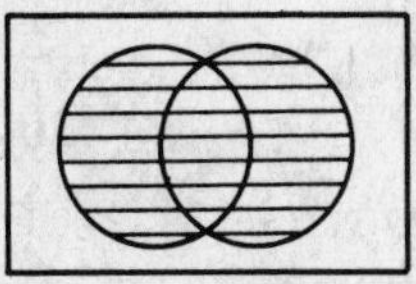

$a \cup b = 0$

b)
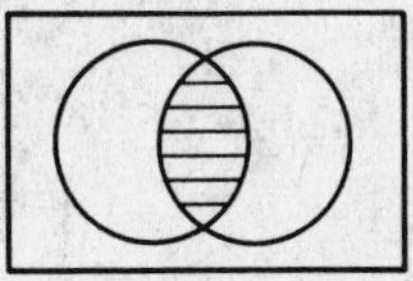

$a \cap b = 0$

c)

$a' \cap b' = 0$

d)
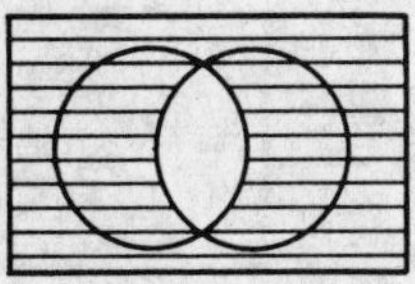

$a' \cup b' = 0$

e)
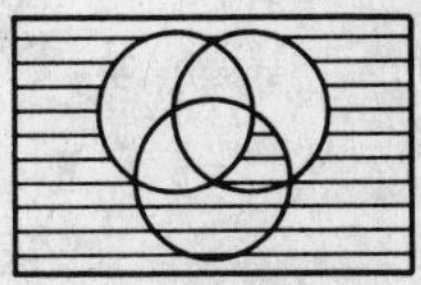

$a' \cap (b' \cup c) = 0$

f)
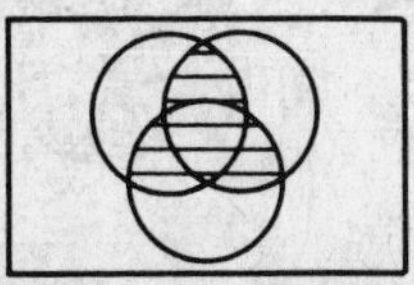

$[b \cap (a \cup c)] \cup (a \cap c) = 0$

g)
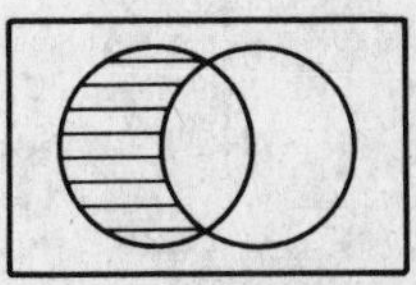

$a \cap b' = 0$

Sets: A = Sports that use a ball {F, G, B}
B = Indoor participant {P, S, R}
C = Fewer than 10 players {P, G, S, R}
D = Outdoor participant {G}

13. $A \cup B = \{F, G, B, P, S, R\}$

14. $B \cap A = 0$

15. $C' \cup A = \{F, G, B\}$

16. $A \cap (D \cup B) = \{G\}$

17. $(A' \cap C) \cup B' = \{F, P, G, S, B, R\} = 1$

Pages 56–58

A = Universal Affirmative; E = Universal Negative; I = Particular Affirmative; O = Particular Negative

1. *A*; 2. *E*; 3. *I* or *O*; 4. *A*; 5. *I*; 6. $MS' = 0$; 7. $EP = 0$;

8. $MT \neq 0$; 9. $FH = 0$; 10. $MC' \neq 0$; 11. $ab' = 0$;

12. $b'a \neq 0$; 13. $a'b' = 0$; 14. $ab'' = 0$; $(ab = 0)$ 15. $ab = 0$;

16. (6) M dist. S undist. (7) E dist. P dist. (8) M undist. T undist. (9) F dist. H dist.

(10) M undist. C dist. 17. Invalid Rule 2 18. Valid 19. Invalid Rule 5

20. Invalid Rule 4 21. Invalid Rule 5 Rule 6 22. Invalid Rule 5 23. Invalid Rule 3

24. $pm' = 0$
$sm = 0$
$\overline{}$
$sp = 0$

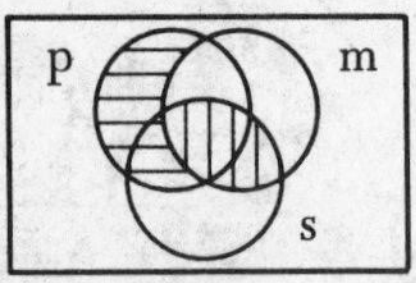

Valid

25. $fm = 0$
$mv \neq 0$
$\overline{}$
$vf' \neq 0$

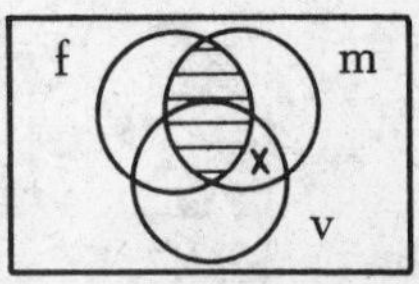

Valid

26. $mp = 0$
$sm' = 0$
$\overline{}$
$sp = 0$

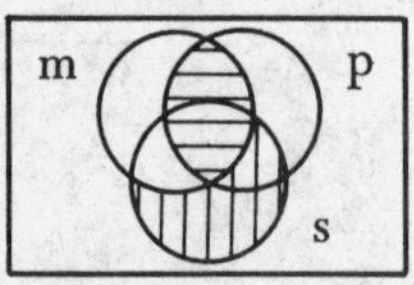

Valid

27. $pm' = 0$
$sm = 0$
$\overline{}$
$sp' \neq 0$

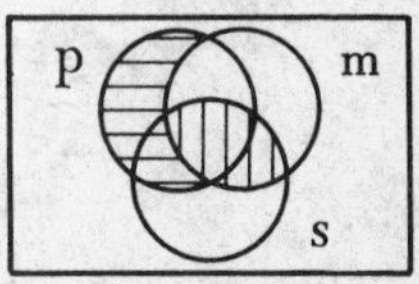

Invalid

28. $pm \neq 0$
$ms' = 0$
$\overline{}$
$sp \neq 0$

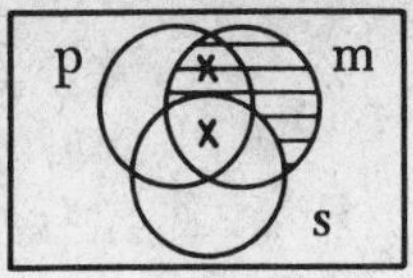

Valid

29. $bg = 0$
$eg' = 0$
$(eb = 0)$
$eb \neq 0$ Valid

30. $gp \neq 0$
$pa' = 0$
$(ag \neq 0)$
$ag = 0$ Valid

31. $mp' = 0$
$sm \neq 0$
$(sp \neq 0)$
$sp = 0)$ Valid

32. $a'p' \neq 0$
$s'a' = 0$
$(sp' \neq 0)$
$sp' = 0$ Valid

33. $gt = 0$
$tp' \neq 0$
$(pg' \neq 0)$
$pg' = 0$ Invalid Rule 4

Pages 66–67

		1.	2.	3.	4.
		② ①	③ ① ② ①	② ①	③ ① ② ①
p	q	$-(p \cdot q)$	$-(-p \cdot q)$	$-(p \supset q)$	$-(p \supset -q)$
T	T	F T	T F F T	F T	T T F F
T	F	T F	T F F F	T F	F T T T
F	T	T F	F T T T	F T	F F T F
F	F	T F	T T F F	F T	F F T T

		5.	6.	7.	8.
		③ ① ② ①	① ② ①	② ①	① ② ①
p	q	$-(p \vee -q)$	$-p \equiv -q$	$-(p \equiv q)$	$p \supset -p$
T	T	F T T F	F T F	F T	T F F
T	F	F T T T	F F T	T F	T F F
F	T	T F F F	T F F	T F	F T T
F	F	F F T T	T T T	F T	F T T

		9.	10.
		① ② ①	① ② ①
p	q	$p \cdot -p$	$p \vee -p$
T	T	T F F	T T F
T	F	T F F	T T F
F	T	F F T	F T T
F	F	F F T	F T T

11. $-V \supset -G$
12. $B \cdot -C$
13. $-(C \vee S)$
14. $-(-W \vee B)$
15. $P \supset M$
16. $M \supset P$
17. $R \supset D$
18. $P \cdot -A$
19. $M \supset (P \cdot S)$
20. $S \vee (-S \supset H)$

Pages 81–82

1. Tautology
2. Tautology
3. Tautology
4. Tautology
5. $\{-q \supset -[(p \vee -r) \cdot (r \supset p)]\} \supset (-p \supset q)$ Neither
6. $[(M \supset J) \cdot (M \cdot H)] \supset (J \cdot H)$ Valid
7. $[-(P \cdot -A) \cdot (-G \vee P) \cdot P] \supset A$ Valid
8. $\{(-W \vee -D \vee T) \cdot -(-W \cdot -D) \cdot [-T \supset (W \cdot D)] \cdot [T \vee -(-W \vee -D)]\} \supset T$ Valid
9. $[(W \supset O) \cdot -(-W \vee N) \cdot (-O \supset T) \cdot (N \vee -T)] \supset O$ Valid
10. $(p \vee q \vee r \vee s) \cdot -(p \cdot q \cdot r \cdot s) \cdot [q \supset (r \cdot -p)] \cdot (s \supset -r) \cdot [-q \supset (s \cdot p)] \cdot [-p \supset (s \cdot -r)]$

All statements are true together on the 7th line of the 16-line Truth Table, that is, when:

Brian is a prince.
Lynn is not a queen.
Cheryl is not a robber.
Timmy is a spook.

Pages 94–97

1. 1) $C \supset B$	Pr.	$/\therefore A$
2) $-C \supset A$	Pr.	
3) $-B$	Pr.	
4) $-C$	1,3, M.T.	
5) A	2,4, M.P.	
2. 1) $R \supset S$	Pr.	$/\therefore P \cdot S$
2) $P \cdot Q$	Pr.	

3) $R \vee -Q$	Pr.	
4) Q	2, Simp.	
5) $- -Q$	4, D.N.	
6) R	3,5, D.D.	
7) S	1,6, M.P.	
8) P	2, Simp.	
9) $P \cdot S$	8,7, Adj.	

3.

1) $N \vee I$	Pr.	$\underline{/\therefore N}$
2) $I \supset C$	Pr.	
3) $E \cdot -C$	Pr.	
4) $-C$	3, Simp.	
5) $-I$	2,4, M.T.	
6) N	1,5, D.D.	

4.

1) $C \supset -A$	Pr.	$\underline{/\therefore -E}$
2) $-R \supset -E$	Pr.	
3) $C \vee -R$	Pr.	
4) A	Pr.	
5) $- -A$	4, D.N.	
6) $-C$	1,5, M.T.	
7) $-R$	3,6, D.D.	
8) $-E$	2,7, M.P.	

5.

1) $R \supset E$	Pr.	$\underline{/\therefore -R}$
2) $A \cdot -D$	Pr.	
3) $-E \vee D$	Pr.	
4) $R \vee A$	Pr.	
5) $-D$	2, Simp.	
6) $-E$	3,5, D.D.	
7) $-R$	1,6, M.T.	

6.

1) $E \cdot A$	Pr.	$\underline{/\therefore -Y}$
2) $S \supset -Y$	Pr.	
3) $S \vee -A$	Pr.	
4) A	1, Simp.	
5) $- -A$	4, D.N.	
6) S	3,5, D.D.	
7) $-Y$	2,6, M.P.	

7.

1) $R \supset S$	Pr.	$\underline{/\therefore -P \cdot T}$
2) $-(P \vee -R)$	Pr.	

	3) $-S \vee T$	Pr.
	4) $-P \cdot --R$	2, D.M.
	5) $--R$	4, Simp.
	6) R	5, D.N.
	7) S	1,6, M.P.
	8) $--S$	7, D.N.
	9) T	3,8, D.D.
	10) $-P$	4, Simp.
	11) $-P \cdot T$	10,9, Adj.
8.	1) $-T \vee R$	Pr. $\underline{/\therefore S}$
	2) $O \cdot -U$	Pr.
	3) $B \supset (L \cdot -E)$	Pr.
	4) $(R \cdot -U) \supset S$	Pr.
	5) $-B \supset U$	Pr.
	6) $L \supset T$	Pr.
	7) $-U$	2, Simp.
	8) $--B$	5,7, M.T.
	9) B	8, D.N.
	10) $L \cdot -E$	3,9, M.P.
	11) L	10, Simp.
	12) T	6,11, M.P.
	13) $--T$	12, D.N.
	14) R	1,13, D.D.
	15) $R \cdot -U$	14,7, Adj.
	16) S	4,15, M.P.
9.	1) $(L \vee O) \supset (G \cdot -I)$	Pr. $\underline{/\therefore -C}$
	2) $-(-I \cdot C)$	Pr.
	3) L	Pr.
	4) $L \vee O$	3, Add.
	5) $G \cdot -I$	1,4, M.P.
	6) $--I \vee -C$	2, D.M.
	7) $-I$	5, Simp.
	8) $---I$	7, D.N.
	9) $-C$	6,8, D.D.
10.	1) $F \supset -A$	Pr. $\underline{/\therefore F \supset (-A \cdot T \cdot C)}$
	2) $C \vee -T$	Pr.
	3) $T \vee -F$	Pr.
	4) $\quad \mid F$	H.P.

	5)	$\quad\mid -A$	1,4, M.P.
	6)	$\quad\mid - -F$	4, D.N.
	7)	$\quad\mid T$	3,6, D.D.
	8)	$\quad\mid - -T$	7, D.N.
	9)	$\quad\mid C$	2,8, D.D.
	10)	$\quad\mid -A \cdot T \cdot C$	5,7,9, Adj.
	11)	$F \supset (-A \cdot T \cdot C)$	4–10, C.P.

11.	1)	$S \supset O$	Pr. $/\therefore -R \supset -S$
	2)	$O \supset -L$	Pr.
	3)	$A \vee R$	Pr.
	4)	$L \vee -A$	Pr.
	5)	$\quad\mid -R$	H.P.
	6)	$\quad\mid A$	3,5, D.D.
	7)	$\quad\mid - -A$	6, D.N.
	8)	$\quad\mid L$	4,7, D.D.
	9)	$\quad\mid - -L$	8, D.N.
	10)	$\quad\mid -O$	2,9, M.T.
	11)	$\quad\mid -S$	1,10, M.T.
	12)	$-R \supset -S$	5–11, C.P.

12.	1)	$-K \supset A$	Pr. $/\therefore T \supset K$
	2)	$N \vee -T$	Pr.
	3)	$-(A \cdot N)$	Pr.
	4)	$\quad\mid T$	H.P.
	5)	$\quad\mid - -T$	4, D.N.
	6)	$\quad\mid N$	2,5, D.D.
	7)	$\quad\mid -A \vee -N$	3, D.M.
	8)	$\quad\mid - -N$	6, D.N.
	9)	$\quad\mid -A$	7,8, D.D.
	10)	$\quad\mid - -K$	1,9, M.T.
	11)	$\quad\mid K$	10, D.N.
	12)	$T \supset K$	4–11, C.P.

13.	1)	$(-T \supset -H) \supset I$	Pr. $/\therefore I$
	2)	$-N \vee K$	Pr.
	3)	$-(-N \cdot -T)$	Pr.
	4)	$K \supset -H$	Pr.
	5)	$\quad\mid -T$	H.P.
	6)	$\quad\mid - -N \vee - -T$	3, D.M.
	7)	$\quad\mid - - -T$	5, D.N.

	8)	$\mid\ --N$	6,7, D.D.
	9)	$\mid\ K$	2,8, D.D.
	10)	$\mid\ -H$	4,9, M.P.
	11)	$-T \supset -H$	5–10, C.P.
	12)	I	1,11, M.P.
14.	1)	$(J \vee M) \supset L$	Pr. $/\therefore H$
	2)	$(D \vee S) \supset E$	Pr.
	3)	$-H \supset (J \vee S)$	Pr.
	4)	$(E \vee L) \supset M$	Pr.
	5)	$-M$	Pr.
	6)	$\mid\ -H$	H.P.
	7)	$\mid\ J \vee S$	6,3, M.P.
	8)	$\mid\ -(E \vee L)$	4,5, M.T.
	9)	$\mid\ -E \cdot -L$	8, D.M.
	10)	$\mid\ -E$	9, Simp.
	11)	$\mid\ -(D \vee S)$	2,10, M.T.
	12)	$\mid\ -D \cdot -S$	11, D.M.
	13)	$\mid\ -S$	12, Simp.
	14)	$\mid\ J$	7,13, D.D.
	15)	$\mid\ -L$	9, Simp.
	16)	$\mid\ -(J \vee M)$	1,15, M.T.
	17)	$\mid\ -J \cdot -M$	16, D.M.
	18)	$\mid\ -J$	17, Simp.
	19)	$\mid\ J \cdot -J$	14,18, Adj.
	20)	$-H \supset (J \cdot -J)$	6–19, C.P.
	21)	$--H$	20, Abs.
	22)	H	21, D.N.
15.	1)	$(L \cdot -A) \supset -(M \vee P)$	Pr. $/\therefore M \cdot S)$
	2)	$-M \supset -S$	Pr.
	3)	$-(-L \vee -S)$	Pr.
	4)	$\mid\ -(M \cdot S)$	H.P.
	5)	$\mid\ -M \vee -S$	4, D.M.
	6)	$\mid\ --L \cdot --S$	3, D.M.
	7)	$\mid\ --S$	6, Simp.
	8)	$\mid\ -M$	5,7, D.D.
	9)	$\mid\ -S$	2,8, M.P.
	10)	$\mid\ -S \cdot --S$	9,7 Adj.
	11)	$-(M \cdot S) \supset (-S \cdot --S)$	4–10, C.P.
	12)	$--(M \cdot S)$	11, Abs.

	13) $M \cdot S$	12, D.N.
16.	1) $D \vee -L$	Pr. $/ \therefore L \supset -M$
	2) $M \supset -D$	Pr.
	3) $\quad -(L \supset -M)$	H.P.
	4) $\quad L \cdot --M$	3, N.I.
	5) $\quad L$	4, Simp.
	6) $\quad --L$	5, D.N.
	7) $\quad D$	1,6, D.D.
	8) $\quad --M$	4, Simp.
	9) $\quad M$	8, D.N.
	10) $\quad -D$	2,9, M.P.
	11) $\quad D \cdot -D$	7,10, Adj.
	12) $-(L \supset -M) \supset (D \cdot -D)$	3–11, C.P.
	13) $--(L \supset -M)$	12, Abs.
	14) $L \supset -M$	13, D.N.
17.	1) $S \vee O$	Pr. $/ \therefore -E \vee M$
	2) $S \supset -E$	Pr.
	3) $O \supset M$	Pr.
	4) $\quad -(-E \vee M)$	H.P.
	5) $\quad --E \cdot -M$	4, D.M.
	6) $\quad --E$	5, Simp.
	7) $\quad -S$	2,6, M.T.
	8) $\quad O$	1,7, D.D.
	9) $\quad M$	3,8, M.P.
	10) $\quad -M$	5, Simp.
	11) $\quad M \cdot -M$	9, 10, Adj.
	12) $-(-E \vee M) \supset (M \cdot -M)$	4–11, C.P.
	13) $--(-E \vee M)$	12, Abs.
	14) $-E \vee M$	13, D.N.
18.	1) $P \supset (F \vee T)$	Pr. $/ \therefore -T \supset (-P \vee S)$
	2) $-F$	Pr.
	3) $\quad -[-T \supset (-P \vee S)]$	H.P.
	4) $\quad -T \cdot -(-P \vee S)$	3, N.I.
	5) $\quad -(-P \vee S)$	4, Simp.
	6) $\quad --P \cdot -S$	5, D.M.
	7) $\quad --P$	6, Simp.
	8) $\quad P$	7, D.N.
	9) $\quad F \vee T$	1,8, M.P.

	10)	$\mid -T$	4, Simp.
	11)	$\mid F$	9,10, D.D.
	12)	$\mid F \cdot -F$	11,2, Adj.
	13)	$-[-T \supset (-P \vee S)] \supset (F \cdot -F)$	3–12, C.P.
	14)	$- -[-T \supset (-P \vee S)]$	13, Abs.
	15)	$-T \supset (-P \vee S)$	14, D.N.
19.	1)	$\{-[(R \vee S) \supset (F \cdot -C)] \supset H\} \vee (-D \cdot S)$	Pr. /∴$-R$
	2)	$-S$	Pr.
	3)	$-H$	Pr.
	4)	$-F$	Pr.
	5)	$-S \vee - -D$	2, Add.
	6)	$- -D \vee -S$	5, Com.
	7)	$-(-D \cdot S)$	6, D.M.
	8)	$-[(R \vee S) \supset (F \cdot -C)] \supset H$	1,7, D.D.
	9)	$- -[(R \vee S) \supset (F \cdot -C)]$	8,3, M.T.
	10)	$(R \vee S) \supset (F \cdot -C)$	9, D.N.
	11)	$-F \vee - -C$	4, Add.
	12)	$-(F \cdot -C)$	11, D.M.
	13)	$-(R \vee S)$	10,12, M.T.
	14)	$-R \cdot -S$	13, D.M.
	15)	$-R$	14, Simp.
20.	1)	$B \supset \{M \supset [-(T \cdot P) \supset -(E \supset C)]\}$	Pr. /∴Y
	2)	$(-B \vee -M) \supset Y$	Pr.
	3)	$C \cdot -T$	Pr.
	4)	$\mid -Y$	H.P.
	5)	$\mid -(-B \vee -M)$	2,4, M.T.
	6)	$\mid - -B \cdot - -M$	5, D.M.
	7)	$\mid - -B$	6, Simp.
	8)	$\mid B$	7, D.N.
	9)	$\mid M \supset [-(T \cdot P) \supset -(E \supset C)]$	1,8, M.P.
	10)	$\mid - -M$	6, Simp.
	11)	$\mid M$	10, D.N.
	12)	$\mid -(T \cdot P) \supset -(E \supset C)$	9,11, M.P.
	13)	$\mid -T$	3, Simp.
	14)	$\mid -T \vee -P$	13, Add.
	15)	$\mid -(T \cdot P)$	14, D.M.
	16)	$\mid -(E \supset C)$	12,15, M.P.
	17)	$\mid E \cdot -C$	16, N.I.

18)	$\quad\vert\; -C$	17, Simp.
19)	$\quad\vert\; C$	3, Simp.
20)	$\quad\vert\; C \cdot -C$	19,18, Adj.
21)	$-Y \supset (C \cdot -C)$	4–20, C.P.
22)	$- -Y$	21, Abs.
23)	Y	22, D.N.

21. $[J \supset (D \supset B)] \supset [(J \supset D) \supset (J \supset B)]$. To show that this is a tautology and therefore a valid argument form, we begin by hypothesizing the antecedent:

1)	$\vert\; J \supset (D \supset B)$	H.P.
2)	$\vert\quad\vert\; J \supset D$	H.P.
3)	$\vert\quad\vert\quad\vert\; J$	H.P.
4)	$\vert\quad\vert\quad\vert\; D \supset B$	1,3, M.P.
5	$\vert\quad\vert\quad\vert\; D$	2,3, M.P.
6)	$\vert\quad\vert\quad\vert\; B$	4,5, M.P.
7)	$\vert\quad\vert\; J \supset B$	3–6, C.P.
8)	$\vert\; (J \supset D) \supset (J \supset B)$	2–7, C.P.
9)	$[J \supset (D \supset B)] \supset [(J \supset D) \supset (J \supset B)]$	1–8, C.P.

Actually, this kind of presentation could be applied to all our previous problems if the premises were to be considered (in conjunction) as the antecedent and the conclusion as the consequent of a Major Implication, as described in the section on Truth Tables. [See Kalish & Montague, *Logic: Techniques of Formal Reasoning* (New York: Harcourt, Brace & World, 1964).]

22.

1)	$P \supset Q$	Pr.	$/\therefore Q \vee S$
2)	$R \supset S$	Pr.	
3)	$P \vee R$	Pr.	
4)	$\quad\vert\; -(Q \vee S)$	H.P.	
5)	$\quad\vert\; -Q \cdot -S$	4, D.M.	
6)	$\quad\vert\; -Q$	5, Simp.	
7)	$\quad\vert\; -P$	1,6, M.T.	
8)	$\quad\vert\; R$	3,7, D.D.	
9)	$\quad\vert\; -S$	5, Simp.	
10)	$\quad\vert\; -R$	2,9, M.T.	
11)	$\quad\vert\; R \cdot -R$	8,10, Adj.	
12)	$-(Q \vee S) \supset (R \cdot -R)$	4–11, C.P.	
13)	$- -(Q \vee S)$	12, Abs.	
14)	$Q \vee S$	13, D.N.	

23.

1)	$C \supset (H \supset -A)$	Pr.	$/\therefore C \supset (H \supset E)$
2)	$(-A \cdot N) \supset -G$	Pr.	
3)	$-E \supset (N \cdot G)$	Pr.	
4)	$\vert\ C$	H.P.	
5)	$\vert\ H \supset -A$	1,4, M.P.	
6)	$\vert\ \vert\ H$	H.P.	
7)	$\vert\ \vert\ -A$	5,6, M.P.	
8)	$\vert\ \vert\ \vert\ -E$	H.P.	
9)	$\vert\ \vert\ \vert\ N \cdot G$	3,8, M.P.	
10)	$\vert\ \vert\ \vert\ G$	9, Simp.	
11)	$\vert\ \vert\ \vert\ -(-A \cdot N)$	2,10, D.N., M.T.	
12)	$\vert\ \vert\ \vert\ - -A \vee \cdot -N$	11, D.M.	
13)	$\vert\ \vert\ \vert\ -N$	12,7, D.N., D.D.	
14)	$\vert\ \vert\ \vert\ N$	9, Simp.	
15)	$\vert\ \vert\ \vert\ N \cdot -N$	14,13, Adj.	
16)	$\vert\ \vert\ -E \supset (N \cdot -N)$	8–15, C.P.	
17)	$\vert\ \vert\ E$	16, Abs., D.N.	
18)	$\vert\ H \supset E$	6–17, C.P.	
19)	$C \supset (H \supset E)$	4–18, C.P.	

24.

1)	$\{(P \cdot Q) \supset [R \supset (H \cdot -S)]\} \supset [(T \cdot -W) \vee -(C \vee -H)]$	Pr.	$/\therefore -W$
2)	$-R \vee (T \cdot H)$	Pr.	
3)	$H \supset C$	Pr.	
4)	$-C \vee -S$	Pr.	
5)	$\vert\ W$	H.P.	
6)	$\vert\ W \vee -T$	5, Add.	
7)	$\vert\ -T \vee W$	6, Com.	
8)	$\vert\ -(T \cdot -W)$	7, D.M., I.S. (D.N.)	
9)	$\vert\ -C \supset -H$	3, Contra.	
10)	$\vert\ C \vee -H$	9, E.I.D., I.E. (D.N.)	
11)	$\vert\ -(T \cdot -W) \cdot (C \vee -H)$	8,10, Adj.	
12)	$\vert\ -[(T \cdot -W) \vee -(C \vee -H)]$	11, D.M., I.S. (D.N.)	
13)	$\vert\ -\{(P \cdot Q) \supset [R \supset (H \cdot -S)]\}$	1,12, M.T.	
14)	$\vert\ (P \cdot Q) \cdot -[R \supset .(H \cdot -S)]$	13, N.I.	
15)	$\vert\ -[R \supset (H \cdot -S)]$	14, Simp.	
16)	$\vert\ R \cdot -(H \cdot -S)$	15, N.I.	

17)	R	16, Simp.
18)	$T \cdot H$	2,17, D.N., D.D.
19)	H	18, Simp.
20)	C	3,19, M.P.
21)	$-S$	4, 20, D.N., D.D.
22)	$-(H \cdot -S)$	16, Simp.
23)	$-H \vee S$	22,D.M., D.N.
24)	S	23,19, D.N., D.D.
25)	$S \cdot -S$	24,21, Adj.
26)	$W \supset (S \cdot -S)$	5–25, C.P.
27)	$-W$	26, Abs.

25. To prove: $[(H \cdot I) \supset C] \supset [H \supset (I \supset C)]$

1)	$(H \cdot I) \supset C$	H.P.
2)	H	H.P.
3)	I	H.P.
4)	$H \cdot I$	2,3, Adj.
5)	C	1,4, M.P.
6)	$I \supset C$	3–5, C.P.
7)	$H \supset (I \supset C)$	2–6, C.P.
8)	$[(H \cdot I) \supset C] \supset [H \supset (I \supset C)]$	1–7, C.P.

Page 115

1.	$(\exists x)(Ax \cdot Bx)$	$-(x) - (Ax \cdot Bx)$
2.	$-(\exists x)(Gx \cdot -Rx)$	$(x)(Gx \supset Rx)$
3.	$-(\exists x)(Px)$	$(x) - (Px)$
4.	$-(\exists x)(Gx)$	$(x) - (Gx)$
5.	$-(\exists x)(Ox \cdot -Nx)$	$(x)(Ox \supset Nx)$
6.	$(\exists x)(Sx \cdot Bx)$	$-(x) - (Sx \cdot Bx)$
7.	$-(\exists x)(Vx \cdot Lx)$	$(x)(Vx \supset -Lx)$
8.	$(\exists x)(Cx \cdot Gx)$	$-(x) - (Cx \cdot Gx)$
9.	$-(\exists x)(Lx \cdot -Cx)$	$(x)(Lx \supset Cx)$
10.	$[(\exists x)(Dx \cdot -Hx) \cdot -(\exists x)(Hx \cdot -Dx)]$	$[-(x)(Dx \supset Hx) \cdot (x)(Hx \supset Dx)]$

11.

1)	$(x)(Ax \supset Bx)$	Pr. $/\therefore (\exists x) - (Ax)$
2)	$(\exists x) - (Bx)$	Pr.
3)	$-B\alpha$	2, E.S.
4)	$A\alpha \supset B\alpha$	1, U.S.
5)	$-A\alpha$	4,3, M.T.
6)	$(\exists x) - (Ax)$	5 E.G.

12. Universe: People

1)	$(\exists x)(-Sx \cdot Px)$	Pr. $\underline{/\therefore (\exists x)(Kx \cdot -Sx)}$
2)	$(x)(Px \supset Ex)$	Pr.
3)	$(x)(-Kx \supset -Ex)$	Pr.
4)	$-S\alpha \cdot P\alpha$	1, E.S.
5)	$P\alpha \supset E\alpha$	2, U.S.
6)	$-K\alpha \supset -E\alpha$	3, U.S.
7)	$P\alpha$	4, Simp.
8)	$E\alpha$	5,7, M.P.
9)	$K\alpha$	6,8, D.N., M.T., D.N.
10)	$-S\alpha$	4, Simp.
11)	$K\alpha \cdot -S\alpha$	9,10, Adj.
12)	$(\exists x)(Kx \cdot - Sx)$	11, E.G.

13.

1)	$(x)[(Mx \cdot Ox) \supset Rx]$	Pr. $\underline{/\therefore (x)(Ox \supset (Ex \cdot Mx)]}$
2)	$(x)(-Ox \vee Ex)$	Pr.
3)	$(x)(-Ex \vee -Rx)$	Pr.
4)	$(Ma \cdot Oa) \supset Ra$	1, U.S.
5)	$-Oa \vee Ea$	2, U.S.
6)	$-Ea \vee -Ra$	3, U.S.
7)	$\vert\ Oa$	H.P.
8)	$\vert\ Ea$	5,7, D.N., D.D.
9)	$\vert\ -Ra$	6,8, D.N., D.D.
10)	$\vert\ -(Ma \cdot Oa)$	4,9, M.T.
11)	$\vert\ -Ma \vee -Oa$	10, D.M.
12)	$\vert\ -Ma$	11,7, D.N., D.D.
13)	$\vert\ Ea \cdot -Ma$	8,12, Adj.
14)	$Oa \supset (Ea \cdot -Ma)$	7–13, C.P.
15)	$(x)[Ox \supset (Ex \cdot -Mx)]$	14, U.G.

14.

1)	$(x)[(Jx \supset -Ex) \supset Tx]$	Pr. $\underline{/\therefore (\exists x)(Tx \cdot Mx)}$
2)	$-(\exists x)[Ex \cdot -(-Sx \vee -Ax)]$	Pr.
3)	$(\exists x) - (-Mx \vee -Sx)$	Pr.
4)	$(x)(-Ax \supset -Jx)$	Pr.
5)	$(x) - [Ex \cdot -(-Sx \vee -Ax)]$	2, Trans.
6)	$-(-M\alpha \vee -S\alpha)$	3, E.S.
7)	$(J\alpha \supset -E\alpha) \supset T\alpha$	1, U.S.
8)	$-A\alpha \supset -J\alpha$	4, U.S.

9)	$-[E\alpha \cdot -(-S\alpha \vee -A\alpha)]$	5, U.S.
10)	$--M\alpha \cdot --S\alpha$	6, D.M.
11)	$\mid J\alpha$	H.P.
12)	$\mid --A\alpha$	8,10, D.N., M.T.
13)	$\mid -E\alpha \vee (-S\alpha \vee -A\alpha)$	9, D.M., I.S. (D.N.)
14)	$\mid (-E\alpha \vee -S\alpha) \vee -A\alpha$	13, Given tautology
15)	$\mid -E\alpha \vee -S\alpha$	14,12, D.D.
16)	$\mid --S\alpha$	10, Simp.
17)	$\mid -E\alpha$	15,16, D.D.
18)	$J\alpha \supset -E\alpha$	11–17, C.P.
19)	$T\alpha$	7,18, M.P.
20)	$--M\alpha$	10, Simp.
21)	$M\alpha$	20, D.N.
22)	$T\alpha \cdot M\alpha$	19,21, Adj.
23)	$(\exists x)(Tx \cdot Mx)$	22, E.G.

15. Universe: Men

1)	$(x)[(Lx \vee Ox) \supset -Gx)]$	Pr. $/\therefore (\exists x) - (Sx)$
2)	$-(\exists x)(Ix \cdot -Cx)$	Pr.
3)	$(\exists x)(Lx \cdot -Cx)$	Pr.
4)	$(x)[Sx \supset (Ix \vee Gx)]$	Pr.
5)	$(x) - (Ix \cdot -Cx)$	2, Trans.
6)	$L\alpha \cdot -C\alpha$	3, E.S.
7)	$(L\alpha \vee O\alpha) \supset -G\alpha$	1, U.S.
8)	$S\alpha \supset (I\alpha \vee G\alpha)$	4, U.S.
9)	$-(I\alpha \cdot -C\alpha)$	5, U.S.
10)	$-I\alpha \vee C\alpha$	9, D.M., I.S. (D.N.)
11)	$-C\alpha$	6, Simp.
12)	$-I\alpha$	10,11, D.D.
13)	$L\alpha$	6, Simp.
14)	$L\alpha \vee O\alpha$	13, Add.
15)	$-G\alpha$	7,14, M.P.
16)	$-I\alpha \cdot -G\alpha$	12,15, Adj.
17)	$-(I\alpha \vee G\alpha)$	16, D.M.
18)	$-S\alpha$	8,17, M.T.
19)	$(\exists x) - (Sx)$	18, E.G.

Pages 128–132

Th. 4. $/(p \supset -q) \supset (q \supset -p)$

1) $(p \vee q) \supset (q \vee p)$ A3

2) $(-p \vee -q) \supset (-q \vee -p)$	1, $-p/p, -q/q$
3) $(p \supset -q) \supset (q \supset -p)$	2, Def. $\supset$

Th. 7. $\underline{/-p \vee p}$

1) $p \supset p$	Th. 5
2) $-p \vee p$	1, Def. $\supset$

Th. 8. $\underline{/p \vee -p}$

1) $(p \vee q) \supset (q \vee p)$	A3
2) $(-p \vee p) \supset (p \vee -p)$	1, $-p/p, p/q$
3) $-p \vee p$	Th. 7
4) $p \vee -p$	2,3, Imp.

Th. 14. $\underline{/(-p \vee -q) \supset -(p \cdot q)}$

1) $p \supset --\mathrm{p}$	Th. 9
2) $(-p \vee -q) \supset --(-p \vee -q)$	1, $(-p \vee -q)/p$
3) $(-p \vee -q) \supset -(p \cdot q)$	2, Def.

Th. 15. $\underline{/-(p \cdot q) \equiv (-p \vee -q)}$

1) $-(p \cdot q) \supset (-p \vee -q)$	Th. 13
2) $(-p \vee -q) \supset -(p \cdot q)$	Th. 14
3) $[-(p \cdot q) \supset (-p \vee -q)] \cdot [(-p \vee -q) \supset -(p \cdot q)]$	1, 2, Adj.
4) $-(p \cdot q) \equiv (-p \vee -q)$	3, Def. $\equiv$

Th. 17. $\underline{/(-q \supset -p) \supset (p \supset q)}$

1) $(p \supset -q) \supset (q \supset -p)$	Th. 4
2) $(q \supset r) \supset [(p \supset q) \supset (p \supset r)]$	Th. 2
3) $[(p \supset --q) \supset (p \supset q)] \supset \{[(-q \supset -p) \supset (p \supset --q)] \supset [(-q \supset -p) \supset (p \supset q)]\}$	2, $(p \supset --q)/q$, $(p \supset q)/r$, $(-q \supset -p)/p$
4) $(--q \supset q) \supset ([p \supset --q) \supset (p \supset q)]$	2, $--q/q, q/r$
5) $--p \supset p$	Th. 11
6) $--q \supset q$	5, q/p
7) $(p \supset --q) \supset (p \supset q)$	4,6, Imp.
8) $[(-q \supset -p) \supset (p \supset --q)] \supset [(-q \supset -p) \supset (p \supset q)]$	3,7, Imp.
9) $(-q \supset -p) \supset (p \supset -q)$	1, $-q/p, p/q$
10) $(-q \supset -p) \supset (p \supset q)$	8,9, Imp.

Th. 18. $\underline{/(-p \supset q) \supset (-q \supset p)}$

1) $(q \supset r) \supset [(p \supset q) \supset (p \supset r)]$	Th. 2
2) $[(-p \supset --q) \supset (-q \supset p)] \supset \{[(-p \supset q) \supset (-p \supset --q)] \supset [(-p \supset q) \supset (-q \supset p)]\}$	1, $(-p \supset --q)/q$, $(-q \supset p)/r$, $(-p \supset q)/p$
3) $(-q \supset -p) \supset (p \supset q)$	Th. 17
4) $(-p \supset --q) \supset (-q \supset p)$	3, p/q, $-q/p$
5) $[(-p \supset q) \supset (-p \supset --q)] \supset [(-p \supset q) \supset (-q \supset p)]$	2, 4, Imp.
6) $(q \supset --q) \supset [(-p \supset q) \supset (-p \supset --q)]$	1, $--q/r$, $-p/p$
7) $p \supset --p$	Th. 9
8) $q \supset --q$	7, q/p
9) $(-p \supset q) \supset (-p \supset --q)$	6,8, Imp.
10) $(-p \supset q) \supset (-q \supset p)$	5,9, Imp.

Th. 20. $\underline{/(p \supset -q) \vee -(q \supset -p)}$

1) $(p \supset -q) \supset (q \supset -p)$	Th. 4
2) $-(p \supset -q) \vee (q \supset -p)$	1, Def. $\supset$
3) $(p \vee q) \supset (q \vee p)$	A3
4) $[-(p \supset -q) \vee (q \supset -p)] \supset [(q \supset -p) \vee -(p \supset -q)]$	3, $-(p \supset -q)/p$, $(q \supset -p)/q$
5) $(q \supset -p) \vee -(p \supset -q)$	4,2, Imp.
6) $(p \supset -q) \vee -(q \supset -p)$	5, p/q, q/p, Sim. Sub.

Page 135

Th. 21. $\underline{/-(p \cdot -p)}$

1) $p \vee -p$	Th. 8
2) $(-p \vee -q) \supset -(p \cdot q)$	Th. 14
3) $-p \vee --p$	1, $-p/p$
4) $(-p \vee --p) \supset -(p \cdot -p)$	2, $-p/q$
5) $-(p \cdot -p)$	4,3, Imp.

Th. 22. $\underline{/[(p \vee q) \vee r] \supset [(p \vee q) \vee (q \vee r)]}$

1) $(q \supset r) \supset [(p \vee q) \supset (p \vee r)]$	A4
2) $[r \supset (q \vee r)] \supset \{(p \vee r) \supset [p \vee (q \vee r)]\}$	1, r/q, $(q \vee r)/r$
3) $q \supset (p \vee q)$	A2
4) $r \supset (q \vee r)$	3, r/q, q/p
5) $(p \vee r) \supset [p \vee (q \vee r)]$	2,4, Imp.
6) $[(p \vee q) \vee r] \supset [(p \vee q) \vee (q \vee r)]$	5, $(p \vee q)/p$

Th. 23. $/p \supset (p \vee q)$

1) $q \supset (p \vee q)$	A2
2) $p \supset (q \vee p)$	1, p/q, q/p, Sim. Sub.
3) $(q \vee p) \supset (p \vee q)$	Th. 6
4) $(q \supset r) \supset [(p \supset q) \supset (p \supset r)]$	Th. 2
5) $[(q \vee p) \supset (p \vee q)] \supset \{[p \supset (q \vee p)] \supset [p \supset (p \vee q)]\}$	4, $(q \vee p)/q$, $(p \vee q)/r$
6) $[p \supset (q \vee p)] \supset [p \supset (p \vee q)]$	5,3, Imp.
7) $p \supset (p \vee q)$	6,2, Imp.

Th. 24. $/-(p \cdot q) \supset -(q \cdot p)$

1) $-(p \cdot q) \supset (-p \vee -q)$	Th. 13
2) $(p \vee q) \supset (q \vee p)$	A3
3) $(-p \vee -q) \supset (-q \vee -p)$	2, $-p/p$, $-q/q$
4) $p \supset --p$	Th. 9
5) $(-q \vee -p) \supset --(-q \vee -p)$	4, $(-q \vee -p)/p$
6) $(q \supset r) \supset [(p \supset q) \supset (p \supset r)]$	Th. 2

Use Steps 1, 3, 6, (substituting $(-p \vee -q)/q$, $(-q \vee -p)/r$, $-(p \cdot q)/p$ in Step 6) to show:

7) $-(p \cdot q) \supset (-q \vee -p)$	—

Then use Steps 7, 5, 6 to show:

8) $-(p \cdot q) \supset --(-q \vee -p)$	—
9) $-(p \cdot q) \supset -(q \cdot p)$	8, Def.

Th. 25. $/[-(p \vee q) \supset -p] \cdot [-(p \vee q) \supset -q]$

1) $p \supset (p \vee q)$	Th. 23
2) $(p \supset q) \supset (-q \supset -p)$	Th. 16
3) $[p \supset (p \vee q)] \supset [(-p \vee q) \supset -p]$	2, $(p \vee q)/q$
4) $-(p \vee q) \supset -p$	3,1, Imp.
5) $q \supset (p \vee q)$	A2
6) $[q \supset (p \vee q)] \supset [-(p \vee q) \supset -q]$	2, q/p, $(p \vee q)/q$
7) $-(p \vee q) \supset -q$	6,5, Imp.
8) $[-(p \vee q) \supset -p] \cdot [-(p \vee q) \supset -q]$	4,7, Adj.

Th. 26. $/-p \supset -(p \cdot q)$

1) $p \supset (p \vee q)$	Th. 23
2) $-p \supset (-p \vee -q)$	1, $-p/p$, $-q/q$
3) $p \supset --p$	Th. 9
4) $(-p \vee -q) \supset --(-p \vee -q)$	3, $(-p \vee -q)/p$
5) $(q \supset r) \supset [(p \supset q) \supset (p \supset r)]$	Th. 2

Use Steps 2, 4, 5 (substituting $(-p \vee -q)/q$ in Step 5) to show:

6) $-p \supset --(-p \vee -q)$	—
7) $-p \supset -(p \cdot q)$	6, Def. $\cdot$

Th. 27. $/(p \supset q) \supset -(p \cdot -q)$

1) $(q \supset r) \supset [(p \supset q) \supset (p \supset r)]$	Th. 2
2) $(q \supset --q) \supset [(p \supset q) \supset (p \supset --q)]$	1, $--q/r$
3) $p \supset --p$	Th. 9
4) $q \supset --q$	3, q/p
5) $(p \supset q) \supset (p \supset --q)$	2,4, Imp.
6) $(p \supset q) \supset (-p \vee --q)$	5, Def. $\supset$
7) $(-p \vee --q) \supset --(-p \vee --q)$	3, $(-p \vee --q)/p$
8) $(-p \vee --q) \supset -(p \cdot -q)$	7, Def. $\cdot$

Use Steps 6, 8, 1 (substituting $(-p \vee --q)/q$ in Step 1) to show:

9) $(p \supset q) \supset -(p \cdot -q)$	—

Th. 28. $/(-p \vee -q) \supset --(-q \vee -p)$

1) $(p \vee q) \supset (q \vee p)$	A3
2) $(-p \vee -q) \supset (-q \vee -p)$	1, $-p/p$, $-q/q$
3) $p \supset --p$	Th. 9
4) $(-q \vee -p) \supset --(-q \vee -p)$	3, $(-q \vee -p)/p$
5) $(q \supset r) \supset [(p \supset q) \supset (p \supset r)]$	Th. 2

Use Steps 2, 4, 5 to show:

6) $(-p \vee -q) \supset --(-q \vee -p)$	—

Th. 29. $/(p \supset q) \equiv -(p \cdot -q)$

1) $-(p \cdot q) \supset (-p \vee -q)$	Th. 13
2) $-(p \cdot -q) \supset (-p \vee --q)$	1, $-q/q$
3) $(q \supset r) \supset [(p \vee q) \supset (p \vee r)]$	A4
4) $(--q \supset q) \supset [(-p \vee --q) \supset (-p \vee q)]$	3, $--q/q$, q/r, $-p/p$
5) $--p \supset p$	Th. 11
6) $--q \supset q$	5, q/p
7) $(-p \vee --q) \supset (-p \vee q)$	4,6, Imp.
8) $(-p \vee --q) \supset (p \supset q)$	7, Def. $\supset$

Use Steps 2, 8, and Theorem 2 to show:

9) $-(p \cdot -q) \supset (p \supset q)$	—
10) $(p \supset q) \supset -(p \cdot -q)$	Th. 27
11) $[(p \supset q) \supset -(p \cdot -q)] \cdot [-(p \cdot -q) \supset (p \supset q)]$	10,9, Adj.

12) $(p \supset q) \equiv -(p \cdot -q)$ 11, Def. $\equiv$

Th. 30. $\underline{/(-p \cdot -q) \supset -(p \vee q)}$

1) $(-p \vee -q) \supset -(p \cdot q)$ Th. 14
2) $(- -p \vee - -q) \supset -(-p \cdot -q)$ 1, $-p/p$, $-q/q$
3) $(q \supset r) \supset [(p \vee q) \supset (p \vee r)]$ A4
4) $p \supset - -p$ Th. 9
5) $q \supset - -q$ 4, q/p
6) $(q \supset - -q) \supset [(- -p \vee q) \supset (- -p \vee - -q)]$ 3, $- -q/r$, $- -p/p$
7) $(- -p \vee q) \supset (- -p \vee - -q)$ 6,5, Imp.
8) $(q \supset r) \supset [(p \supset q) \supset (p \supset r)]$ Th. 2

Use Steps 7, 2, 8 (substituting $(- -p \vee - -q)/q$ in Step 8) to show:

9) $(- -p \vee q) \supset -(-p \cdot -q)$ —
10) $(q \vee p) \supset (p \vee q)$ Th. 6
11) $(q \vee - -p) \supset (- -p \vee q)$ 10, $- -p/p$

Use Steps 11, 9, 8 to show:

12) $(q \vee - -p) \supset -(-p \cdot -q)$ —
13) $(p \supset - -p) \supset [(q \vee p) \supset (q \vee - -p)]$ 3, p/q, $- -p/r$, q/p, Sim. Sub.
14) $(q \vee p) \supset (q \vee - -p)$ 13,4, Imp.

Use Steps 14, 12, 8 to show:

15) $(q \vee p) \supset -(-p \cdot -q)$ —
16) $(p \vee q) \supset (q \vee p)$ A3

Use Steps 16, 15, 8, to show:

17) $(p \vee q) \supset -(-p \cdot -q)$ —
18) $(p \supset -q) \supset (q \supset -p)$ Th. 4
19) $[(p \vee q) \supset -(-p \cdot -q)] \supset [(-p \cdot -q) \supset -(p \vee q)]$ 18, $(p \vee q)/p$, $(-p \cdot -q)/q$
20) $(-p \cdot -q) \supset -(p \vee q)$ 19,17, Imp.

Page 135–Polish Notation

1) $(p \supset -q) \cdot -(p \vee q)$
2) $p \vee \{r \cdot [s \equiv (t \supset u)]\}$
3) $(p \supset - -p) \equiv -(-q \vee -q)$
4) $(-q \supset q) \supset q$
5) $\{[(p \cdot -q) \supset (-r \cdot s)] \supset [(-p \vee -r) \cdot s]\} \supset q$
6) *ECCpqrCpCqr*
7) *CAApqrAApqAqr*

8) $CCCpNNqCNqNpCCCpqCpNNqCCpqCNqNp$
9) $AKNcNChbNKNgNp$
10) $NKpNANqNr$

Pages 141–145

Th. 4. $\underline{/a+a=a}$

1) $a+0=a$	A2
2) $a+(a\times a')=a$	1, A8, I.S.
3) $a+(b\times c)=(a+b)\times(a+c)$	A6
4) $a+(a\times a')=(a+a)\times(a+a')$	3, a/b, a'/c
5) $(a+a)\times(a+a')=a$	2,4, I.S.
6) $(a+a)\times 1=a$	5, A8, I.S.
7) $a\times 1=a$	A3
8) $(a+a)\times 1=(a+a)$	7, $(a+a)/a$
9) $a+a=a$	6,8, I.S.

Th. 6. $\underline{/a\times 0=0}$

1) $a\times a'=0$	A8
2) $a+0=a$	A2
3) $a'+0=a'$	2, a'/a
4) $a\times(a'+0)=0$	1,3, I.S.
5) $a\times(b+c)=(a\times b)+(a\times c)$	A7
6) $a\times(a'+0)=(a\times a')+(a\times 0)$	5, a'/b, $0/c$
7) $(a\times a')+(a\times 0)=0$	4,6, I.S.
8) $0+(a\times 0)=0$	7,1, I.S.
9) $a+b=b+a$	A4
10) $a+0=0+a$	9, $0/b$
11) $0+a=a$	2,10, I.S.
12) $0+(a\times 0)=a\times 0$	11, $(a\times 0)/a$
13) $a\times 0=0$	8,12, I.S.

Th. 7. $\underline{/a=a}$

1) $a+a=a$	Th. 4
2) $a=a+a$	1, I.C.
3) $a=a$	2,1, I.S.

Th. 9. $\underline{/0=1'}$

1) $a\times 1=a$	A3
2) $1'\times 1=1'$	1, $1'/a$
3) $a\times a'=0$	A8
4) $1\times 1'=0$	3, $1/a$

5) $a \times b = b \times a$	A5
6) $1' \times 1 = 1 \times 1'$	5, $1'/a$, $1/b$
7) $1 \times 1' = 1'$	2,6, I.S.
8) $0 = 1'$	4,7, I.S.

Th. 13. $\underline{/a \subset 1}$

1) $a + 1 = 1$	Th. 5
2) $a \subset 1$	1, Def. $A \subset B$

Th. 15. $\underline{/(a \subset 0) \supset (a = 0)}$

1) $a \subset 0$	Hypothesis
2) $a + 0 = 0$	1, Def $A \subset B$
3) $a + 0 = a$	A2
4) $a = 0$	2,3, I.S.
5) $(a \subset 0) \supset (a = 0)$	1–4, Rule 6

Page 161

1.

a)

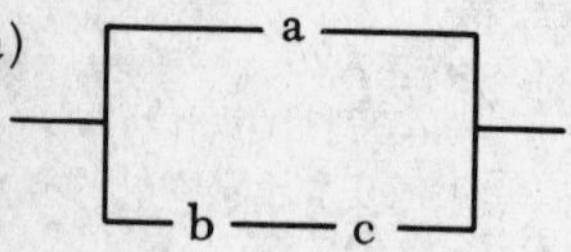

b)

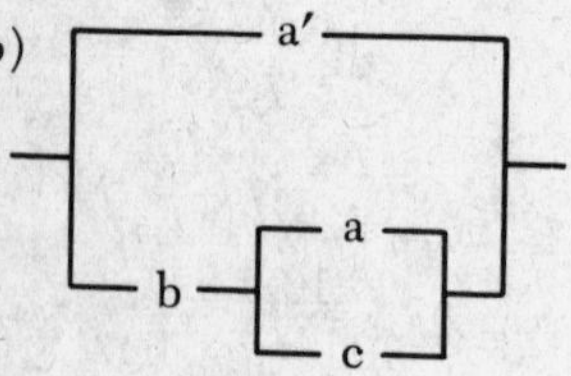

c)

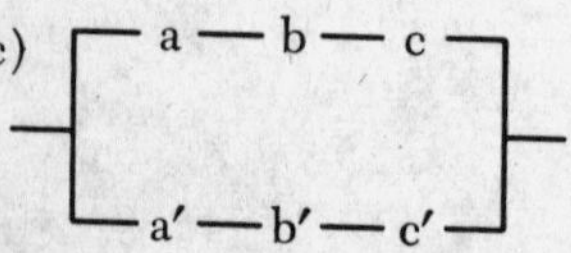

d)

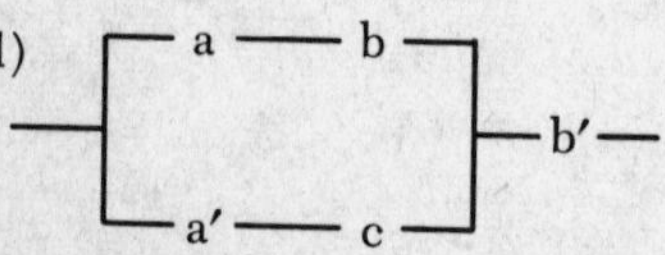

e)

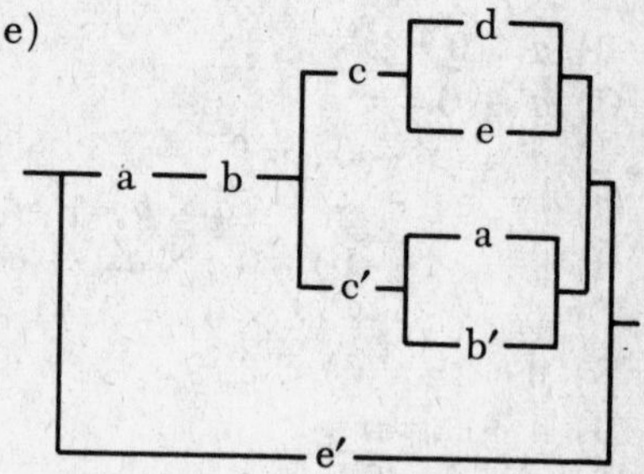

f)

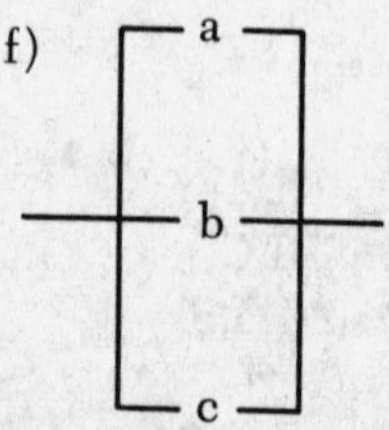

2. a) $a(bc'+b'c)$
   b) $x+y(z+x')+y'z'$
   c) $xy(z'+x'+y')z$
   d) $a(b+a'+b')+c$

3. a)

②			③	①	②	①
a	b	c	a	(bc'	+	b'c)
0	0	0	0	0	0	0
0	0	1	0	0	1	1
0	1	0	0	1	1	0
0	1	1	0	0	0	0
1	0	0	0	0	0	0
1	0	1	1	0	1	1
1	1	0	1	1	1	0
1	1	1	0	0	0	0
			≡			

b)

③	①		④	②	①	③	②
x	y	z	x +	y	(z + x')	+	y'z'
0	0	0	1	0	1	1	1
0	0	1	0	0	1	0	0
0	1	0	1	1	1	1	0
0	1	1	1	1	1	1	0
1	0	0	1	0	0	1	1
1	0	1	1	0	1	0	0
1	1	0	1	0	0	0	0
1	1	1	1	1	1	1	0
			≡				

c)

		②	①	②	①	③
x	y	z	xy	(z'	+ x' +	y')z
0	0	0	0	0	1	0
0	0	1	0	0	1	0
0	1	0	0	0	1	0
0	1	1	0	0	1	0
1	0	0	0	0	1	0
1	0	1	0	0	1	0
1	1	0	1	1	1	0
1	1	1	1	0	0	0
						≡

d)

②	①	③	③	②	①	④
a	b	c	$a\,(b$	$+\,a'$	$+\,b')$	$+\,c$
0	0	0	0	1	1	0
0	0	1	0	1	1	1
0	1	0	0	1	1	0
0	1	1	0	1	1	1
1	0	0	1	1	1	1
1	0	1	1	1	1	1
1	1	0	1	1	0	1
1	1	1	1	1	0	1

4. $ad+(b+c)(c'+b)+ad'$
$ad+ad'+(b+c)(b+c')$
$a(d+d')+b+cc'$
$a(1)+b+0$
$a+b$

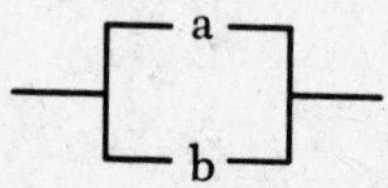

Pages 165–166

1. $a+bc+bc'$
$a+b(c+c')$
$a+b(1)$
$a+b$

2. $abc(d+a'+b'+c')$
$abcd+aa'bc+abb'c+abcc'$
$abcd+0+0+0$
$abcd$

3. $a(a'+b)$
$aa'+ab$
ab

4. $bc'+(a+b)(a+b')+bc$
$b(c+c')+a+ab+ab'$
$b+a(1+b+b')$
$a+b$

5. $[(a+b)+(a+c)(b+c')]a'+a'c$
$(a+b+ab+bc+ac')a'+a'c$
$a'b+a'bc+a'c$
$a'[b+bc+c]$
$a'[b(1+c)+c]$
$a'(b+c)$

6. $a(b+c)+[b'(a+c')+c']$
$ab+ac+ab'+b'c'+c'$
$a(b+b'+c)+c'(b'+1)$
$a+c'$

7. $z+(x+z)(x+z')(y+z)(y+z')$
$z+(x+zz')(y+zz')$
$\underline{\underline{z+xy}}$

8. $a+(b+c)(c'+b)+a'b+a'b'$
$a+bc'+cc'+bb+bc+a'(b+b')$
$a+a'+c'(b+c)+b(b+c)$
$1+c'(b+c)+b(b+c)$
$\underline{\underline{1}}$

9. $[a(b'+c')+a'c(a'+b+c')]b$
$[ab'+ac'+a'c+a'bc]b$
$0+abc'+a'bc+a'bc$
$abc'+a'bc$
$\underline{\underline{b(ac'+a'c)}}$

10. $a'bcd'+bd+b'cd+a'b'c+b'c'd$
$b'd(c+c')+a'c(b'+bd')+bd$
$b'd+a'c[(b'+b)(b'+d')]+bd$
$d(b+b')+a'c(b'+d')$
$d+a'c(b'+d')$
$(d+a'c)(d+b'+d')$
$(d+a'c)(1)$
$\underline{\underline{d+a'c}}$

Pages 174–175

1. a) $xy+xy'+x'y'$
b) $ab'+ab$
c) $x'yz+x'yz'+x'y'z+x'y'z'+xyz+xyz'+xy'z'$
d) $abc'+abc+ab'c$
e) $x'yz+x'y'z+x'yz'$
f) $a'b'c'+abc+ab'c$
g) $abcd+abcd'+abc'd+abc'd'+ab'cd+ab'cd'$
$+ab'c'd+ab'c'd'+a'b'cd+a'b'c'd+a'b'c'd'$
h) $x'yz+x'yz'+x'y'z+x'y'z'+xyz$

2. Simplification: $a(b+c)$

a	b	c	$a(b+c)$		
0	0	0	0	0	
0	0	1	0	1	
0	1	0	0	1	
0	1	1	0	1	
1	0	0	0	0	
1	0	1	1	1	*
1	1	0	1	1	*
1	1	1	1	1	*
			≡		

* Current flows in the circuit at $ab'c$ or abc' or abc as stated in the expression for 1(*d*).

3. a) $(a'+b)(a'+b')(a+b)$
   b) $(x+y)(x+y')$
   c) $(x+y+z)(x+y+z')(x+y'+z)(x+y'+z')$
   $(x'+y'+z)$
   d) $(a+b+c)$
   e) $(a+b'+c)(a+b+c')(a'+b+c')$
   f) $(x+y+z)(x'+y'+z')$

4. a) $z'(x+y)$
   b) $x(y'+z')$
   c) $x+(y+z)(y'+z')$
   d) $xz'+y$

5.

a	b	c	$c'(a'b+ab')$
0	0	0	0
0	0	1	0
0	1	0	1
0	1	1	0
1	0	0	1
1	0	1	0
1	1	0	0
1	1	1	0

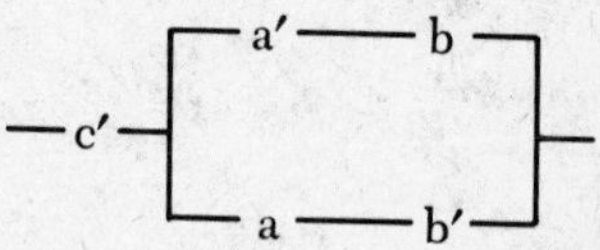

DNF $a'bc'+ab'c'$
CNF $(a+b+c)(a+b+c')(a+b'+c')(a'+b+c')$
$(a'+b'+c)(a'+b'+c')$

Index

Index